Schmollers Jahrbuch

Journal of Applied Social Science Studies

Zeitschrift für Wirtschafts- und Sozialwissenschaften

Herausgegeben von

Gert G. Wagner und Joachim Wagner
Stefan Bach, Richard V. Burkhauser, Ulrich Kaiser,
Regina T. Riphahn, Timothy M. Smeeding, Holly Sutherland

128. Jahrgang 2008 Heft 1

Neighbourhood Effects Studies on the Basis of European Micro Data

Edited by C. Katharina Spiess, Simon Burgess,
and Hartmut Häussermann

Duncker & Humblot · Berlin

Schmollers Jahrbuch

Journal of Applied Social Science Studies
Zeitschrift für Wirtschafts- und Sozialwissenschaften

Schmollers Jahrbuch is supported by the
German Council for Social and Economic Data (RatSWD)

All correspondence regarding the content of the journal should be directed to:
Gert G. Wagner, Rat für Sozial- und Wirtschaftsdaten, Mohrenstraße 58,
10117 Berlin / Germany
email: schmollers_jahrbuch@ratswd.de

The journal is published four times a year with a total of 672 pages. As of the first issue 2008 the journal is also available as electronic edition. The price for a yearly subscription for institutions is € 188.00, for individual subscribers € 98.00 and for students € 60.00, single issue price is € 26.00. All prices are exclusive of mailing costs and suggested retail prices. The subscription price for institutions includes unlimited electronic access. Individual subscribers get electronic access via user name and password. Orders may be directed to any bookstore or directly to the publisher. Cancellations must be made at least 6 weeks before the end of the year.

Verlag Duncker & Humblot GmbH, Carl-Heinrich-Becker-Weg 9,
12165 Berlin / Germany
phone: +49-30/79 00 06-0 fax: +49-30/79 00 06-31
home page: http://www.duncker-humblot.de

ISSN 1439-121X (print edition)
ISSN 1865-5742 (electronic edition)
ISBN 978-3-428-12761-0

Separate articles are offered for download by www.gbi.de (since 2000) and www.atypon-link.com (since 2008).

Bibliografische Information der Deutschen Nationalbibliothek

Die Deutsche Nationalbibliothek verzeichnet diese Publikation in der Deutschen Nationalbibliografie; detaillierte bibliografische Daten sind im Internet über http://dnb.d-nb.de abrufbar.

Contents

Authors' Addresses

Roger Andersson, Uppsala University, Institute for Housing & Urban Research, Sweden
E-mail: Roger.Andersson@ibf.uu.se

Danuta Biterman, Centre for Epidemiology, The National Board of Health and Welfare, 106 30 Stockholm, Sweden
E-mail: danuta.biterman@ssocialstyrelsen.se

Simon Burgess, Centre for Market and Public Organisation, University of Bristol, UK
E-Mail: Simon.Burgess@bristol.ac.uk

Steven Cummins, Department of Geography, Queen Mary, University of London, UK
E-mail: s.c.j.cummins@qmul.ac.uk

Anita Drever, University of Tennessee, 408 Burchfield Geography Building, 37996 Knoxville, Tennessee, USA
E-mail: adrever@utk.edu

Anne Ellaway, MRC Social and Public Health Sciences Unit, University of Glasgow, UK
E-mail: a.ellaway@sphsu.mrc.ac.uk

Jürgen Friedrichs, University of Cologne, Research Institute for Sociology, Greinstr. 2, 50939 Cologne, Germany
E-Mail: friedrichs@wiso.uni-koeln.de

George C. Galster, Clarence Hilberry Professor of Urban Affairs, Wayne State University, Detroit, MI 48202, USA
E-mail: aa3571@wayne.edu

Björn Gustafsson, University of Göteborg, Department of Social Work, P.O. Box 720, SE 405 30 Göteborg, Sweden
E-mail: Bjorn.Gustafsson@socwork.gu.se

Gundi Knies, Institute for Social and Economic Research, University of Essex, Wivenhoe Park, Colchester CO4 3SQ, UK
E-Mail: gknies@essex.ac.uk

Sally Macintyre, MRC Social and Public Health Sciences Unit, University of Glasgow, UK
E-mail: s.macintyre@sphsu.mrc.ac.uk

Torun Österberg, University of Göteborg, Department of Social Work, P.O. Box 720, SE 405 30 Göteborg, Sweden
E-mail: torun.osterberg@socwork.gu.se

Carol Propper, Centre for Market and Public Organisation, University of Bristol, UK
E-Mail: Carol.Propper@bristol.ac.uk

Amanda Sacker, International Institute for Society and Health, Department of Epidemiology & Public Health, University College London, UK
E-mail: a.sacker@ucl.ac.uk

Mai Stafford, Department of Epidemiology & Public Health, University College London, 1 – 19 Torrington Place, London, WC1E 6BT, UK
E-mail: m.stafford@ucl.ac.uk

Wenda van der Laan Bouma-Doff, Delft University of Technology, OTB Research Institute for Housing, Urban and Mobility Studies, P.O. Box 5030, 2600 GA Delft, The Netherlands
E-mail: w.vanderlaanbouma-doff@tudelft.nl

Dick Wiggins, Department of Sociology, City University London, UK
E-mail: R.D.Wiggins@city.ac.uk

Schmollers Jahrbuch 128 (2008), 1
Duncker & Humblot, Berlin

Editorial

With the first issue of *Schmollers Jahrbuch* in 2008 (Volume 128), a major restructuring goes into effect. Richard Hauser and Dietmar Petzina, who have both played a major role as editors since the relaunch of the journal in 2000, have retired. As professors emeritus, they of course have the right to do so. We would like to thank them sincerely for all their help and extend our best wishes to both of them for the future.

We are delighted – and very grateful – that new editors have stepped up to join *Schmollers Jahrbuch.* Through the contribution of their personal expertise, they will sharpen the journal's profile. Their involvement will also significantly expand the expertise of the editors, making it no longer necessary to have an editorial board. *Schmollers Jahrbuch* has benefitted greatly from the advice of the board and gratefully acknowledges their support.

Among the new editors, Stefan Bach (DIW Berlin) will be responsible for public finance. He stands for applied economics with a special emphasis on German issues, a field in which we receive many successful submissions.

Ulrich Kaiser (University of Southern Denmark) will take responsibility for submissions in industrial organisation. Submissions in this area have been increasing steadily in recent years. Ulrich Kaiser will also strengthen the international component within the group of editors.

This international perspective will be enhanced further by Holly Sutherland (Essex University). We hope that she will attract more submissions in the field of micro-simulation and distributional issues.

Our aim is not only to increase the quality of the referee process but also – with the help of our new editors – to accelerate this process even more.

The changes in the group of editors provide a good occasion to underscore our language policy: German is welcome if a paper deals with German issues. However, papers that are more theoretical or more general in their approach should be written in English.

In closing, we would like to express our thanks to the German Council for Social and Economic Data (*Rat für Sozial- und Wirtschaftsdaten*) for supporting our editorial office and homepage. This support is provided because of the great success of the „European Data Watch" section, making *Schmollers Jahrbuch* an important platform for the aims and tasks of the council.

Berlin and Lueneburg, February 2008

Gert G. Wagner and
Joachim Wagner

Schmollers Jahrbuch 128 (2008), 3 – 6
Duncker & Humblot, Berlin

Introduction: „Neighbourhood Effects Studies on the Basis of European Micro-data“

The beginning of neighbourhood studies can be dated to the begining of the 20th century when the first studies based on theoretical approaches related to a social ecological approach were undertaken at the University of Chicago. At this time it was difficult to disentangle context effects from effects due to the composition of the residents of a particular context. Meanwhile, new statistical methods and better data allow us to distinguish much better between these two effects. At the beginning of the 21st century neighbourhood studies are an important field in social sciences. The neighbourhood focus is increasingly an important issue in explaining a variety of outputs and outcomes in various disciplines and research questions. The availability of better micro-data allowing us to take neighbourhood effects into account are another reason for this. However, European countries still offer very different micro-data sets in respect to neighbourhood research. On the one hand, Sweden and other Scandinavian countries describe and define the neighbourhood on a very small regional level, while other European countries are still far behind the Scandinavian countries, although they make some progress in respect to the data they offer.

Given these challenges for neigbourhood research it was the aim of a conference, which took place in spring 2007 at the Humboldt University of Berlin, to bring together Europe's „Neighbourhood Effects“ researchers, and to encourage further analysis of the existing European data by looking at research in different countries, undertaken in different academic disciplines. The conference was jointly organized by CMPO at the University of Bristol, the Georg-Simmel-Zentrum für Metropolenforschung, at the Humboldt-University Berlin and the Socio-Economic Panel Study (SOEP) at the DIW Berlin.

This special issue summarizes some of the papers presented at this conference, to make sure that the spirit of the conference – to encourage further neighbourhood research – is lasting. These contributions deal with methodological issues and data problems on the one hand, and on the other hand, almost all of them focus on one particular research question embedded in the neighbourhood context.

The papers presented at the conference nicely illustrate the problems and the rich potential of neighbourhood studies at this time. As Galster reflects, it is now widely known that identification of causal relationships is difficult.

Other papers acknowledge this and grapple with the implications. On the other hand, the conference highlighted that all over Europe exciting new datasets are becoming available with neighbourhood identifiers and characteristics. There is no single message to emerge from the conference other than this: neighbourhoods are potentially important in peoples' lives, and the data are becoming available to document and understand this.

This volume starts with three contributions which deal with more general questions of neighbourhood research taking national studies as examples. The first contribution by *George C. Galster,* deals with six major challenges which confront researchers attempting to quantify accurately the independent effect of neighbourhood context on individuals. Galster describes these challenges, prior attempts to meet them, and their respective shortcomings. Moreover, he suggests some promising approaches, techniques and finally data improvements to deal with theses shortcomings. Essentially he sets out his agenda for future neighbourhood research initiatives which might not only be discussed on the European level.

Roger Anderson's contribution summarizes some of the basic questions that appear both in the neighbourhood effect literature and in planning practices and policy discourses. He draws on a series of studies using Swedish data. The paper attempts to answer questions on the strength of the relation between housing mix and social mix, on the relation between the population composition of neighbourhoods and residents' social interaction, on the relationship of social opportunities of individual residents and their neighbourhood context and to the extend in which this is produced through local social interaction. He also addresses the questions: what population mix matters, what scale matters and what time span matters.

Jürgen Friedrich's contribution deals with the impact of neighbourhood characteristics, such as poverty rates, on the attitudes and behaviour of residents. His contribution explores the feasibility of three existing large German date sets for such a purpose. He concludes that the data cannot be regionalized in a sufficient manner, so he describes an alternative strategy, a „puzzle strategy" to combine data from different existing data sets.

The following set of contributions focus on one particular question of neighbourhood research and try to answer this based on one particular national micro-data set. The contribution by *Gundi Knies, Simon Burgess* and *Carol Popper* is based on German micro data. It is an example of a study making use of new attempts by the provider of micro-data to improve their data sets for neighbourhood research. The authors test whether people's life satisfaction depends on their relative income position in the neighbourhood. They find no negative and no statistically significant associations between neighbourhood income and life satisfaction, but they find positive associations between neighbourhood income and happiness.

The contribution of *Mai Stafford, Amanda Sacker, Anne Ellaway, Steven Cummins, Dick Wiggins* and *Sally Macintyre* is an example of a neighbourhood study from the field of health research. Using obesity as an example, they theorised a model of the potential causal pathways linking neighbourhood characteristics, through diet and physical activity, to obesity. Using data from England and Scotland, their structural model highlights certain neighbourhood characteristics which are important for understanding the increasing problem of obesity and others which are of no significant importance.

Another set of contributions focus on segregation issues, one important part of neighbourhood research. The study by *Danuta Biterman, Bjorn Gustafsson* and *Torun Österberg,* investigates certain issues of economic and ethnic segregation from the perspective of children in the three metropolitan regions of Sweden. Their main focus is on child income. They find that residential polarisation and ethnic residential polarisation increased, while they report a relatively large overlap between economic and ethnic polarisation. They conclude that increased returns to parental education have forcefully contributed to larger economic polarisation among children in Swedish metropolitan regions.

The contribution by *Wenda van der Laan Bouma-Doff* focuses on the associations between ethnic concentration and labour market participation. This research is based on a data set on the four largest ethnic groups in the Netherlands and the ethnic composition of the neighbourhood. Based on this data she investigates whether ethnic minorities living in ethnically concentrated neighbourhoods participate less in the labour force, and if so, which mechanisms are behind this relationship. The results show that, Moroccans living in such neighbourhoods show a lower participation rate. This relationship might be explained by the fact, that Moroccans are a highly marginalized, stigmatized and discriminated ethnic category, as a result of which they are confronted with barriers on both the housing *and* the labour market.

The contribution by *Anita I. Drever* takes another approach, in contrast to other research on segregation. Her research does not focus on the effects on minority residents of living in an ethnic neighbourhood, but rather she explores how living within an ethnic neighbourhood affects members of the dominant ethnic group rather than the minorities that define it. She uses micro-data for Germany. Her results indicate that Germans living within ethnic neighbourhoods are for instance less well off financially than their peers in other parts of the city. The analysis did not however suggest that Germans living in ethnic neighbourhoods have fewer social contacts, or that they are more likely to be unemployed. Indeed, Germans living within ethnic neighbourhoods reported levels of satisfaction with their housing and standard of living equal to Germans elsewhere.

Finally, it is our pleasure to thank the participants of the conference, and the authors and referees of this Special Issue. We thank the Volkswagen Foundation for their financial support of the conference, without this it would not have been so successful. And last but not least we want to thank Gundi Knies, who substantially contributed to the success of the conference, in the phase of its preparation, during its processing and post-processing.

Berlin and Bristol, January 2008

C. Katharina Spiess,
Simon Burgess, and
Hartmut Häussermann

Schmollers Jahrbuch 128 (2008), 7 – 48
Duncker & Humblot, Berlin

Quantifying the Effect of Neighbourhood on Individuals: Challenges, Alternative Approaches, and Promising Directions

By George C. Galster*

Abstract

Six major challenges confront statistical researchers attempting to quantify accurately the independent effect of neighbourhood context on individuals: (1) defining the scale of neighbourhood; (2) identifying mechanisms of neighbourhood effect; (3) measuring appropriate neighbourhood characteristics; (4) measuring exposure to neighbourhood; (5) measuring appropriate individual characteristics; and (6) endogeneity. The paper describes these challenges, prior attempts to meet them, and their respective shortcomings. It notes several approaches on the horizon that offer the promise of surmounting these challenges: experiments with varied scales of bespoke neighbourhoods; databases with multi-domain measures of neighbourhood characteristics; statistical models testing for non-linear neighbourhood effects that are stratified by residential group, density of local social interactions, and duration of residency; and econometric devices involving instrumental variables and residuals. It argues that further progress can be made on this front if we take advantage of natural quasi-experiments and push toward fielding a major, new social survey employing a people / place panel design.

JEL Classifications: B40, R00, C9, C01, C49

1. Introduction

In both Western Europe and the United States, the scholarly and political salience of quantifying the effects of neighbourhood context on individuals has grown rapidly in the past two decades. In academic circles, the number of research papers on this subject has expanded exponentially; compare Gephart (1997), van Kempen (1997), Friedrichs (1998), Leventhal / Brooks-Gunn (2000); Sampson / Morenoff / Gannon-Rowley (2002); Friedrichs / Galster / Musterd (2003); Ellen / Turner (2003); Galster (2005). In political circles, de-

* The author wishes to thank Simon Burgess, Hartmut Häussermann, Gundi Knies, Katharina Spiess, and other participants in the Humboldt University workshop "Neighbourhood Effects studies on the Basis of European Micro-Data" for helpful suggestions on an earlier draft, and Richard Ban for production assistance.

bates have intensified over the degree to which policies for increasing the "social mix" of neighbourhoods can be justified on the basis of the evidence; for examples, see: Galster / Zobel (1998); Atkinson / Kintrea (2001); Ostendorf / Musterd / de Vos (2001); Friedrichs (2002); Kearns (2002); Musterd (2003); Kleinhans (2004); Delorenzi (2006); Joseph (2006); Joseph / Chaskin / Webber (2006); and Galster (2002, 2007a, b). Given the saliency of the issue, accurately quantifying neighbourhood effects emerges as a concern of more than pedantic, methodological interest.

In this paper I attempt to respond to this concern. I begin by forwarding a model of neighbourhood effects that establishes a framework within which methodological challenges can be understood. Second, I discuss what I consider to be the six paramount challenges facing scholars who seek to obtain unbiased estimates of the independent effect of neighbourhood on individuals. These are: (1) defining the scale of neighbourhood; (2) identifying mechanisms of neighbourhood effect; (3) measuring appropriate neighbourhood characteristics; (4) measuring exposure to neighbourhood; (5) measuring appropriate individual characteristics; and (6) endogeneity. Third, I review and evaluate the various methods that researchers have employed in their attempts to confront the aforementioned challenges. Fourth, I note for each of the six challenges emerging strategies and directions that I view as promising. Finally, I advance two suggestions for new sources of data that could significantly advance the field of measuring neighbourhood effects. Throughout I attempt to bring to bear methodological sensitivities and studies emanating from a variety of disciplines and continents.

2. A General Model of Neighbourhood Effects on Individuals

In general terms, one can specify that the outcome of interest (O) observed at time t for individual i residing in neighbourhood j in metropolitan area k can be expressed:

[1] $$O_{it} = \alpha + \beta[P_{it}] + \gamma[P_i] + \varphi[UP_{it}] + \partial[UP_i] + \theta[N_{jt}] + \mu[M_{kt}] + \varepsilon$$

where:

$[P_t]$ = observed personal characteristics that can vary over time (e.g., marital or fertility status, educational attainment)

$[P]$ = observed personal characteristics that do not vary over time (e.g., year and country of birth)

$[UP_t]$ = unobserved personal characteristics that can vary over time (e.g., psychological states, interpersonal networks and relationships)

$[UP]$ = unobserved personal characteristics that do not vary over time (e.g., IQ, prior experiences, certain values and beliefs)

$[N_t]$ = observed characteristics of neighbourhood where individual resides during t

$[M_t]$ = observed characteristics of metropolitan area in which individual resides during t (e.g., area unemployment rates)

ε = a random error term with statistical properties discussed below

i = individual

j = neighbourhood

k = metropolitan area

t = time period (typically a year)

All Greek letters represent parameters to be estimated through some sort of multivariate statistical technique.

The six central empirical challenges facing analysts attempting to measure neighbourhood effects accurately (i.e., get a precise, unbiased measure of θ) can been seen through the framework of equation [1].

- What is the appropriate geographic scale(s) that define $[N]$?
- What are the causal processes that underlie the relationship θ between $[N]$ and O?
- What are the appropriate characteristics to measure when operationalizing $[N]$?
- What is the intensity and duration of individual i's exposure to $[N]$? Does $[N]$ affect O immediately, with a lag, or cumulatively?
- How can we comprehensively operationalize and measure the key components of $[P]$ and $[P_t]$? Given that one cannot do so for $[UP]$ and $[UP_t]$, what can be done to minimize bias in estimated θ from omitted individual variables associated with neighbourhood selection?
- What are endogenous relationships between $[N]$ and $[P_t]$, and what can be done to minimize bias in estimated θ from such relationships?

3. The Six Paramount Challenges

The methodological concerns associated with empirical investigation of the behavioral and psychological impacts of neighbourhoods have been the subject of several excellent treatises; see especially Manski (1993, 1995, 2000); Duncan / Connell / Klebanov (1997); Duncan / Raudenbush (1999); Sampson / Morenoff / Gannon-Rowley (2002); Durlauf / Cohen-Cole (2004). I draw liberally from these works, while providing supplements and syntheses.

3.1 Defining the Scale of Neighbourhood

In an earlier survey of the neighbourhood literature, I noted the multiplicity of conceptualizations of neighbourhood (Galster, 2001). Many scholars have employed a purely ecological perspective, while others have attempted to integrate social and ecological perspectives. The upshot is that, whatever "neighbourhood" is, it undoubtedly has distinct social, economic, and psychological meanings at various geographic scales. The first to recognize this was Suttles (1972), who argued that households engaged indistinct social relationships within four scales of neighbourhood, which he labeled: (1) "block face;" (2) "community of limited liability;" (3) "expanded community of limited liability:" and (4) "sector of a city." Suttles' and subsequent empirical work has confirmed the ability of households to recognize multiple scales of neighbourhood; see, e.g., Birch et al. (1979). I have since formulated theories of nested scales of neighbourhood based on the nature of the spatial variations in externalities of amenities impinging on a household (Galster, 1986) and of the geographic nature of the various attributes of the bundle comprising neighbourhood (Galster, 2001).

The challenge for empirical researchers of neighbourhood effects that logically follows from the above is daunting: [*N*] should be operationalized at *multiple scales.* However, such can easily produce variables that are too highly correlated across scales to produce distinct estimates of θ at various scales. Even more fundamentally, often there is a great deal of interpersonal variance in the boundaries of neighbourhoods, both within and across scales. This means that data gathered from administratively defined spaces may not correspond well or consistently to the "neighbourhood" experienced by households residing in these spaces.

3.2 Identifying Mechanisms of Neighbourhood Effect

There have been several comprehensive reviews of the potential theoretical links between neighbourhood processes and individual outcomes; see especially Jencks / Mayer (1990); Duncan / Connell / Klebanov (1997); Gephart (1997); Friedrichs (1998); Dietz (2002); Sampson / Morenoff / Gannon-Rowley (2002); and Ioannides / Loury (2004). I therefore will list these mechanisms and describe them only briefly here. I employ the useful distinction introduced by Manski (1995; 2000) between endogenous, correlated, and exogenous effects.

Three Types of Neighbourhood Effect Mechanisms

To be sure, it is feasible to estimate equation [1] without consideration of the causal mechanisms that underlie the correlations. However, such a mechanical approach is to be avoided. As I shall amplify below, the proper specification of neighbourhood variables comprising [*N*] and the appropriate scale of geography over which they are measured can only be accomplished by consideration of these mechanisms.

Endogenous Neighbourhood Effects. Endogenous neighbourhood effects are those that occur when the behaviors or attitudes of one neighbourhood resident has a direct influence on (at least a portion of) his or her neighbors. This mechanism can be thought of as a social externality. Numerous versions of endogenous effects have been forwarded:

- Socialization: Behaviors and attitudes of all individuals may be changed (for better or worse) by contact with role models or peers who may be neighbors. When these changes occur they are often referred to as "contagion effects." For example, the actions by some to informally police and clean common neighbourhood spaces may encourage all others in the area to do the same.
- Epidemic / Social Norms: This is a special subset of socialization effects that are characterized by a minimum threshold being achieved before noticeable consequences ensue from collective socialization. The need for some subset of the neighbourhood population to reach a critical mass before their social norms begin to influence others to conform is a case in point. Another is the influence of local acts of crime and violence: when neighbors finally perceive the neighbourhood as too dangerous they will restrict their activities outside the home.
- Selective Socialization: This process is another special type of socialization process wherein neighbors are not all equally affected by others. Employed residents are often viewed as positive role models encouraging (only) their unemployed neighbors to find work, for example. Conversely, secondary school dropouts may discourage only their same-age peers from attending school.
- Social Networks: Though one may say that socialization proceeds through social networks, I specify this as a distinct process involving the interpersonal communication of information and resources. One local group may intensify the density and multi-nodal structure of their social networks (create "strong ties") by clustering, thereby increasing the sources of assistance in times of need. On the other hand, such situations may lack the "weak ties" that offer the prospect of bringing new information and resources into the community, thereby increasing social isolation.
- Competition: Under the premise that certain local resources are limited and not public goods, this theory posits that groups within the neighbourhood will compete for these resources amongst themselves. Because the context is a zero-sum game, social conflict will arise as one group more successfully competes. The control of a local public park for the specialized group activities provides one example.

- Relative Deprivation: This mechanism suggests that residents who have achieved some socioeconomic success will be a source of disamenities for their less-well off neighbors. The latter will view the successful with envy or will make them perceive their own relative inferiority as a source of dissatisfaction.
- Stigmatization: Endogenous stigmatization of a place transpires when important institutional, governmental or market actors negatively stereotype all residents of a place and / or reduce the flows of resources flowing into the place because of its household composition. This might occur as the percentage of households in some disadvantaged ethnic group in the neighbourhood exceeds the threshold of where they are perceived by these external actors as "dominant."
- Exposure to Violence: Neighbors who engage in visibly violent and abusive behaviors can create negative externalities in the form of psychological damage to others nearby, especially if these people are themselves victimized.
- Economic Development Spillovers: Changes in the neighbourhood income distribution may be reflected in the density of retail and entertainment employment opportunities in or near the locale potentially available to residents.

Correlated Neighbourhood Effects. Correlated neighbourhood effect mechanisms do not vary by alterations in neighbourhood household composition, but rather are determined by larger structural forces in the metropolitan area, like locations of jobs and geographic disamenities and the structures of local government. These external forces may impinge differentially of different neighbourhoods, but within any given neighbourhood they affect all residents roughly equally, producing thereby correlations in neighbors' outcomes. Several such mechanisms have been forwarded in the literature:

- Spatial mismatch: certain neighbourhoods have little accessibility (in either spatial proximity or as mediated by transportation networks) to job opportunities appropriate to the skills of their residents
- Local institutional resources: certain neighbourhoods have access to fewer and / or weaker private, non-profit, or public institutions and organizations
- Public services: certain neighbourhoods are located within local political jurisdictions that offer inferior services and facilities
- External stigma: certain neighbourhoods may be stigmatized regardless of their current population, because of their history, environmental or topographical disamenities, style, scale and type of dwellings, or condition of their commercial districts and public spaces
- Environmental contamination and pollution

Exogenous Neighbourhood Effects. Exogenous neighbourhood effects occur if the behaviors or attitudes of one neighbor depend on the exogenous characteristics of the individual's neighbors, such as ethnicity, religion, or race. For example, a recent immigrant may feel a special comfort and security because of proximity to another from the same national background, what is often termed "ethnic solidarity." Or, expressed in a less positive version, one may have an aversion to proximity to a neighbor because of racial or religious differences and may therefore behave differently in the neighbourhood context. Yet another version of this mechanism may be termed "social cohesion:" the notion that residential contact among groups that differ in their exogenous characteristics will increase their social interactions and thereby reduce intergroup prejudices and misapprehensions.

The Likelihood of Non-Linear Neighbourhood Effects

Several of the aforementioned potential mechanisms of neighbourhood effect in all probability should manifest themselves in a non-linear, or threshold-like fashion. Indeed, because there are compelling theoretical reasons for such manifestations in certain cases, one can in principle deduce from the observation of non-linearities what the underlying causal mechanism might be (Galster, 2005). The challenge confronting researchers is therefore to experiment with statistical methods that will allow non-linear relationships to emerge from the data (for a review of these methods, see Galster / Quercia / Cortes, 2000).

There are several, not mutually exclusive, behavioral mechanisms suggested by extant theory through which a non-linear, threshold-like relationship between neighbourhood characteristics and individual outcomes measured as continuous variables may be produced. Some rely upon collective actions and social intercourse to create thresholds; others involve more atomistic attitudes and behaviors. There is also another source of non-linearity that inherently arises when considering individual outcomes that are measured in discrete, dichotomous terms. Consider each.

Collective socialization theories focus on the role that social groups exert on shaping an individual's attitudes, values and behaviors (e.g., Simmel, 1971; Weber, 1978). Such an effect can occur to the degree that: (1) the individual comes in social contact with the group, and (2) the group can exert more powerful threats or inducement to conform to its positions than competing groups. These two preconditions may involve the existence of a threshold. Given the importance of interpersonal contact in enforcing conformity, if the individuals constituting the group in question were scattered innocuously over urban space, they would be less likely to be able either to convey their positions effectively to others with whom they might come in contact or to exert much pressure to conform. It is only when a group reaches some critical mass of density or power over a predefined area that it is likely to become effective in shaping the behaviors of others. Past this threshold, as more members are recruited, the group's power to sanction non-conformists probably grows non-linearly. This is especially likely when the position of the group becomes so dominant as to become normative in the area.[1]

The basic tenet of contagion models is that if decision makers live in a community where some of their neighbors exhibit non-normative behaviors, they will be more likely to adopt these behaviors themselves. In this way, social problems are believed to be contagious, spread through peer influence. Crane (1991) proposes a formal contagion model to explain the incidence and spread of social problems. He contends that the key implication of the contagion model is that there may be critical levels of incidence of social problems in neighbourhoods. He states that if "the incidence of problems stays below a critical point, the frequency or prevalence of the problem tends to gravitate toward some relatively low-level equilibrium. But if the incidence surpasses a critical point, the process will spread explosively. In other words, an epidemic may occur, raising the incidence to an equilibrium at a much higher level" (p. 1227).

Gaming models assume that, in many decisional situations involving neighbourhoods, the personal costs and benefits of alternative courses of action are uncertain, depending on how many other actors choose various alternatives. The individual's expected payoff of an alternative varies, however, depending on the number or proportion of others who make a decision before the given actor does. Thus, the concept of a threshold amount of observed prior action is central in this type of model. The well-known prisoners' dilemma is the simplest form of gaming model (Schelling, 1978), but more sophisticated variants have been developed and applied to a variety processes occurring in neighbourhoods (Granovetter, 1978; Granovetter / Soong, 1986).

Logic also suggests that neighbourhood effect of stigmatization operates through a threshold. Opinions held by the larger community about the residents and reputation of a particular neighbourhood are unlikely to altered in a linear fashion by marginal changes in the population of the neighbourhood group that is the prime basis of the stigmatization. It is only when a critical mass of this group has been attained that public opinion is likely to turn against this place and its inhabitants.

Finally, non-linearities can arise out of the very nature of the dichotomous choice process being investigated. For example, individual choices to move, switch housing tenures, or participate in the labour market are conventionally

---

1 More modern sociological treatises closely related to collective socialization also suggest thresholds, such as Wilson's (1987) contention that as a critical mass of middle class families leave the inner-city, low-income blacks left behind become isolated from the positive role models that the erstwhile dominant class offered. Economists also have developed several mathematical treatises involving collective socialization effects in which thresholds often emerge as solutions to complex decision problems under certain assumptions (Akerlof, 1980; Galster, 1987: ch. 3; Brock / Durlauf, 2001).

modeled with a logit or probit functional relationship. This fact will have important methodological implications, as I explain below.

3.3 Measuring Appropriate Neighbourhood Characteristics

It is one thing to identify several neighbourhood processes that we posit have behavioral impacts. It is entirely another matter to ascertain how these processes can be adequately measured (Raudenbush / Sampson, 1999).

Different categories of potential neighbourhood effect mechanisms are likely more straightforward to operationalize than others. For example, many correlated effects have been readily measured with off-the-shelf administrative data that are freely available from governmental agencies, such as job accessibility variables used to operationalize spatial mismatch. Other correlated effects could be measured in obvious ways but likely require accessing administrative data that are not easily available, such as institutional resources and public services. At the other extreme, measuring endogenous effect mechanisms directly will always involve detailed, multi-item social surveys conducted with residents of neighbourhoods under investigation and (in the case of endogenous stigmatization) those outside of these places as well.

I am confident that we have developed sufficiently sophisticated survey instruments to accurately measure such things as networks, peer groups, role models, feelings of relative deprivation and competition, and stereotypes. The research challenge is one of resources; "off-the-shelf" information of the type needed above is rarely, if ever, provided by governmental social surveys. This implies the assembling of substantial resources to conduct purposive surveys of the requisite depth and breadth to measure directly the various potential neighbourhood effect mechanisms (I will suggest such a survey below). As a second-best response, one needs to develop robust proxy measures for these mechanisms involving only prosaic data, a daunting challenge indeed.

3.4 Measuring Exposure to Neighbourhood

Researches can readily identify the neighbourhoods in which subjects reside, but it is a far greater challenge to identify the degree to which they are exposed to the processes thought to convey neighbourhood effects, whether these processes work instantaneously to generate outcomes for individuals or with substantial lag or cumulative impact. As is the case with so much of research design in the context of neighbourhood effects, what is appropriate depends on which underlying process is assumed to operate.

If, e.g., endogenous stigmatization were the predominant mechanism through which neighbourhood effects transpired, one could reasonably posit that the effect would apply equally to all residents of the popularly demarcated place that is stigmatized and that the stigmatization effect would occur immediately upon a new resident's arrival. If socialization via role models were the predominant mechanism, however, the intensity of exposure to such an influence would depend on the degree to which the individual's social networks were contained within the neighbourhood. Moreover, the degree to which such a socialization process would change the individual's behavior would be directly related to the duration of the individual's exposure to these role models. Thus, within the context of the socialization mechanism we would expect neighbourhood effects to be strongest for those who have only intra-neighbourhood social relationships and who have lived there on extended time. The empirical challenge is to operationalize these exposures and duration effects and allow for the measured neighbourhood effect to be contingent upon them.

3.5 Measuring Appropriate Individual Characteristics

As is clear from equation [1], the researcher should to the extent feasible control for all time-varying [P_t] and time-invariant [P] characteristics of the sampled individuals that may be correlated with the outcome in question O_{it}. To the extent that any of these personal characteristics are correlated with both O_{it} and [N_{it}], failure to control for them will bias the estimate of θ. Of course, virtually every database available to neighbourhood research is incomplete in its coverage of desired [P_{it}] and [P_i]

The research challenge for neighbourhood researchers is to devise databases where such gaps are minimized.

But even in the most comprehensive databases the specter of [UP_{it}] and [UP] lurks. A special case of this specter results in selection biases in estimated θ.

The most basic selection issue is that certain types of individuals who have certain (unmeasured) characteristics will move from / to certain types of neighbourhoods. Any observed relationship between neighbourhood conditions and outcomes for such individuals may therefore be biased because of this systematic spatial selection process, *even if all the observable characteristics of are controlled* (Manski, 1995, 2000; Duncan / Connell / Klebanov, 1997). This selection problem can be formulated as a type of omitted variables bias. Is the observed statistical relationship between individual outcomes and neighbourhood indicative of a neighbourhood's independent effect, or merely [UP_{it}] and / or [UP] that truly affected individuals' outcomes but also (spuriously, in the extreme) led to their neighbourhood choices as well? The direction of this bias has been the subject of debate, with Jencks / Mayer (1990) and Tienda (1991) arguing that measured neighbourhood impacts are biased upwards, and Brooks-Gunn / Duncan / Aber (1997) arguing the opposite. The challenge is to overcome this selection / omitted variables bias, whatever its direction.

3.6 Endogeneity

The central challenge related to endogeneity is that some individual characteristics [P_{it}] and associated neighbourhood characteristics [N_{it}] may be mutually causal. Elsewhere I have argued (Galster, 2003; Galster, Marcotte et al., forthcoming a) that individuals jointly make decisions about [*N*], whether to own or rent their dwelling, and how long they plan on residing there. To illustrate the argument, those who wish to buy a home and remain in it an extended time will try to avoid neighbourhoods with a poor quality of life and gloomy prospects for home appreciation.

One obvious empirical implication is that certain variables comprising [P_{it}] and [N_t] may suffer from multicollinearity. Another is more subtle. If neighbourhood, tenure, and household residential mobility are simultaneously determined, and all have effects upon *O*, to what extent is the measured ij an estimate of the *independent* impact of [N_t]?

3.7 Interrelationships Among the Challenges

Even though the foregoing discussion considered six challenges to the precise, unbiased estimation of θ as if they were independent, it is readily apparent that the first four are closely interrelated. Different mechanisms through which neighbourhood effects transpire are likely associated with distinct differences in: (1) the geographic scale over which they operate; (2) how they are appropriately measured; (3) the degree to which residents are equally exposed; and (4) the speed at which exposure affects outcomes. At this point yet another complication can be introduced: different neighbourhood processes are likely to have differential consequences over a variety of interesting outcomes. Unfortunately, in most cases our theory is insufficiently developed to permit us to know with certainty which mechanisms generate which outcomes. The upshot is that researchers are challenged to investigate, for any given *O*, a wide set of potential causal mechanisms, each holding an associated suite of implications for measurement, including scale, exposure, and duration.

4. Efforts to Meet the Six Paramount Challenges

In this section I do not attempt a comprehensive review of the empirical neighbourhood effects literature. Such would not only be beyond the scope of this paper but would be redundant, given the large number of reviews extant; see Gephart (1997); van Kempen (1997); Friedrichs (1998); Robert (1999); Leventhal / Brooks-Gunn (2000); Earls / Carlson (2001); Sampson / Morenoff / Gannon-Rowley (2002); Friedrichs / Galster / Musterd (2003); Ellen / Turner

(2003); and Galster (2005). Instead, I illustrate representative responses from the literature that attempt to address the six paramount challenges.

4.1 Defining the Scale of Neighbourhood

The literature is replete with alternative specifications of neighbourhood geography because data are collected at various scales by different institutions. The U.S.-based studies typically employ the census tract, an area bounded by local planners who employ transportation routes and / or topographical features to create as demographically homogeneous areas as possible containing roughly 4,000 inhabitants, on average. Western European-based studies evince a greater variety of scales. For example, U.K.-based work has used administrative data from wards (similar to tracts), lower super output areas (roughly 1,400 inhabitants), and school catchment areas (various sizes); e.g., see Buck (2001, 2007) and Bramley / Karley (2007). Postal code areas have often been employed, though these vary from 9,000 – 17,000 inhabitants in Germany (e.g., Drever, 2004; 2007) to 1,700 in the Netherlands (e.g., Van der Laan Bouma-Doff, 2007a). Still other work has employed "city districts" of various sizes (cf. Blasius / Friedrichs, 2007; Oberwittler, 2007). Farwick (2007) has considered the "apartment complex" as neighbourhood. The challenge in examining this work is in deducing the influence of different neighbourhood scales, when so much is different across these studies.

The most direct way of answering the question "what scale(s) of neighbourhood matter in generating individual outcomes" is to conduct parallel analyses of a particular outcome where [*N*] is measured at different scales and estimates of ij are compared. Several studies have taken this tack: Buck (2001), Bolster et al. (2004) and Knies (2007). All find statistically significant relationships at various scales, but stronger correlations between outcomes and neighborhood variables when the latter are measured at smaller spatial scales.

4.2 Identifying Mechanisms of Neighbourhood Effect

As noted above, extant theory has identified numerous potential mechanisms that might explain the observed correlations between neighbourhood characteristics and a variety of individual outcomes. So what, in fact, is going on in the "black box" of neighbourhood? While current empirical evidence is not decisive, it is certainly strongly suggestive of several mechanisms described above (Van Kempen, 1997; Dietz, 2002; Sampson / Morenoff / Gannon-Rowley, 2002; Ellen / Turner, 2003; Galster, 2005). Four kinds of empirical studies have emerged that may be distinguished by their approaches: (1) studies of intra- and inter-group relations in neighbourhoods; (2) regression models of linear neighbourhood effects; (3) regression models of non-linear neighbourhood effects; and (4) miscellaneous studies. The first and fourth sets attempt to measure the mechanism directly; the others attempt to draw inferences about underlying mechanisms.

Studies of Intra- and Inter-Group Relations in Neighbourhoods

There have been numerous investigations into social processes within neighbourhoods, most of which have employed ethnographic and other qualitative approaches. One set has examined processes among low-income residents of disadvantaged neighbourhoods and another between low-income and higher-income residents of more diverse neighbourhoods. Though revealing and remarkably consistent in their findings, these studies provide circumscribed help in answering the question above because their qualitative nature cannot tell us about the relative importance of alternative mechanisms present.

Studies that have examined the social relationships in disadvantaged U.S. neighbourhoods typically have emphasized the importance of peer and role model influences (see Sullivan, 1989, Anderson, 1990, 1991; Diehr et al., 1993; South and Baumer, 2000; and Ginther, Haveman and Wolfe, 2000). One of the most notable because of its sophisticated efforts to avoid statistical bias is Case and Katz's (1991) investigation of youth in low-income Boston neighbourhoods. They find that neighbourhood peer influences among youth are strong predictors of a variety of negative behaviors, including crime, substance abuse, and lack of labor force participation.

The other set of U.S. studies has focused upon the social relationships among low-income households who are located among predominantly higher-income neighbors, often as the result of some sort of innovation, experiment, or court-mandated modification to an assisted housing program. Examples include: racial desegregation rental housing vouchers (Rosenbaum, 1991, 1995; Rosenbaum et al., 1991; Rosenbaum / Reynolds / DeLuca, 2002; Mendenhall, 2004), Moving To Opportunity class desegregation housing vouchers (Popkin / Harris / Cunningham, 2002; Rosenbaum / Harris / Denton, 2003), scattered-site public housing (Briggs, 1997, 1998; Kleit, 2001a, 2001b, 2002, 2005), and mixed-income public or private developments (Schill, 1997; Clampet-Lundquist, 2004)

In sum, these studies consistently show that the social relationships among members of different economic groups are quite limited, even within the same neighbourhood or housing complex. Members of the lower-status group often do not take advantage of propinquity to broaden their "weak ties" and enhance the resource-producing potential of their networks, instead often restricting their networks to nearby members of their own group or to those remaining in the "old neighbourhood". This suggests that social networking may be a powerful neighbourhood force *among* members of a given group, but less so in an inter-group context, where perhaps the role model and social control mechanisms operate more strongly. These studies also are noteworthy for what they did *not* find: evidence of relative deprivation or competition that led to worse outcomes for the less-advantaged neighbors.

Regression Coefficients from Models of Linear Neighbourhood Effects

A second source of information about neighbourhood effect mechanisms can be gleaned inferentially from regression analyses of non-experimental data for individual households and their neighbourhoods, typically based on a nationally representative, longitudinal sample. The notion is that if particular sorts of descriptors within a neighbourhood's population profile prove to be statistically and economically significant predictors of outcomes, these may be suggestive of the underlying processes shaping given outcomes.

Here the U.S. literature suggests that both the "advantaged" and the "disadvantaged" aspects of the neighbourhood's population need to be included in predicting most outcomes (though the latter seems more important for most outcomes), and different neighbourhood aspects predict different outcomes. On this point, the theoretical and empirical research on neighbourhood effects summarized in Brooks-Gunn / Duncan / Aber (1997) seems particularly compelling. They argue that some measure of the of "high risk" neighbors is important, where "risk" is typically operationalized in U.S. empirical work as neighbourhood rates of poverty, single-parent households, idleness among adults, or welfare benefit receipt. So, too, are measures of a conceptually distinct effect: the absence or presence of more affluent, middle-class neighbors, operationalized as adults with college degrees or adults in "middle class" occupations. More recent studies have reached similar conclusions in several international contexts; see Kohen et al. (2002); Kauppinen (2004), Musterd / Andersson (2005), and Andersson et al. (2007).

But is it the socioeconomic composition of neighbourhood *per se* that matters, or the lack of social order and cohesion that might be associated with it, as first suggested by Aneshensel / Sucoff (1996)? It appears that it is not social mix alone or directly that may influence outcomes but, rather, the internal social dynamics of the place that often is only partly measured by its socioeconomic status (see the review in Sampson / Morenoff / Gannon-Rowley, 2002; and Turley, 2003). This theme has been emphasized in a number of studies by Sampson and his colleagues (Sampson, 1992; 1997; Sampson / Groves, 1989; Sampson / Raudenbush / Earls, 1997; Sampson / Morenoff / Earls, 1999; Morenoff / Sampson / Raudenbush, 2001). To understand the effects of disadvantaged neighbourhoods on mental distress and criminality, they argue, one must understand their degree of social organization, which entails the context of community norms, values and structures enveloping residents' behaviors (what has been labeled as "collective efficacy"). This raises the issue, addressed further below, of how well readily available proxies measure the social processes underlying neighbourhood effects.

Regression Coefficients from Regression Models of Non-Linear Neighbourhood Effects

Different types of intra-neighbourhood processes yield distinctive, typically non-linear functional forms for the relationship between the percentage of disadvantaged residents in a neighbourhood and the amount of externality being generated (Galster, 2007a). This can be used to draw out implications for underlying mechanisms of neighbourhood effects if the statistical procedures used to investigate the relationship between a neighbourhood indicator and an individual outcome permit the estimation of non-linear relationships.

Unfortunately, few extant empirical studies test for non-linear relationships between neighbourhood poverty conditions and various individual outcomes. The key U.S.-based exceptions include: Krivo / Peterson (1996), Vartanian (1999a, b), and Weinberg / Reagan / Yankow (2004). A prior analysis (Galster, 2002) suggests that the independent impacts of neighbourhood poverty rates in encouraging negative outcomes for individuals like criminal behavior, school leaving, and duration of poverty spells appear to be nil unless the neighbourhood exceeds about 20 % poverty, whereupon the externality effects grow rapidly until the neighbourhood reaches approximately 40 % poverty. Subsequent increases in the poverty population appear to have little marginal external effect. Analogously, the independent impacts of neighbourhood poverty rates in discouraging positive behaviors, such as employment, appear to be nil unless the neighbourhood exceeds about 15 % poverty, whereupon the effects grow rapidly until the neighbourhood reaches roughly 30 % poverty. Again, subsequent increases in poverty appear to have little marginal effect.

As far as non-linear relationships between individual outcomes and neighbourhood percentages of affluent residents in the U.S., the work of Crane (1991), Duncan / Connell / Klebanov (1997), and Chase-Lansdale et al. (1997) is relevant. Unfortunately, though they all suggest the existence of a threshold of affluence they differ on where this occurs. Crane's (1991) analysis finds strong evidence of epidemic-like effects on both secondary school leaving and teenage childbearing associated with the share of affluent (professional-managerial occupation) neighbors dropping below five percent. For the same outcome, Duncan et al. (1997) find that the effect of percentage of affluent neighbors becomes dramatically stronger when the percentage exceeds the national mean for the neighbourhood. Chase-Lansdale et al. (1997) find that the percentage of affluent neighbors is positively associated with higher intellectual functioning scores for black children and female children only when the percentage exceeds the 25th percentile and is less than the 75th percentile; for other children the effect is linear. Both the Duncan et al. (1997) and Chase-Lansdale et al. (1997) findings support the notion of collective socialization.

Turley (2003) analyzes behavioral and psychological test scores for youth as measured in a special supplement of the U.S. Panel Study of Income Dynamics. She relates these scores to the median family income of the census tract, so one cannot be certain whether the observed relationship is being generated by the relative share of affluent or poor residents. She tests for nonlinearities by employing a quadratic version of neighbourhood income and finds that it is statistically significant and negative for the self-esteem outcome, implying that improving the economic environment of youth has a much greater impact for those initially in disadvantaged circumstances.

The European evidence related to potential non-linear neighbourhood effects is even more limited and often contradictory (see the review in Galster, 2007b). Most relevant evidence focuses on individual economic outcomes as they relate to percentages of disadvantaged neighbors. Here the findings regarding nonlinearities are inconsistent in the extreme; cf. Ostendorf / Musterd / de Vos, (2001); Buck (2001); Musterd / Ostendorf / de Vos (2003); Van der Klaauw / van Ours (2003); Gordon / Monastiriotis (2006); Musterd / Andersson (2005); Oberwittler (2007). The two studies using European data to investigate potential nonlinear effects of affluent neighbors on children's education both find increasing marginal positive effects; Kauppinen (2004) and Gordon / Monastiriotis (2006). Van der Laan Bouma-Doff (2007a) discovers that the labor force participation of ethnic minorities in Rotterdam is inversely related to the percentage of own-group neighbors only when that percentage exceeds 20 percent. In a separate study (2007b), she finds that ethnic minorities have substantial social interactions with native Dutch neighbors only after the share of Dutch neighbors exceeds 60 percent. Buck (2007) observes a variety of non-linearities and thresholds associated with relationships between measures of social capital and an index of deprivation in U.K. neighbourhoods. Galster et al. (2007) use Swedish register data to explore the relationships between neighbourhood income mix and subsequent earnings of adults. They find a wide variety of nonlinear neighbourhood effects, which they claim are consistent with negative role modeling and job information network mechanisms.

Miscellaneous Studies of Neighbourhood Mechanisms

This last category of studies cannot be easily labeled either by focus or method, and addresses a variety of prospective mechanisms. One group, for example, establishes support for a variety of correlated neighbourhood effects mechanisms. Numerous studies (see reviews by Kain, 1992; Ihlanfeldt, 1999) have investigated the issue of differential accessibility to work (the "spatial mismatch" hypothesis) in the U.S. context. This literature generally suggests that mismatch can be an important aspect of opportunity differentials in at least some American metropolitan areas, though it seems of less importance than the social conditions of neighbourhoods (O'Regan / Quigley, 1996; Weinberg et al. 2004).

Other studies have documented the differences in both public services and private institutional resources serving different U.S. neighbourhoods (e.g., Kozol, 1991; Wolman et al., 1991; Card / Krueger, 1992; Drier / Mollenkopf / Swanstron, 2004). Still others have shown how the internal workings of institutions serving poor communities shape expectations and life chances of their clientele (Rasmussen, 1994, Bauder, 2001). Although the evidence linking these differences to various outcomes for children has been subject to challenge (e.g., Burtless, 1996; Morenoff / Sampson / Raudenbush, 2001; Popkin / Harris / Cunningham, 2002), there is increasing evidentiary prominence of some institutions, such as the public schools, serving as important mediators of neighbourhood effects in the U.S. (Ennett et al., 1997; Teitler / Weiss, 1996). The comparative influences of neighbourhood and school effects in the U.K. has been investigated by Bramley / Karley (2007).

Other literature, both qualitative and quantitative, has documented how exposure to violence may produce serious and long lasting emotional trauma for young children (e.g., Martinez / Richters, 1993; Richters / Martinez, 1993; Aneshensel / Sucoff, 1996). The U.S Moving To Opportunity (MTO) demonstration study and the Yonkers Family and Community Survey also provided strong support for the perceived importance of this factor, since safety concerns were cited as a prime reason for participating in these mobility programs by most public housing families (Briggs, 1997; Goering / Feins, 2003).

Galster / Santiago (2006) provide a unique study of parental perceptions of neighbourhood effect mechanisms. Findings indicate that low-income parents perceive the following primary neighbourhood mechanisms at these frequencies: (1) the degree (or lack) of social norms and collective efficacy (24 %); (2) influence of children's peers (12 %); (3) exposure to crime and violence (11 %); and (4) the presence and quality of institutional resources (3 %). Approximately one-third of all parents reported that their neighbourhood had no impact at all on their children, citing that their children were either "too young" to be affected by these mechanisms or that parents had sufficient resources to buffer any deleterious effects of the neighbourhood. Parents residing in high-poverty neighbourhoods were much more likely to perceive a neighbourhood effect, however.

Finally, U.S.-based studies have observed that inter-ethnic group tolerance and subsequent social contacts have been enhanced with greater interracial neighbourhood contacts, especially earlier in life (Allport, 1954; Ihlanfeldt / Scafidi, 2002; Emerson / Kimbro / Yancey, 2002). This implies that there may be some case for the social solidarity neighbourhood effect mechanism. The picture is less clear from Western European evidence (e.g., see Farwick, 2007).

4.3 Measuring Appropriate Neighbourhood Characteristics

There have been many efforts on both sides of the Atlantic to measure directly the social processes within neighbourhoods that, in theory, produce endogenous neighbourhood effects. These efforts have taken the form of purposive social surveys administered at a high sampling density within a limited number of neighbourhoods. These surveys often employ multi-item scales to operationalize sophisticated measures of such things as social networks, inter-group interactions and stereotypes, perceptions of disorder and anti-social behavior, neighbourhood evaluations, etc. Notable examples of these efforts include Sampson / Raudenbush / Earls (1997); Friedrichs / Blasius (2003); Farwick (2007), Oberwittler (2007), Blasius / Friedrichs (2007), and Permentier / Bolt / Ham (2007). Unfortunately, these efforts involve resource-intensive data collection activities, and thus are rarely (if ever) replicated in the same neighbourhoods.

More common, neighbourhood-effects researchers have relied upon more general social surveys (sometimes in a panel format) that have been collected by other entities for different or wider-ranging purposes. This raises the question of whether these databases may contain reasonable proxies for the unmeasured social processes. Several notable efforts to discover such have been conducted.

Potential Proxies for Intra-Neighbourhood Social Processes

There are several studies that find strong evidence that U.S. census tract-level socioeconomic and demographic indicators (often collapsed into factor indices) are strongly related to various intra-neighbourhood social processes, networks, and subjective impressions held by neighbors, as measured by surveys of residents. However, the studies are not perfectly consistent, and suggest that tract-level socioeconomic-demographic indicators are, at best, imperfect proxies (Sampson / Morenoff / Gannon-Rowley, 2002).

Sampson / Raudenbush / Earls (1997) interviewed residents in 343 Chicago "neighbourhood clusters" composed of about 8,000 people each. They developed multi-item scales of "informal social control" and "social cohesion and trust," which they found so highly correlated that they could be combined into a single index of "collective efficacy." The collective efficacy index was, in turn, regressed on three composite factor-score indexes based on aggregate, census data for the neighbourhoods: "concentrated disadvantage," "immigrant concentration", and "residential stability". The authors find that all were highly statistically significant predictors of collective efficacy (stability was positively correlated). All three aggregate level indicators also proved strongly correlated with residents' perceptions of neighbourhood violence, and in Sampson (1997) the level of youth delinquency.

A companion study related these same three neighbourhood factors to three different aspects of social organization within the neighbourhood, using a sample of 238 British communities (Sampson / Groves, 1989). They found that: neighbourhood residential stability was directly related to local friendship networks, neighbourhood socioeconomic status was inversely related to unsupervised peer groups and directly related to organizational participation, and neighbourhood ethnic heterogeneity was directly related to unsupervised peer groups.

In related work, Sampson / Morenoff / Earls (1999) statistically relate three dimensions of social capital for children's well-being to 1990 census tract information:

- "intergenerational closure" [degree to which adults and children in community are linked]
- "reciprocated exchange" [intensity of inter-family and -adult interaction with respect to child rearing]
- "expectations for informal social control of children" [whether adults expect each other to intervene on behalf of children]

Both the first two were strongly related to neighbourhood stability and concentrated affluence, not concentrated poverty; the last was negatively related to concentrated poverty.

Cook / Shagle / Degirmencioglu (1997) conducted interviews of parents in 137 census tracts in Prince George's County, MD, and their 11 – 15 year-old offspring in their local middle schools. A comprehensive array of subjective multi-item scales related to "social process" were developed from these surveys, ranging from social control and cohesion, to neighbourhood resources, satisfaction, and participation rates; they were aggregated to the tract level. These scales were then analyzed in light of ten census tract variables. They found that they were able to use tract demographic variables to predict "very high percentages of the neighbourhood-level variation in social process" [p. 109 – 110]. Correlations among the neighbourhood social process variables and the tract demographics averaged .37. The combination of percentage white (or black), median income, and percentage in professional-technical occupations alone produced a multiple R of .77 when predicting variation in a global neighbourhood social process measure. Their principal components analysis resulted in one dominant factor, wherein virtually all the social process and tract demographic variables loaded heavily. They conclude that they "do not find clear demarcation into process and demographic factors" [p. 113].

Elliott et al. (1996) gathered statistical and interview information from neighbourhoods in Chicago and Denver. From aggregating parents' responses about their neighbourhoods they created three measures of neighbourhood organization: informal control, social integration, and informal networks. Interviews with youths in these areas produced three constructs related to their outcomes: "pro-social competence" (personal efficacy, educational performance, activities, and expectations, commitment to conventionality); "conventional friends" (proportions of friends who are pro-social, and proportion who are delinquents); "problem behaviors" (variety of criminal behaviors and drug usage types). They found that tract-level factor-score "neighbourhood disadvantage" was strong by negatively correlated with informal control in both sites and social integration in Denver, but was unrelated to informal social networks in either site.

Coulton / Korbin / Su (1999) interviewed parents in 20 different block groups in Cleveland and derived neighbourhood-level subjective measures of neighbourhood quality, facilities, disorder, and control over children. These were then correlated with three factor-analyzed objective indices of neighbourhood structure available from administrative databases: impoverishment, child care burden, and residential instability. Only two pairs of measures (out of a possible 12) proved statistically significantly related: perceived quality and neighbourhood impoverishment score and perceived disorder and neighbourhood impoverishment score.

Kohen / Brooks-Gunn / Leventhal / Hertzman (2002) examined a national sample of Canadian youth and their neighbourhoods during the 1990s. They found that the neighbourhood statistical variables: percent poor, percent affluent and percent female heads all correlated to a significant degree (rho in absolute value between .24 – .30) with respondents' subjective assessments of social disorder. The neighbourhood percent poor was correlated with the subjective assessment of social cohesion at .21.

Potential Proxies for Extra-Neighbourhood Processes

Unfortunately, in contrast to intra-neighbourhood social processes, there is little to suggest appropriate proxy measures of such extra-neighbourhood processes as stigmatization. To my knowledge, only one study has attempted to statistically relate perceptions of key actors about neighbourhoods to socio-economic or demographic indicators measured in those places. Permentier / Bolt / Ham (2007) ask households and real estate agents to evaluate a variety of neighbourhoods in their city of Utrecht in which they do not live, on multiple grounds. They find that neighbourhood reputations are significantly correlated with their socio-economic characteristics, while their physical and functional features are of less importance. Other correlated effects typically have seen measured directly, if incompletely, as noted above.

Conclusions about Proxies for Neighbourhood Processes

U.S. evidence suggests that readily available, census tracts data on socio-economic and demographic of composition administrative may serve as reasonable operationalizations of intra-neighbourhood social processes, though a wide range of such variables should be used, and the set varies depending on the outcome in question being modeled. However, these indicators are imperfect measures, so there remains a crucial need for future research efforts to measure such social process variables directly (Gephart, 1997; Friedrichs, 1998; Raudenbush / Sampson, 1999; Sampson / Morenoff / Gannon-Rowley, 2002). Besides those noted above, the development of proxy measures of institutional resources, organizational participation, collective supervision of youth, clarity and consensus regarding group norms, intra- and extra-neighbourhood social networks for adults and children, are especially salient. In addition, much more needs to be done to measure perceptions held by external actors that may affect opportunities of neighbourhood residents and, thereby, their behaviors.

The Methodological Importance of Non-Linear Effects of Neighbourhood Characteristics

Even if neighbourhood social processes were directly and precisely measured, it still may not be possible to distinguish statistically the source of some observed correlation between [*N*] and *O*, what Manski (1993, 2000) has called the "reflection problem." Manski (1993, 2000) demonstrates that it is mathematically impossible to distinguish endogenous and exogenous processes if both are related in a linear fashion to a continuous variable measuring behavioral outcomes.

There are several potential avenues out of this bind (Manski, 2000). For our purposes, however, one of the most useful is non-linearity. If the endogenous effect occurs in a non-linear fashion it is possible to identify it empirically. Of course, the prior theoretical and empirical sections suggest strongly that this is precisely the case for a wide range of behaviors of interest. Moreover, Brock / Durlauf (2001) have explored the non-linearity associated with a dichotomous outcome, and have developed a discrete choice model of social interactions wherein the endogenous effect can be clearly identified. In sum, exploring non-linearity in neighbourhood effects is not merely an academic curiosity; it may be considered a fundamental empirical requirement in advancing the field.

Moreover, non-linearity permits the unambiguous clarification of whether neighbourhood effects are primarily generated by endogenous or exogenous intra-neighbourhood processes. Such clarification holds important implications for the expected magnitude of a potential policy impact. Endogenous processes imply social multipliers among neighbors. Thus, a policy that positively affects one individual or household may end up yielding a multiplied benefit as the altered behavior of the direct beneficiary of the policy is spread to neighbors (Dietz, 2002).

Considerably more attention therefore needs to be paid to exploring non-linear relationships between *O* and [*N*] in future investigations on both sides of the Atlantic, regardless of how [*N*] is measured. However, it would indeed be surprising were these investigations to reveal cross-national similarities in non-linear neighbourhood effects, given the differences in welfare states, labour markets, race and class segregation, and housing policies (Musterd, 2002). Indeed, the aforementioned brief review of U.S. and Western European evidence confirms this suspicion.

4.4 Measuring Exposure to Neighbourhood

It is rare for a study to model the magnitude of the endogenous neighbourhood effect as contingent upon the spatial extent of the individual's social networks. In an exceptional study, Farwick (2007) investigates the probability of Turkish immigrants having native German friends as a function of ethnic composition of the apartment building. He finds an inverse relationship between this probability and the proportion of non-Germans in the building, but only if most of the Turkish individuals' social networks were limited to their buildings.

There have been a few attempts to measure neighbourhood duration effects. Wheaton / Clarke (2003) use a cross-nested, random effects model applied to National Survey of Children data to assess current and past neighbourhood effects on children's health outcomes. They find a lagged effect of neighbourhood socioeconomic indicators on early adult mental health, which they see as supporting hypotheses of cumulative mediating effect of and chronic ambient stress in the neighbourhood. Galster / Marcotte et al. (2007) use neighbourhood poverty rate averaged over all years of childhood as a predictor of multiple outcomes for young adults. Compared with otherwise identical children raised by otherwise identical parents in a neighbourhood with a low average poverty rate of five (5) percent, children experiencing an average 40 percent rate are predicted through their simulation with estimated parameters to have a: (1) 24 percentage-point greater chance of having a child before age 18; (2) 14 percentage-point lower probability of graduating from high school; (3) 10 percentage-point lower probability of graduating from college; and (4) $13,334 lower annual earnings, all else equal.

4.5 Measuring Appropriate Individual Characteristics

There have been three general approaches adopted in response to the challenge of selection bias following from omitted individual characteristics. The first two use experimental or natural designs to generate random or quasi-random assignments of households to neighbourhoods. The last approach consists of a variety of econometric techniques applied to non-experimentally generated data.

Experimental Evidence from Random Assignment

Data on outcomes that can be produced by an experimental design whereby individuals or households are randomly assigned to different neighbourhoods clearly is the preferred method for avoiding biases from selection. In this regard, the U.S. Moving To Opportunity (MTO) demonstration has been touted conventionally as *the* study from which to draw conclusions about the magnitude of neighbourhood effects (e.g., Ludwig / Duncan / Pinkston, 2000; Katz / Kling / Liebman, 2001; Ludwig / Ladd / Duncan, 2001; Ludwig / Duncan / Hirschfield, 2001; Rosenbaum / Harris, 2001; Goering / Feins, 2003). Although the research design indeed randomly assigns those public housing residents who volunteer to one of three experimental groups (controls remaining in public housing in disadvantaged neighbourhoods; recipients of rental vouchers; recipients of rental vouchers and relocation assistance who had to move to neighbourhoods with less than 10 percent poverty rates), it does not fully control the assignment of neighbourhood characteristics of the two experimental groups receiving tenant-based rental subsidies, and thus does not fully purge the relationship between neighbourhood characteristics and unmeasured individual characteristics (Sampson / Morenoff / Gannon-Rowley, 2000). Of course, the group that receives only a rental subsidy with no mobility counseling and no geographic restrictions can select from a wide range of neighbourhoods. But even the treatment group receiving intensive mobility counseling and assistance, though constrained to move initially to a neighbourhood with less than 10 percent poverty rates, has the ability nevertheless to choose neighbourhoods varying on their school quality, home ownership rates, racial composition, local institutional resources, etc. Moreover, subsequent to their initial, constrained location they are free after one year to move to different, higher-poverty neighbourhoods should they choose; indeed, 85 percent have done so (Kingsley / Pettit, 2007).

Thus, MTO does not fully finesse the selection bias issue. Unless a social experiment is designed wherein the precise neighbourhood conditions are randomly assigned to participants and then these locations fixed for a substantial period, data gathered will still need to be analyzed using one of the econometric methods described below.

Quasi-Random Assignment Natural Experiments

It is sometimes possible to observe interventions into households' residential locations that mimic random assignment. In this way they may be viewed as second-best options for removing selection effects.

There are several prominent examples of such opportunistic research that have provided valuable insights into U.S. neighbourhood impacts. The Gautreaux (Chicago) and Yonkers (NY) court-ordered, public housing racial-ethnic desegregation programs (Rosenbaum, 1995; Rubinowitz / Rosenbaum, 2000;

Briggs, 1997, 1998; Fauth / Leventhal / Brooks-Gunn, 2003a, b) are illustrative. The Gautreaux study compares two groups of Black tenants originally residing public housing who moved out to private apartments using rental vouchers: movers to low-poverty, low-minority suburban neighbourhoods and movers to low-minority but higher-poverty, city neighbourhoods. The Yonkers study compares a combined sample of Black and Latino movers to low-minority, low-poverty neighbourhoods in Yonkers (NY), to a similar sample of those who had applied to move out of high-poverty, predominantly minority-occupied neighbourhoods in the city but were not randomly selected to do so. In other national contexts, Oreopolis (2003) compared outcomes for young adults whose families had been assigned to public housing in Toronto and those whose parents occupied private-sector housing. Edin / Fredricksson / Aslund (2003) and Aslund / Fredricksson (2005) analyze neighbourhood effects for immigrants relocated across Sweden as part of a government-sponsored settlement plan.

Although these natural experiments may indeed provide some exogenous variation in neighbourhood locations, the selection problems are unlikely to be avoided completely. There typically is selection involved in who chooses to participate in these programs. In some cases (Gautreaux, e.g.), participants have some non-trivial latitude in which locations they choose, both initially and subsequently. In other cases (Yonkers, e.g.), there are limitations in the range of neighbourhoods to which participants moved. Finally, many programs must contend with low take-up rates, which likely reduce the power to identify program experimental effects.

There are several prominent examples of such opportunistic research that have provided valuable insights into the mechanisms of neighbourhood impact that are less likely to be tainted by selection, however. Rosenbaum / Reynolds / DeLuca (2002) recently probed qualitatively how the neighbourhoods of *Gautreaux* program movers into Chicago suburbs have enhanced their self-efficacy. Similarly, Briggs (1997, 1998) assessed social relationships through interviews with poor, minority youth who moved to scattered-site public housing in white, middle class neighbourhoods under the auspices of the *Yonkers* (NY) desegregation consent decree. Kleit (2001a, b, 2002) conducted insightful social network analysis of low-income residents of mixed-income housing developments mandated by inclusionary zoning regulations in Montgomery County, MD.

Econometric Models Based on Non-Experimental Data

Most American and Western European studies of neighbourhood effects have used cross-sectional or longitudinal data collected from surveys of individual households residing in a variety of neighbourhoods as a result of mundane factors, not random assignment or idiosyncratic public policies. They use multiple regression or other multivariate analysis techniques to control for $[P_i]$ and $[P_{it}]$ to ascertain the relationship between $[N]$ and a variety of outcomes.

Several methods have been used to deal with the omitted variables-selection issue; only the first two are applicable to both panel and cross-sectional databases; the others require at least one repeated observation per individual.

Instrumenting Neighbourhood. A core technique for dealing with selection bias is using instrumental variables (IV). It can be implemented with either cross-sectional or panel data. In the first stage of this technique, a regression is estimated wherein the characteristic of neighbourhood in question is regressed on one or more explanatory variables that, ideally, are highly correlated with the neighbourhood characteristic but uncorrelated with unmeasured individual characteristics and are not causally related to the outcome in question (Murray, 2006). The predicted values for the neighbourhood characteristic yielded by this first stage regression, which presumably are purged of spurious correlation with unmeasured parental characteristics, are employed as the IV in a second-stage regression explaining outcomes. These IV's ideally capture the exogenous variation in the [N]. The challenge of this method, of course, is identifying first-stage variables that reasonably meet the aforementioned criteria.

In the seminal example of instrumental variables applied to residential neighbourhood, Foster / McLanahan (1996) used city-wide labor market conditions as identifying variables instrumenting for neighbourhood high school dropout rates in a model predicting individual children's school dropout probabilities. These city-wide instruments have several shortcomings, however. First, not only the neighbourhood context but also the city context may influence outcomes for a given neighbourhood's residents. Put differently, the "opportunity structure" has several spatial scales of potential importance (Galster / Killen, 1995). Thus, the neighbourhood variable instrumented in the above fashion will embody an amalgam of both spatial scales; the distinct impacts of the neighbourhood scale cannot be discerned. Second, if families choose their city on the basis of the average quality of its neighbourhoods (or particular neighbourhoods of intended residence), the instrument will not be completely purged of unmeasured parental characteristics. Third, the city-level variable's correlation with the corresponding tract-level variable may be modest, raising the specter of a weak instrument (Murray, 2006).

More recent applications of IVs have been more persuasive. For example, Moschion (2007) analyzes the relationship between an individual French woman's probability of participating in the labor market as a function of the labor force participation rates of her nearest female neighbors. She instruments for the latter with the gender mix of these neighbors' children (for those neighboring women who have two or more children).

Modeling Selection Explicitly. This strategy also involves a two-step process. In the first, a model is estimated where elements of [N_{it}] are regressed on individual characteristics [P_{it}], [P_i]. The (transformations of) predicted values of these selection equations are then added to equation [1] to control explicitly for selection. To my knowledge, this strategy has not been applied in the neighbourhood effects literature, probably because of its limitations. First, datasets often do not provide sufficient data on individuals to precisely estimate the selection equation. Second, such predictors must include some powerful ones that do not include $[P_i]$ and $[P_{it}]$ employed in the second-stage model [1]. Third, if measures for $[UP_i]$ and $[UP_{it}]$ are unavailable for [1] they will be unavailable for the first-stage selection equation, and the fundamental problem is not skirted.

Differencing. When observations of neighbourhood and individual outcomes occur at two points in time, a differencing approach can be applied. The panel structure of the data allows one to write analogues of equation [1] for both times t and $t + 1$. Taking the difference in these two equations, thereby expressing all variables as changes over time, eliminates the unobserved fixed (time-invariant) effect [*UP*]. However, it does not remove the potential role of unobserved, time-varying effects $[UP_t]$ and $[UP_{t+1}]$. This approach has been used by Bolster et al. (2004) and Galster, Andersson et al. (2007) in the study of neighbourhood effects. The potential problem with this approach is that the variation in the key variables of interest (*O*, [*N*]) is likely reduced by differencing, making it more challenging statistically to obtain precise parameter estimates.

Fixed Effects. A fixed-effect approach requires a panel dataset with multiple observations of all variables in equation [1] over time. Under these circumstances, $[UP_i]$ can be collapsed into a set of person-specific dummy variables. This strategy has been applied by Weinberg / Reagan / Yankow (2004) and Knies (2007), for example. The first shortcoming of this approach is that it consumes substantial degrees of freedom. The second is that it does not control for time-varying individual characteristics $[UP_{it}]$.

Sibling Studies. Sibling studies investigate the effect of neighbourhoods on children by exploiting longitudinal datasets with large samples of siblings (Aaronson, 1997, 1998; Plotnick / Hoffman, 2000). Assuming that families do not move across neighbourhoods in response to differences in unmeasured characteristics of children, one can use the inter-temporal variations in neighbourhood conditions experienced by the family to assess impacts on siblings. The central logic is that estimating a model of the *differences* in outcomes between siblings allows the researcher to eliminate the unobserved parental fixed effect [*UP*] and thus more accurately discern the impacts of different neighbourhood environments the siblings may have experienced at different ages.

To estimate this specification accurately, however, several concerns must be addressed (Aaronson, 1998). First, if parents' effectiveness in parenting evolves over time, younger children may be exposed to a different unobserved effect than their older siblings. The analysis should therefore control for birth order. Second, outcomes may be affected by *changes* in family circumstances (unemployment, divorce, etc.) that also may affect neighbourhood choice. This implies that the analysis must control to the extent possible for such measured changes, and assume that they are changing consonant with unmeasured characteristic changes [UP_t]. Third, there remains a concern that typically there is limited variation in the characteristics of neighbourhoods that families move among under circumstances *not* associated with major changes in family circumstances (Levine / Painter, 2000), resulting in imprecise estimates (Aaronson, 1998). Fourth is the problem of small samples of siblings typically available even in the largest datasets

4.6 Endogeneity

The literature is replete with examples of efforts to estimate econometric models of elements of the joint neighbourhood / ownership status / residential mobility expectation selection that underpins the endogeneity problem. The modeling of housing ownership and mobility as a joint decision has, for example, become quite conventional; see Zorn (1988), and Ioannides / Kan (1996) for seminal work. Similarly, modeling tenure choice jointly with expected future mobility has been undertaken for some time; see Boehm (1981), Ioannides (1987) and Rosenthal (1988). In a recent and noteworthy work, Kan (2000) models three simultaneous equations predicting: current year's housing ownership choice, current year's mobility choice, and expected future mobility behavior. Only one work to my knowledge has modeled the joint housing ownership / neighbourhood choice process: Deng / Ross / Wachter (2003). More to the point, none has tried to use these predictions in a two-stage selection-adjustment strategy (described above) to control for endogeneity in a model estimating the effect of neighbourhood choice on subsequent individual outcomes

5. Promising New Directions

5.1 Defining the Scale of Neighbourhood

In this realm I think that further efforts that conduct within-sample tests of the effect on θ from varying the scale at which [N] is measured hold a good deal of promise. As noted above, a few studies have already done so, with interesting consequences. A particularly fertile approach is one that defines concentric circle ("bespoke") neighbourhoods of varying radii centered on each sampled individual, using geographical information system techniques. With this technique one can readily compare estimates of θ across a wide variety of "neighbourhoods" defined at various radii around the individual. Seminal illustrations of this are provided by Bolster et al. (2004) and Andersson /

Musterd (2006). A more technically challenging but potentially intriguing advance here would be to overlay street and topographical patterns around the individual instead of concentric circles, given the evidence that such human-made and natural structures shape the spatial patterns of social interactions (Grannis, 1998).

The data requirements for explorations using bespoke neighbourhoods are intensive, however. It is most feasible when it can be applied to a database containing information about all households in the geographic area under investigation, as is the case in social register-based datasets in Sweden and the Netherlands, for example.

5.2 Identifying Mechanisms of Neighbourhood Effect

Qualitative and ethnographic research has and will hopefully continue to provide invaluable insights into the processes that lead to neighbourhood effects. I thus add my voice to others encouraging such efforts previously (Ellen / Turner, 2003). However, such studies will, I fear, inevitably fall short in helping us *quantify* which particular mechanisms may dominate the causal processes in which circumstances. Here is where I think that further explorations with econometric analyses that employ non-linear relationships between [N] and O and stratify by advantaged and disadvantaged groups (so that the nature of the inter-neighbor externalities can be more clearly seen) hold great promise. For fuller explanation, see Galster (2007a, b). An example of how this can be done is provided by Galster / Andersson, et al. (2007).

5.3 Measuring Appropriate Neighbourhood Characteristics

Raudenbush / Sampson (1999) have already provided a comprehensive and creative analysis of how the measurement of neighbourhood characteristics can fruitfully be advanced, so I will not attempt to tread heavily here. In sum, they argue that survey-based neighbourhood assessments can usefully be constructed by aggregating over multiple-item responses of multiple informants in that place. They experiment with measures derived from interviews, direct observations, and videotapes of streetscapes, and then relate them to theoretically related measures obtained from official administrative data from the same areas.

Following Raudenbush / Sampson (1999) there remains a crucial need for neighbourhood effects researchers to measure variables related to organizational participation, collective supervision of youth, clarity and consensus regarding group norms, and intra- and extra-neighbourhood social networks for adults and children. The same is true for robust measures of neighbourhood institutional resources and extra-neighbourhood processes involving, e.g., stigmatizing of neighbourhood by key actors. This probably will require the merging of information from a variety of sources, ranging from administrative databases to purposive social surveys.

5.4 Measuring Exposure to Neighbourhood

In responding to this challenge there are several directions I would suggest. First, theory and limited evidence suggests that neighbourhood effects should be stronger for those whose social worlds are more comprehensively bound up in them. This, in turn, suggests that the sociological literature on the individual correlates of the geographic extent of social relationships offers a rich vein of useful information. At a heuristic level, if this literature suggests that individual characteristic Z strongly discriminates among those with different geographic extents of social relationships, our sample for estimating equation [1] might well be stratified according to Z. In a more precise way, the literature may provide parameters of a strongly predictive multivariate equation of geographic extents of social relationships. These, in turn, could be used to develop "propensity scores" of the same for each individual in our sample, presuming that we do not have direct measures of the geographic extents of their social relationships but do have measures of their predictive variables. Finally, these propensity scores could be interacted with the $[N]$ variables in our model [1], as per theory.

To test for timing and duration effects, I believe it may be fruitful to focus in a panel study on a subset of individuals who do not move over some extended period. For them one can estimate a series of models like [1] for some outcome O in year t, except that the period over which $[N]$ is measured differs in each. In one variant, $[N]$ might be measured for t only; in another, $t-1$; in another, $t-2$. Other variants could test for duration effects by comparing $[N]$ measured as average scores over $t-1, \ldots, 1-2$, or $t-1, \ldots, 1-n$. Still other variants might flag the *extreme* values of $[N]$ experienced during the period, to assess this sort of exposure mechanism.

5.5 Measuring Appropriate Individual Characteristics

Recall that a central methodological hurdle that quantitative studies of neighbourhood impact must surmount relates to unobserved individual (or parental) characteristics that simultaneously may be guiding both neighbourhood choice and individual (or child and youth) outcomes. Obviously, if we can measure directly a wider array of such individual (or parental) characteristics as motivations (or parenting behaviors), the issue of selection can be dealt with in a straightforward manner with control variables, instead of the more challenging econometric approaches discussed above. Thus, the challenge is to gather data that directly allow us to measure comprehensively key characteristics of individuals (or their parents) in ways that minimize the need for econometric fixes. Below I will suggest such a data collection exercise.

Short of this, there are two promising strategies for dealing with unobserved individual characteristics that can produce selection bias. The first involves confining the panel analysis to the subset of individuals who do not move during a period, thereby removing the element of selection that may be associated with both time-invariant effects $[UP_i]$ and time-varying effects $[UP_{it}]$. If such a period were reasonably lengthy, one would expect to observe sufficient exogenous variation in neighbourhood characteristics, which by definition cannot be correlated with either fixed- or time-varying unobserved personal characteristics. Thus, for each set of non-movers one can estimate a form of [1], without fear of obtaining a biased estimate of θ. The shortcoming of this non-moving sample approach is the potential lack of generality of this subset of households. This strategy has recently been employed by Knies (2007).

A second promising approach computes a "residual" proxy variable for both $[UP_i]$ and $[UP_{it+1}]$ through a two-step method. This approach requires observations from (at least) two periods. It first estimates equation [1] for period t; the residuals (R) from this regression can be expressed:

[2] $$R_i = O_{it}^{actual} - O_{it}^{predicted} = \varphi[UP_{it}] + \partial[UP_i] + \varepsilon\ .$$

Now to the extent that R_i is correlated with both $[UP_i]$ and $[UP_{it+1}]$, its inclusion in a second regression of form [1] but with all other variables measured for period $t+1$ will presumably help reduce the omitted variable bias when this equation is estimated. To my knowledge, this method has been tried only by Musterd et al (forthcoming). Consistent with the foregoing arguments about reducing bias from omitted variables, they found that its inclusion reduced the measured magnitude of the neighborhood income mix on immigrant adult earnings in Sweden. The technique still needs to be subjected to rigorous simulation and mathematical experiments to discern its statistical properties before its use can be recommended unequivocally.

5.6 Endogeneity

Galster / Marcotte, et al. (2007) have recently attempted to tackle the endogeneity problem directly in their investigation of the cumulative impact of neighbourhood poverty rates upon children. They specify structural equations for the endogenous variables: housing ownership choice, neighbourhood choice (poverty rate), expected mobility during the next year, and actual mobility during the next year. The exogenous predictors in all of these equations serve as grist for constructing an IV for neighbourhood poverty rate for each year of the observed children's lives. First, using the 1968 – 1974 birth cohorts from the US Panel Study of Income Dynamics they estimate an OLS regression based on observations of individual child-years wherein the left-hand side is the observed value of the census tract poverty rate in a given child's neighbourhood in a particular year and the right-hand side contains observed values of every exogenous variable in the system of equations. These exogenous variables include contemporaneous values of *countywide* characteristics corresponding to the endogenous variables and dummy variables for calendar year. In this first step, the regression is estimated based on all observations from age 1 to 18 of each child. In the second step, the aforementioned regression is employed to generate predicted values of neighbourhood poverty for each of the first 18 years of each child's life, based on values of all exogenous variables appropriate for the given year. In the third step they compute the *average* of these predicted values over all observed years of childhood, the IV for neighbourhood poverty experienced during childhood. Unfortunately, this procedure did not produce a sufficiently strong, precisely measured instrument for the authors to place much confidence in the estimates it yielded. Nevertheless, the conceptual approach holds promise, I believe, if better fist-stage exogenous predictors can be employed.

6. A Call for Two New Sources of Data

In this section I argue for efforts to acquire data from two types of sources. I believe that these sources offer fertile ground for overcoming many, if not all, of the aforementioned challenges associated with precisely and accurately measuring the effect of neighbourhood conditions on individuals. The first source of data comes from natural experiments, the second from a new, two-wave, people / place panel survey.

6.1 Toward A Renewed Focus on Natural Experiments

As noted above, in the past there have been a few investigations employing "natural quasi-experiments:" idiosyncratic public policy initiatives in various locales that create exogenous variation in neighbourhood environments for the individual households involved. These can be considered, at best, quasi-experimental designs insofar as tenants being observed may still have some latitude in choosing neighbourhoods, although their choices typically are limited by the program design. However, I believe that the potential of self-selection to bias conclusions regarding the *mechanisms* of neighbourhood impact are considerably less serious than in the case of measuring *magnitude* of effects.

More efforts along these lines would prove fruitful. Either classic anthropological case study, control vs. experimental group, or pre-post longitudinal designs (including retrospective comparisons) could be contemplated. There are ample opportunities emerging in the U.S. public policy arena, including HOPE VI mixed-income redevelopments of distressed public housing complexes, court-ordered public housing authority desegregation consent decrees, and innovative local housing authority initiatives. My colleague, Anna Santiago, and I are currently gathering retrospective data from one such natural experiment involving scattered-site public housing in Denver, CO. In the Western European context, several nations are adopting policies for increasing the income and / or tenure diversity of large social housing estates, which may offer additional opportunities for testing neighbourhood impacts in a quasi-experimental context (Kearns, 2002; Musterd, 2002).

6.2 Towards a New Sort of Database

A second initiative I recommend is the initiation of a new, large-scale survey that would be purposively designed to test neighbourhood effects and provide ways for overcoming the aforementioned methodological challenges. I call it a *people / place panel design.* In overview, it would combine the depth, comprehensiveness, and spatial specificity that characterize many sociological, cross-sectional surveys of individuals in specific neighbourhoods, and the crucial inter-temporal but a-spatial features of many ongoing, representative panel surveys of individuals. The former is required for adequate measurement of neighbourhood social processes and physical environments within particular places; the latter is required for observing exposure effects and providing econometric ammunition for overcoming selection and endogeneity biases. The design must include at least two waves of interviews in several neighbourhoods in (preferably) several cities. The minimum elements of the proposed survey would be:

- *Wave 1 person-in-place:* in-depth, comprehensive questionnaire administered to spatially clustered samples of households; multiple clusters within each city; multiple cities sampled; assesses baseline characteristics of individuals and (via aggregation of these individuals' responses) of neighbourhoods sampled

- *Wave 2 person:* comprehensive questionnaire administered to the households originally living at addresses as in wave 1 but now have moved; assesses characteristics of original individuals sampled who moved since wave 1

- *Wave 2 place:* comprehensive questionnaire administered to the households now living at same addresses as in wave 1; assesses later-period characteristics of sampled neighbourhoods and individuals who did not move

Such an endeavor would clearly require a significant investment of resources from a large governmental, institutional, or philanthropic concern(s).[2] Nevertheless, I believe that such an investment in a person / place panel design is necessary if we are to convincingly quantify neighbourhood effects.

7. Conclusions

In order to advance the quantitative investigation of the impact of neighbourhood on a variety of individual human outcomes, researchers must surmount six methodological challenges. These are: (1) defining the scale of neighbourhood; (2) identifying mechanisms of neighbourhood effect; (3) measuring appropriate neighbourhood characteristics; (4) measuring exposure to neighbourhood; (5) measuring appropriate individual characteristics; and (6) endogeneity. Prior attempts to meet these challenges, though representing vast methodological strides in a short period, nevertheless have been only partially successful. The result is that the answer to the increasingly important question: *How much independent causal effect does the neighbourhood have on individuals?* still remains uncertain within broad parameters.

There are, however, several approaches on the horizon that offer the promise of surmounting these challenges. These include: (1) experiments with varied scales of bespoke neighbourhoods; (2) databases with multi-domain measures of neighbourhood characteristics; (3) statistical models testing for non-linear neighbourhood effects that are stratified by household group, density of local social interactions, and duration of residency; and (4) econometric devices involving instrumental variables and residuals. Further progress can be made on this front if we take advantage of natural quasi-experiments and push toward a major, new social survey employing a people / place panel design.

References

Aaronson, D. (1997): Sibling estimates of neighbourhood effects, in: J. Brooks-Gunn / G. Duncan / J. Aber (eds.), Neighbourhood Poverty: Policy Implications in Studying Neighbourhoods, Vol. II, 80 – 93.

Aaronson, D. (1998): Using sibling data to estimate the impact of neighbourhoods on children's educational outcomes, Journal of Human Resources 33 (4), 915 – 946.

Akerlof, G. (1980): A theory of social custom, of which unemployment may be one consequence, Quarterly Journal of Economics 94, 749 – 775.

Allport, G. (1954): The Nature of Prejudice. Cambridge (MA).

---

2 In many respects the survey recently completed as part of the European Commission-funded URBEX program may be seen as a prototype of the one I am suggesting (Musterd, 2007). However, my proposal differs importantly in its people / place panel design.

Anderson, E. (1990): Streetwise: Race, Class and Change in an Urban Community, Chicago.

Anderson, E. (1991): Neighbourhood Effects on Teenage Pregnancy, in: C. Jencks / P. Peterson (eds.), The Urban Underclass, Washington (DC), 375 – 398.

Andersson, R. / *Musterd,* S. / *Galster,* G. / *Kauppinen,* T. (2007): What Mix Matters for Whom? Exploring the Relationships between Individuals' Income and Different Measures of their Neighbourhood Context, Housing Studies 22 (5), 637 – 660.

Aneshensel, C. S. / *Sucoff,* C. A. (1996): The Neighbourhood Context and Adolescent Mental Health, Journal of Health and Social Behavior 37, 293 – 310.

Aslund, O. / *Fredricksson,* P. (2005): Ethnic Enclaves and Welfare Cultures: Quasi-Experimental Evidence, Unpublished manuscript, Department of Economics, Uppsala University.

Atkinson, R. / *Kintrea,* K. (2001): Area Effects: What Do They Mean for British Housing and Regeneration Policy?, European Journal of Housing Policy 2 (2), 147 – 166.

Bauder, H. (2001). You're Good with Your Hands, Why Don't You Become an Auto Mechanic: Neighbourhood Context, Institutions and Career Development, International Journal of Urban and Regional Research 25 (3), 593 – 608.

Birch, D. / *Brown,* E. / *Coleman,* R. et al. (1979): The Behavioral Foundations of Neighborhood Change, Washington (DC).

Blasius, J. / *Friedrichs,* J. (2007): Internal heterogeneity of a deprived urban area and its impact on residents' perception of deviance, Housing Studies 22 (5), 753 – 780.

Boehm, T. (1981): Tenure choice and expected mobility: A synthesis, Journal of Urban Economics 10, 375 – 389.

Bolster, A. / *Burgess,* S. / *Johnston,* R. / *Jones,* K. / *Propper,* C. / *Sarker,* R. (2004) Neighborhoods, Households and Income Dynamics, Bristol, UK: University of Bristol, CMPO Working Paper Series No. 04 / 106.

Bramley, G. / *Karley,* N. (2007): Home-ownership, poverty and educational achievement: school effects as neighbourhood effects, Housing Studies 22 (5), 693 – 722.

Briggs, X. (1997): Moving up versus moving out: researching and interpreting neighbourhood effects in housing mobility programs, Housing Policy Debate 8, 195 – 234.

Briggs, X. (1998): Brown kids in white suburbs: Housing mobility and the many faces of social capital, Housing Policy Debate 9, 177 – 221.

Brock, W. / *Durlauf,* S. (2001): Interactions-based models, in: J. Heckman / E. Learner (eds.) Handbook of Econometrics 5, Amsterdam, 3297 – 3380.

Brooks-Gunn, J. / *Duncan,* G. / *Aber,* J. (eds.) (1997): Neighbourhood Poverty: Context and Consequences for Children, Vol. 1, New York.

Buck, N. (2001): Identifying Neighborhood Effects on Social Exclusion, Urban Studies 38, 2251 – 2275.

Buck, N. (2007): Spatial mobility, social mobility, and the neighbourhood: Evidence form the British Household Panel Survey, Paper presented at the workshop: Neighbourhood Effects Studies on the Basis of European Micro-data, Humboldt University, Berlin.

Burtless, G. (1996): Introduction and Summary, in: G. Burtless, (ed.), Does Money Matter? The Effect of School Resources on Student Achievement and Adult Success. Washington (DC), 147–166.

Card, D. / *Krueger,* A. (1992): Does School Quality Matter? Journal of Political Economy 100, 1–40.

Case, A. / *Katz,* L. (1991): The Company You Keep: The Effects of Family and Neighbourhood on Disadvantaged Youth. NBER Working Paper 3705. Cambridge (MA).

Chase-Lansdale, P. / *Gordon,* R. / *Brooks-Gunn,* J. / *Klebanov,* P. (1997): Neighbourhood and Family Influences on the Intellectual and Behavioral Competence of Preschool and Early School-Age Children, in: J. Brooks-Gunn / G. J. Duncan / J. L. Aber (eds.), Neighbourhood Poverty: Context and Consequences for Children, Vol. I, New York, 79–118.

Clampet-Lundquist, S. (2004): HOPE VI Relocation: Moving to New Neighbourhoods and Building New Ties, Housing Policy Debate 15, 415–447.

Cook, T. / *Shagle,* S. / Degirmencioglu, S. / Coulton, C. / Korbin, J. / Su, M. (1997): Capturing social process for testing mediational models of neighbourhood effects, in: J. Brooks-Gunn / G. Duncan / L. Aber (eds.) Neighbourhood Poverty: Policy Implications in Studying Neighbourhoods, Vol. II, New York, 94–119.

Coulton, C. / *Korbin,* J. / *Su,* M. (1999): Neighbourhoods and child maltreatment: A multi-level study, Child Abuse and Neglect 23, 1019–1040.

Crane, J. (1991): The epidemic theory of ghettos and neighbourhood effects on dropping out and teenage childbearing, American Journal of Sociology 96, 1226–1259.

Delorenzi, S. (2006): Introduction, in: S. Delorenzi, (ed.) Going Places: Neighbourhood, Ethnicity and Social Mobility, London: Institute for Public Policy Research, 1–11.

Deng, Y. / *Ross,* S. / *Wachter,* S. (2003): Racial Differences in Homeownership: The Effect of Residential Location, Regional Science and Urban Economics 33, 517–556.

Diehr, P. / *Koepsel,* T. / *Cheadle,* A. / *Psaty,* B. / *Wagner,* E. / *Curry,* S. (1993): Do Communities Differ in Health Behaviors? Journal of Clinical Epidemiology 46, 1141–1149.

Dietz, R. (2002): The Estimation of Neighbourhood Effects in the Social Sciences, Social Science Research 31, 539–575.

Dreier, P. / *Mollenkopf,* J. / *Swanstrom,* T. (2004): Place Matters, Lawrence, KS, 2nd ed.

Drever, A. (2004): Separate Spaces, Separate Outcomes? Neighborhood Impacts on Minorities in Germany, Urban Studies 41 (8), 1423–1439.

Drever, A. (2007): Mixed neighbourhoods, parallel lives? Residential proximity and inter-ethnic group contact, Paper presented at the workshop: Neighbourhood Effects Studies on the Basis of European Micro-data, Humboldt University, Berlin.

Duncan, G. / *Connell,* J. / *Klebanov,* P. (1997): Conceptual and methodological issues in estimating causal effects of neighbourhoods and family conditions on individual development, in: J. Brooks-Gunn / G. Duncan / J. Aber (eds.), Neighbourhood Poverty: Context and Consequences for Children, Vol. 1, New York, 219–250.

Duncan, G. / *Raudenbush,* S. (1999): Assessing the effect of context in studies of child and youth development, Educational Psychology 34, 29–41.

Durlauf, S. / *Cohen-Cole.* E. (2004): Social Interaction Models. Madison: University of Wisconsin, Social Systems Research Institute Working Paper #8.

Earls, F. / *Carlson,* M. (2001): The social ecology of child health and well-being, Annual Review of Public Health 22, 143 – 166.

Edin, P. / *Fredricksson,* P. / *Aslund,* O. (2003): Ethnic Enclaves and the Economic Success of Immigrants: Evidence from a Natural Experiment, Quarterly Journal of Economics 113, 329 – 357.

Ellen, I. / *Turner,* M. (2003): Do Neighbourhoods Matter and Why?, in: Goering, J. / Feins, J., (eds.), Choosing a Better Life? Evaluating the Moving To Opportunity Experiment, Washington (DC), 313 – 338.

Elliott, D. / *Wilson,* W. / *Huizinga,* D. / *Elliott,* A. / *Rankin,* B. (1996): The effects of neighbourhood disadvantage on adolescent development, Journal of Research in Crime and Delinquency 33 (4), 389 – 426.

Emerson, M. / *Kimbro,* R. / *Yancey,* G. (2002): Contact Theory Extended. Social Science Quarterly 83 (3), 7445 – 761.

Ennett, S. T. / *Flewelling,* R. L. / *Lindrooth,* R. C. / *Norton,* E. C. (1997): School and Neighbourhood Characteristics Associated with School Rates of Alcohol, Cigarette, and Marijuana Use, Journal of Health and Social Behavior 38, 55 – 71.

Fauth, R. / *Leventhal,* T. / *Brooks-Gunn,* J. (2003a): Short-term Effects of Moving from Public Housing in Poor to Affluent Neighbourhoods on Low-Income, Minority Adults' Outcomes, Unpublished paper, National Center for Children and Families, Columbia University.

Fauth, R. / *Leventhal,* T. / *Brooks-Gunn,* J. (2003b): They're Moving Out, Are They Moving Up? Early Impacts of Moving to Low-Poverty Neighbourhoods on Low-Income Youth, Unpublished paper, National Center for Children and Families, Columbia University.

Foster, E. / *McLanahan,* S. (1996): An illustration of the use of instrumental variables: Do neighbourhood conditions affect a young person's chance of finishing high school? Psychological Methods 1, 249 – 260.

Friedrichs, J. (1998): Do poor neighbourhoods make their residents poorer? Context effects of poverty neighbourhoods on their residents, in: H. Andress (ed.), Empirical Poverty Research in a Comparative Perspective, Aldershot, 77 – 99.

Friedrichs, J. (2002): Response: Contrasting U.S. and European Findings on Poverty Neighbourhoods, Housing Studies 17 (1), 101 – 106.

Friedrichs, J. / *Galster,* G. / *Musterd,* S. (2003): Neighbourhood effects on social opportunities: The European and American research and policy context, Housing Studies 18 (6), 797 – 806.

Galster, G. (1987): Homeowners and Neighbourhood Reinvestment, Durham (NC).

Galster, G. (2002): An economic efficiency analysis of deconcentrating poverty populations, Journal of Housing Economics 11, 303 – 329.

Galster, G. (2003): Investigating behavioral impacts of poor neighbourhoods: Towards new data and analytic strategies, Housing Studies 18 (3), 893 – 914.

Galster, G. (2005): Neighbourhood Mix, Social Opportunities, and the Policy Challenges of an Increasingly Diverse Amsterdam, Amsterdam, Netherlands: University of Amsterdam, Department of Geography, Planning, and International Development Studies. available at: http: // www.fmg.uva.nl / amidst / object.cfm / objectid=7C149 E7C-EC9F-4C2E-91DB7485C0839425.

Galster, G. (2007a): Neighbourhood social mix as a goal of housing policy: A theoretical Analysis, European Journal of Housing Policy 7 (1), 19 – 43.

Galster, G. (2007b): Should policymakers strive for neighbourhood social mix? An analysis of the Western European evidence base, Housing Studies 22 (4), 523 – 545.

Galster, G. / *Andersson,* S. / *Musterd,* S. / *Kauppinen,* T. (2007): The effect of neighborhood income mix on adult earnings. Detroit (MI): unpublished paper, Department of Geography and Urban Planning, Wayne State University.

Galster, G. / *Killen,* S. (1995): The geography of metropolitan opportunity: A reconnaissance and conceptual framework, Housing Policy Debate 6 (1), 7 – 43.

Galster, G. / *Marcotte,* D. / *Mandell,* M. / *Wolman,* H. / *Augustine,* N. (2007): The influence of neighbourhood poverty during childhood on fertility, education and earnings outcomes, Housing Studies 22 (5), 723 – 752.

Galster, G. / *Quercia,* R. / *Cortes,* A. (2000): Identifying Neighbourhood Thresholds: An Empirical Exploration, Housing Policy Debate 11, 701 – 732.

Galster, G. / *Santiago,* A. (2006): What's the 'Hood Got to Do with It? Parental Perceptions about How Neighbourhood Mechanisms Affect Their Children, Paper presented at Urban Affairs Association Annual Meetings, Montreal.

Galster, G. / *Zobel,* A. (1998): Will dispersed housing programmes reduce social problems in the US?, Housing Studies 13 (5), 605 – 622.

Gephart, M. (1997): Neighbourhoods and communities as contexts for development, in: J. Brooks-Gunn / G. Duncan / J. Aber (eds.): Neighbourhood Poverty: Context and Consequences for Children, vol. I, New York, 1 – 43.

Ginther, D. / *Haveman,* R. / *Wolfe,* B. 2000. Neighbourhood Attributes as Determinants of Children's Outcomes. Journal of Human Resources. 35, 603 – 642.

Goering, J. / *Feins,* J., (eds.) (2003): Choosing a Better Life? Evaluating the Moving To Opportunity Experiment, Washington (DC).

Gordon, I. / *Monastiriotis,* V. (2006): Urban Size, Spatial Segregation and Inequality in Educational Outcomes, Urban Studies 43 (1), 213 – 236.

Granovetter, M. (1978): Threshold models of collective behavior, American Journal of Sociology 83, 1420 – 1443.

Granovetter, M. / *Soong,* R. (1986): Threshold models of diversity: Chinese restaurants, residential segregation, and the spiral of silence, The Journal of Sociology 18, 69 – 104.

Grannis, R. (1998): The Importance of Trivial Streets, American Journal of Sociology 103 (6), 1530 – 1564.

Ihlanfeldt, K. (1999): The Geography of Economic and Social Opportunity within Metropolitan Areas, in: A. Altshuler / W. Morrill / H. Wolman / F. Mitchell (eds.), Governance and Opportunity in Metropolitan America, Washington (DC), 213 – 252.

Ihlanfeldt, K. / *Scafidi,* B. (2002): The Neighbourhood Contact Hypothesis, Urban Studies 39, 619 – 641.

Ioannides, Y. (1987): Residential mobility and housing tenure choice, Regional Science and Urban Economics 17, 265 – 287.

Ioannides, Y. / *Kan,* K. (1996): Structural estimation of residential mobility and housing tenure choice, Journal of Regional Science 36 (3), 335 – 363.

Ioannides, Y. / *Loury,* L. (2004): Job Information Networks, Neighbourhood Effets, and Inequality, Journal of Economic Literature 42, 1056 – 1093.

Jenks, C. / *Mayer,* S. (1990): The social consequences of growing up in a poor neighbourhood, in: L. Lynn / M. McGeary (eds.), Inner-city Poverty in the United States, Washington (DC), 111 – 186.

Joseph, M. (2006): Is mixed-income development an antidote to urban poverty?, Housing Policy Debate 17 (2), 209 – 234.

Joseph, M. / *Chaskin,* R. / *Webber,* H. (2006): The theoretical basis for addressing poverty through mixed-income development, Urban Affairs Review 42 (3), 369 – 409.

Kain, J. (1992): The Spatial Mismatch Hypothesis: Three Decades Later, Housing Policy Debate 3 (2), 371 – 460.

Kan, K. (2000): Dynamic modeling of housing tenure choice, Journal of Urban Economics 48, 46 – 69.

Katz, L. / *Kling,* J. / *Liebman,* J. (2001): A Moving to Opportunity in Boston: Early results of a randomized mobility experiment, Quarterly Journal of Economics 116, 607 – 654.

Kauppinen, T. M. (2004): Neighbourhood Effects in a European City: The Educational Careers of Young People in Helsinki, Paper presented at European Network for Housing Research meetings, Cambridge (England).

Kearns, A. (2002): Response: From residential disadvantage to opportunity? Reflections on British and European policy and research, Housing Studies 17 (1), 145 – 150.

Kingsley, T. / *Pettit,* K. (2007): Destination Neighbourhoods of Multi-Move Families in the Moving To Opportunity Demonstration, Paper presented at the Urban Affairs Association annual meeting, Seattle.

Kleinhans, R. (2004): Social implications of housing diversification in urban renewal: a review of recent literature, Journal of Housing and the Built Environment 19, 367 – 390.

Kleit, R. (2001a): The Role of Neighbourhood Social Networks in Scattered-Site Public Housing Residents' Search for Jobs, Housing Policy Debate 12 (3), 541 – 573.

Kleit, R. (2001b): Neighbourhood Relations in Scattered-Site and Clustered Public Housing, Journal of Urban Affairs 23, 409 – 430.

Kleit, R. (2002): Job Search Networks and Strategies in Scattered-Site Public Housing, Housing Studies 17 (1), 83 – 100.

Kleit, R. (2005): HOPE VI New Communities: Neighbourhood Relationships in Mixed-Income Housing, Environment and Planning A 37 (8), 1413 – 1441.

Knies, G. (2007): Keeping Up With the Schmidts: Do better-off Neighbours Make People Unhappy?, Paper presented at the workshop: Neighbourhood Effects Studies on the Basis of European Micro-data, Humboldt University, Berlin.

Kohen, D. / *Brooks-Gunn,* J. / *Leventhal,* T. / *Hertzman,* C. (2002): Neighbourhood Income and Physical and Social Disorder in Canada: Associations with Young Children's Competencies, Child Development 73 (6), 1844 – 1860.

Kozol, J. (1991): Savage Inequalities (NY).

Krivo, L. J. / *Peterson,* R. D. (1996): Extremely disadvantaged neighbourhoods and urban crime, Social Forces 75, 619 – 650.

Leventhal, T. / *Brooks-Gunn,* J. (2000): The neighbourhoods they live in, Psychological Bulletin 126 (2), 309 – 337.

Levine, D. / *Painter,* G. (2000): How Much of School Effects is Just Sorting? Identifying Causality in the National Education Longitudinal Survey, Unpublished manuscript, University of Southern California.

Ludwig, J. / *Duncan,* G. / *Hirschfield,* P. (2001): Urban poverty and juvenile crime: Evidence from a randomized housing-mobility experiment, Quarterly Journal of Economics 116 (2), 655 – 679.

Ludwig, J. / *Ladd,* H. / *Duncan,* G. (2001): The effects of urban poverty on educational outcomes: Evidence from a randomized experiment, in: W. Gale / J. R. Pack (eds.), Brookings-Wharton Papers on Urban Affairs, Washington (DC), 147 – 201.

Ludwig, J. / *Duncan,* G. / *Pinkston,* J. (2000): A Neighbourhood Effects on Economic Self-Sufficiency: Evidence from a Randomized Housing-Mobility Experiment, JCPR Working Paper 159. [http: // www.jcpr.org / wp / Wpprofile.cfm?ID=165].

Manski, C. (1993): Identification of endogenous social effects: The reflection Problem, Review of Economic Studies 60, 531 – 542.

Manski, C. (1995): Identification Problems in the Social Sciences, Cambridge (MA).

Manski, C. (2000): Economic analysis of social interactions, Journal of Economic Perspectives 14, 115 – 136.

Martinez, J. / *Richters,* P. (1993): The NIMH Community Violence Project: II. Children's Distress Symptoms Associated with Violence Exposure. Psychiatry 56, 22 – 35.

Mayer, N. (1981): Rehabilitation decisions in rental housing, Journal of Urban Economics 10, 7694.

Mendenhall, R. (2004): Black Women in Gautreaux's Housing Desegregation Program, Unpublished doctoral dissertation, Human Development and Social Policy, Northwestern University.

Morenoff, J. / *Sampson,* R. / *Raudenbush,* S. (2001): Neighbourhood Inequality, Collective Efficacy, and the Spatial Dynamics of Homicide, Criminology 39 (3), 517 – 560.

Moschion, J. (2007): The Social Multiplier and the Labour Market Participation of Mothers, Paper presented at the workshop: Neighbourhood Effects Studies on the Basis of European Micro-data, Humboldt University, Berlin.

Murray, M. (2006): Avoiding Invalid Instruments and Coping with Weak Instruments, Journal of Economic Perspectives 20, 111 – 132.

Musterd, S. (2002): Response: Mixed housing policy: A European (Dutch) perspective, Housing Studies 17 (1), 139 – 144.

Musterd, S. (2003): Segregation and Integration: A Contested Relationship, Journal of Ethnic and Migration Studies 29 (4), 623 – 641.

Musterd, S. (ed.) (2007): Poverty Neighbourhoods, London.

Musterd, S. / *Andersson,* R. (2005): Housing Mix, Social Mix and Social Opportunities, Urban Affairs Review 40 (6), 761 – 790.

Musterd, S. / *Andersson,* R. / *Galster,* G. / *Kauppinen,* T. (forthcoming): Are co-ethnic clusters good or bad? Environment and Planning A.

Musterd, S. / *Ostendorf,* W. / *de Vos,* S. (2003): Neighborhood Effects and Social Mobility, Housing Studies 18 (6), 877 – 892.

O'Regan, K. M. / *Quigley,* J. M. (1996): Spatial Effects Upon Employment Outcomes. New England Economic Review, Special Issue: Earnings Equality, 41 – 64.

Oberwittler, D. (2007): The effects of neighbourhood poverty on adolescent problem behaviours: A multi-level analysis differentiated by gender and ethnicity, Housing Studies 22 (5), 781 – 804.

Oreopolis, P. (2003): The Long-Run Consequences of Living in a Poor Neighborhood, Quarterly Journal of Economics 118 (4), 1533 – 1575.

Ostendorf, W. / *Musterd,* S. / *de Vos,* S. (2001): Social mix and the neighbourhood effect: Policy ambition and empirical support, Housing Studies 16 (3), 371 – 380.

Permentier, M. / *Bolt,* G. / *Ham,* M. (2007): Comparing residents' and non-residents' assessments of neighbourhood reputations, paper presented at the American Association of Geographers meetings, San Francisco.

Plotnick, R. / *Hoffman,* S. (1999): The effect of neighbourhood characteristics on young adult outcomes: Alternative estimates, Social Science Quarterly 80 (1), 1 – 18.

Popkin, S. / *Harris,* L. / *Cunningham,* M. (2002): Families in Transition: A Qualitative Analysis of the MTO Experience, Washington (DC): Urban Institute Report prepared for the U.S. Department of Housing and Urban Development.

Rasmussen, D. W. (1994): Spatial Economic Development, Education and the New Poverty, International Regional Science Review 14, 107 – 117.

Raudenbush, S. / *Sampson,* R. (1999): 'Ecometrics:' Toward a science of assessing ecological settings, with application to the systematic social observation of neighbourhoods, Sociological Methodology 29, 1 – 41.

Richters, P. / *Martinez,* J. E. (1993): The NIMH Community Violence Project: I. Children as Victims of and Witnesses to Violence, Psychiatry 56, 7 – 21.

Robert, S. (1999): Socioeconomic position and health: The independent contribution of community socioeconomic context, Annual Review of Sociology 25, 489 – 516.

Rosenbaum, E. / *Harris,* L. / *Denton,* N. (2003): New Places, New Faces: An Analysis of Neighbourhoods and Social Ties Among MTO Movers in Chicago, in: Goering, J. / Feins, J. (eds.), Choosing a Better Life? Evaluating the Moving To Opportunity Experiment, Washington (DC), 275 – 310.

Rosenbaum, J. (1991): Black Pioneers: Do Moves to the Suburbs Increase Economic Opportunity for Mothers and Children?, Housing Policy Debate 2, 1179 – 1213.

Rosenbaum, J. (1995): Changing the geography of opportunity by expanding residential choice: Lessons from the Gautreaux program, Housing Policy Debate 6 (1), 231 – 269.

Rosenbaum, J. / *Harris,* L. (2001): Residential mobility and opportunities: Early impacts of the moving to opportunity demonstration program in Chicago, Housing Policy Debate 12 (2), 321 – 346.

Rosenbaum, J. / *Popkin,* S. / *Kaufman,* J. / *Rusin,* J. (1991): Social integration of Low-income Black Adults in Middle Class Suburbs, Social Problems 38, 448 – 61.

Rosenbaum, J. / *Reynolds,* L. / *DeLuca,* S. (2002): How do places matter? The geography of opportunity, self-efficacy, and a look inside the black box of residential mobility, Housing Studies 17 (1), 71 – 82.

Rosenthal, S. (1988): A residence time model of housing markets, Journal of Public Economics 36, 87 – 109.

Rubinowitz, L. / *Rosenbaum,* J. (2000): Crossing the Class and Color Lines: From Public Housing to White Suburbia. Chicago (IL).

Sampson, R. J. (1992): Family Management and Child Development, in: J. McCord (ed.), Advances in Criminological Theory 3, New Brunswick (NJ), 63 – 93.

Sampson, R. J. (1997): Collective regulation of adolescent misbehavior: Validation results for eighty Chicago neighbourhoods, Journal of Adolescent Research 12 (2), 227 – 244.

Sampson, R. / *Groves,* W. B. (1989): Community structure and crime: Testing social disorganization theory, American Journal of Sociology 94 (4), 774 – 802.

Sampson, R. / *Morenoff,* J. / *Earls,* F. (1999): Beyond social capital: Spatial dynamics of collective efficacy for children, American Sociological Review 64, 633 – 660.

Sampson, R. / *Morenoff,* J. / *Gannon-Rowley,* T. (2002): Assessing 'neighbourhood effects': Social processes and new directions in research, Annual Review of Sociology 28, 443 – 478.

Sampson, R. / *Raudenbush,* S. / *Earls,* F. (1997): Neighbourhoods and violent crime: A multilevel study of collective efficacy, Science 277, 918 – 924.

Schelling, T. (1978): Micromotives and Macrobehavior, New York.

Schill, M. (1997): Chicago's New Mixed-Income Communities Strategy: The Future Face of Public Housing?, in: W. Van Vliet (ed.) Affordable Housing and Urban Redevelopment in the United States, Thousand Oaks (CA), 135 – 157.

Simmel, G. (1971): Georg Simmel on Individuality and Social Forms, University of Chicago, 135 – 157.

South, S. / *Baumer,* E. (2000): Deciphering Community and Race Effects on Adolescent Pre-Marital Childbearing, Social Forces 78, 1379 – 1407.

Sullivan, M. (1989): Getting Paid: Youth Crime and Work in the Inner City, Ithaca (NY).

Suttles, G. (1972): The Social Construction of Communities. Chicag (IL).

Teitler, J. / *Weiss,* C. (1996): Contextual Sex: The Effect of School and Neighbourhood Environments on the Timing of First Intercourse. Paper presented at the Annual Meetings of the Population Association of America, New Orleans.

Tienda, M. (1991): Poor people and poor places: Deciphering neighbourhood effects of poverty outcomes, in: J. Haber (ed.) Macro-Micro Linkages in Sociology, Newbury Park, 244 – 262.

Turley, R. (2003): When Do Neighbourhoods Matter? The Role of Race and Neighbourhood Peers, Social Science Research 32, 61 – 79.

Van der Klaauw, B. / *Van Ours,* J. (2003): From Welfare to Work: Does the Neighborhood Matter? Journal of Public Economics 87, 957 – 85.

Van der Laan Bouma-Doff, W. (2007a): Spatial Concentration and the Labour Market Participation of Ethnic Minority Women. Paper presented at the workshop: Neighbourhood Effects Studies on the Basis of European Micro-data, Humboldt University, Berlin.

Van der Laan Bouma-Doff, W. (2007b): The neighbourhood barrier: Effects of spatial isolation of ethnic minorities in the Netherlands, Paper presented at NETHUR School on Neighbourhood Effects, Technical University of Delft.

Van Kempen, E. (1997): Poverty Pockets and Life Chances, American Behavioral Scientist 41 (3), 430 – 449.

Vartanian, T. (1999a): Adolescent Neighbourhood Effects on Labor Market and Economic Outcomes, Social Service Review 73, 142 – 67.

Vartanian, T. (1999b): Childhood Conditions and Adult Welfare Use: Examining Neighbourhood and Family Factors, Journal of Marriage and the Family 61, 225 – 37.

Weber, M. (1978): Economy and Society, Berkeley (CA).

Weinberg, B. / *Reagan,* P. / *Yankow,* J. (2004): Do Neighbourhoods Affect Work Behavior? Evidence from the NLSY79, Journal of Labor Economics 22 (4), 891 – 924.

Wheaton, B. / *Clarke,* P. (2003): Space Meets Time: Integrating Temporal and Contextual Influences on Mental Health in Early Adulthood, American Sociological Review 68 (5), 680 – 706.

Wilson, W. J. (1987): The Truly Disadvantaged, Chicago (IL).

Wilson, W. J. (1996): When Work Disappears, New York.

Wolman, H. / *Lichtman,* C. / *Barnes,* S. (1991): The Impact of Credentials, Skill Levels, Worker Training, and Motivation on Employment Outcomes, Economic Development Quarterly 5, 140 – 151.

Zorn, P. (1988): An analysis of household mobility and tenure choice, Journal of Urban Economics 24, 113 – 128.

Schmollers Jahrbuch 128 (2008), 49 – 63
Duncker & Humblot, Berlin

Neighbourhood Effects and the Welfare State. Towards a European Research Agenda?

By Roger Andersson

Abstract

This paper raises four broad questions related to the neighbourhood effect issue.

(1) Is there really a strong relation between housing mix and social mix? (2) How does the social composition of neighbourhoods affect residents' social interaction and behaviour? (3) Are social opportunities of individual residents related to their neighbourhood context? (4) If there is such a relation, to what extent is this produced through local social interaction?

While the answer to the first question is often taken for granted, not only by planners but also by urban research, the following three have been much discussed over the last decade on both sides of the Atlantic. Most researchers hypothesise that neighbourhood effects would be less pronounced in countries like Sweden, where planning practices, social class differences, segregation patterns, and welfare state regulations substantially differ from those found in the U.S. However, recent empirical studies – based on large longitudinal datasets – confirm the existence of neighbourhood effects also in Sweden. Future European research should not only further explore the above four questions but needs also to systematically engage with issues concerning how neighbourhoods should be defined (scale issues), the importance of time of residency in particular neighbourhoods, and how mix should be operationalised (class, ethnicity etc).

JEL Classifications: D62, I39, J68

1. Introduction

Over the past couple of decades, studies on the impact of neighbourhood compositions on the life chances of individuals are gaining interest and also provide new insights (for an updated overview, see Galster, 2007 and an issue of Housing Studies, 2007, no 5). Most of the empirical research and theoretical inputs so far come from the Unites States, a country that have had a much longer history of racial segregation compared to European countries, but in the wake of increasing immigration to Europe, and fear of social exclusion, issues related to residential segregation have moved high up the urban policy debates in many European countries. The neighbourhood effect issue is one such topic.

This paper takes its point of departure in one particular country, Sweden, a country that has pursued a social mix policy since the mid 1970s as an instrument to avoid further segregation. (Andersson, 2007) One may doubt the efficiency and criticise the lack of strong commitment by planners and local politicians in relation to this general aim but the country is an interesting case for researching some of the underlying assumptions about neighbourhood compositions and social outcomes. It is interesting from a policy perspective but also due to the existence of internationally unique types of data, which enable researchers to conduct large scale longitudinal studies on individuals (in fact the entire population). Empirically, this paper will make use of results from a series of published and yet unpublished papers using the Swedish data resources.[1] The paper will address four broad questions indicated in figure 1.

1. Is there really a strong relation between housing mix and social mix? This is a fundamental issue since planning for social mix is based on the assumption that the micro structures of the housing stock in terms of tenure, housing types, size and cost of dwellings etc are thought to strongly influence the population composition of neighbourhoods.
2. How does population composition of neighbourhoods affect residents' social interaction and behaviour?
3. Are social opportunities of individual residents related to their neighbourhood context?
4. If there is such a relation, to what extent is this produced through local social interaction? The idea is that social opportunities might be directly or indirectly affected by residency.

Three equally important questions arise if one wants to study these relations: What population mix matters? What scale matters? What time matters? I will deal with these latter questions after having discussed figure 1 more in detail.

2. Housing Mix and Social Mix

Combining basic individual rights – such as the right for people to make a choice where to live in a city – with aims such as striving for population mix in neighbourhoods is easier said than done. The idea behind mix is to create positive social externalities (a collective assett) but the tools cannot be allowed to conflict with the right for people to decide where to live. Hence, no legal opportunities exist that allow politicians to create social mixes directly (see

1 Andersson (2001); Andersson / Bråmå (2004); Andersson / Musterd (2005, 2006); Musterd / Andersson (2005, 2006); Andersson / Musterd / Galster / Kauppinen (2007); Musterd / Andersson / Galster / Kauppinen (2007); Galster / Kauppinen / Musterd / Andersson (fc).

Borevi, 2002, chapter 6, who analyses Swedish housing mix policies since 1975). Therefore, politicians tend to use housing and planning policy tools (i.e. supply measures) instead to reach their goals. In short, the idea is that housing mix (a mix of housing types and tenure types) will create social mix (a mix of households according to their socio-economic position) and that this will create better social opportunities for individuals. In fact, these strategies are based on two crucial assumptions. The first is that social mix really enhances the individual opportunities (i.e. relations 3 and / or 4 in figure 1 are true). The second is that there is a strong relation between social mix and housing mix (relation 1 is true).

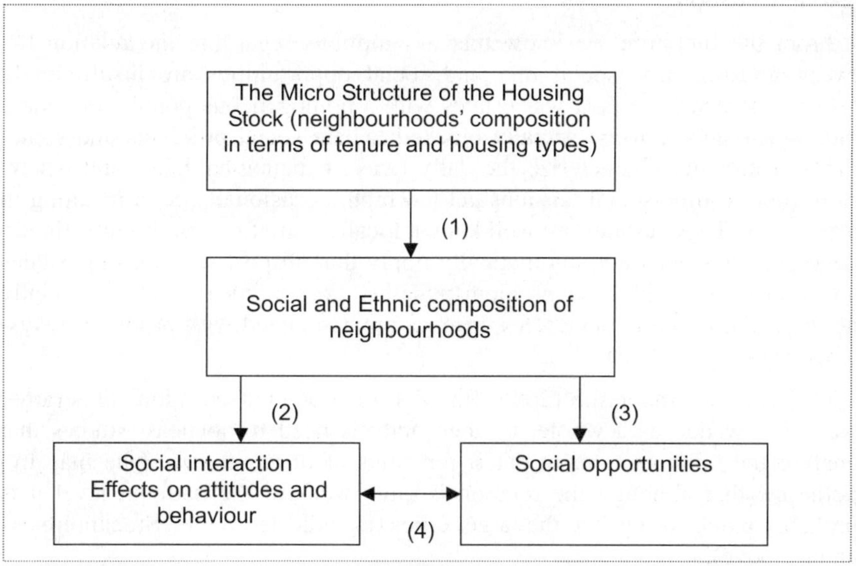

Source: Author.

Figure 1: A research programme on neighbourhood mix and neighbourhood effects

These issues are obviously firmly related to the actual plans and activities around the restructuring of certain areas in cities. Today, at least in many European cities, a large share of urban restructuring plans is aimed at transforming large-scale post-war housing estates (van Kempen et al., 2006). The areas in which these estates can be found tend to be rather homogeneous in terms of the type and tenure of the dwellings. They are also often attracting households with a rather weak social position and many immigrants. The dominant idea is that there is housing (type and tenure) homogeneity that creates social homogeneity (concentration of poor people) that reduces social opportunities for those who are living there. So, the same set of assumptions applies for these estates and the people living in them. It is worth noting that homogenous high-income areas are never considered to constitute problems for individuals or policy makers. As Andersson (2000) shows in a countrywide analysis on housing segregation in Sweden, the geographical concentration of the rich is much stronger than that of the poor. And in Sweden, as probably elsewhere, the majority of all homogenous areas are dominated by home ownership. In the Stockholm region 288,000 people live in neighbourhoods having more than 90% of the population in home ownership. As a contrast, only 52,000 live in neighbourhoods having a similarly strong dominance of rental dwellings. If more mix as such is wanted, mixing the former seems to be an appropriate recommendation.

From the literature we know that assumptions regarding the relation between housing mix, social mix and social opportunities are insufficiently tested. There will be post-war estates with a homogeneous population where individuals appear to be socially blocked; where social problems and sometimes criminality characterize the daily lives of their inhabitants and where, from time-to-time social tensions get too high, occasionally even resulting in urban riots. These estates are well known locally and often also highly stigmatized. Yet, this does not automatically imply that all post-war housing estates are associated with these problems; neither does it mean that all socially homogeneous (and poor) estates or areas are associated with problems (Musterd / Andersson, 2005)

Musterd and Andersson (2005) find that relation (1) (see figure 1) is rather weak in Sweden as a whole. Further study is needed, not least studies that analyse the relation more in detail for cities of different size. One may hypothesize that although the relation is quite weak at the national level it is probably much stronger in the larger cities (as indicated by the Stockholm example above).

3. Social and Ethnic Mix and Neighbourhood Effects

Many researchers make use of Charles Manski's (2000) distinction between three types of neighbourhood effects: endogenous, contextual (exogenous) and correlated (see Galster, 2006). If we face endogenous interactions, the propensity of an agent to behave in some way varies with the behaviour of the group. In contextual interactions, the propensity of an agent to behave in some way varies with exogenous characteristics of the group members. Correlated effects concern situations when agents in the same group tend to behave similarly because they have similar individual characteristics or face similar institutional environments. As concluded by Manski: "Endogenous and contextual interactions express distinct ways that agents might be influenced by their social environments, while correlated effects express a non-social phenomenon." (Manski, 2000, 127).

Many versions of endogenous effects have been forwarded, including effects related to socialization, social networks, local competition over finite resources, and relative deprivation. Exogenous neighbourhood effects occur if the behaviours or attitudes of one neighbour depend on the exogenous (or predetermined, fixed) characteristics of the individual's neighbours, such as ethnicity, religion, or race. For my purpose the distinction between endogenous and exogenous effects are not of immediate importance. Both sets of effects relate to the population composition of a neighbourhood and both relate to the fact that people interact locally and potentially have influence on each other (relation 2 and 4 in figure 1). Manski's third type of possible effects, the correlated neighbourhood effect, is however interesting as it does not presuppose ideas about "contagion effects" or mechanisms related directly to the composition of households. Correlated neighbourhood effects typically do not vary by alterations in neighbourhood household composition, but rather are determined by larger structural forces in the metropolitan area, like locations of jobs and geographic dis-amenities and the structures of local government. These external forces may impinge differentially on different neighbourhoods, but within any given neighbourhood they affect all residents roughly equally, producing thereby correlations in neighbours' outcomes (Galster, 2006; Andersson et al., 2007). Such aspects of peoples' environment are not 'non-social' – and certainly not non-political – but they do not stem from local human to human interaction. Of course, the real effect of the external forces on individuals is depending on individual resources and dispositions.

4. What Mix Matters?

In a Swedish-Dutch collaboration, Roger Andersson and Sako Musterd have produced a series of papers using the statistical database GeoSweden as the empirical foundation. GeoSweden contains yearly demographic, socioeconomic, educational and geographical information on all people residing in Sweden 1990–2004 (later to be updated with information for 2005 and 2006). The first two papers (Musterd / Andersson, 2005 and 2006 respectively) are based on the 1991 to 1999 period, and both attempts to analyse the existence and magnitude of neighbourhood effects on (un)employment careers. Both these papers confirm the existence of such effects. Figure 2 gives an overview of the relation between the percentage of unemployed in the 500m by 500m neighbourhoods (entire country) and the percentage of all unemployed in 1991 who remain unemployed also in 1995 and 1999. The levels are different according to national origin and educational groups but all categories experience a clear impact of the residential context (horizontal axis). The effects seem to be rather linear as unemployment increases from 2 to about 15 percent.

In an enlarged collaboration, including also George Galster and Timo Kauppinen, Swedish data are used for examining several important issues in the neighbourhood effects discourse. In Andersson / Musterd / Galster / Kauppinen (2007) the authors address the crucial question "What mix matters"? This paper explores the degree to which a wide variety of 1995 neighbourhood conditions in Sweden are statistically related to earnings for all adult metropolitan and non-metropolitan men and women during the 1996 – 1999 period, controlling for a wide variety of personal characteristics. They find that the extremes of the neighbourhood income distribution, operationalised by the percentages of adult males with earnings in the lowest 30th and the highest 30th percentiles, hold greater explanatory power than domains of household mix related to education, ethnicity, or housing tenure. Separating the effects of having substantial shares of low and high income neighbours, they find that it is the presence of the former that means most for metropolitan and non-metropolitan men and women, with the largest effects for metropolitan men.

According to research findings in a recently finished EU-funded project, Urban Governance, Inclusion and Sustainability (UGIS), both area-based policies and most mix policies are now partly driven by the fear of ethnic clustering (Andersson, 2003; Beaumont et al., 2003; Palander, 2006). Our findings do not support the hypothesis that the ethnic dimension is the most crucial one in relation to employment and income prospects. On the contrary, we find that the socioeconomic composition of neighbourhoods is the most important dimension, at least in terms of individuals' incomes. It is however important to note that although these results clearly point at the conclusion that mix of income groups is the most important aspect, this is not necessarily true for other types of social outcomes (educational achievements, crime, social cohesion etc.).

A special aspect of the 'what mix matters' issue relates to local concentration of immigrants. A Musterd / Andersson / Galster / Kauppinen (fc) paper addresses the role of ethnic clusters in relation to immigrants' income development. Differences in immigrant economic trajectories have been attributed to a wide variety of factors. One of these is the local spatial context where immigrants reside. This spatial context assumes special salience in light of expanding public exposure to and scholarly interest in "ethnic enclaves". Does concentrating immigrants aid or retard their chances for improving their economic standing? In this paper the authors contribute clear statistical evidence relevant to answering this question. They develop multiple measures of the spatial context in which immigrants reside and assess their contribution to average earnings of immigrant individuals in the three large Swedish metropolitan areas, controlling for individual and regional labour market characteristics. They use longitudinal information about Swedish immigrants during the 1995 – 2002 period. They find no evidence (with one exception) that own-group ethnic enclaves in Sweden typically enhance the income prospects of its resident immigrants, unless individuals use the enclave for a short-term place from which to launch themselves quickly into different milieus.

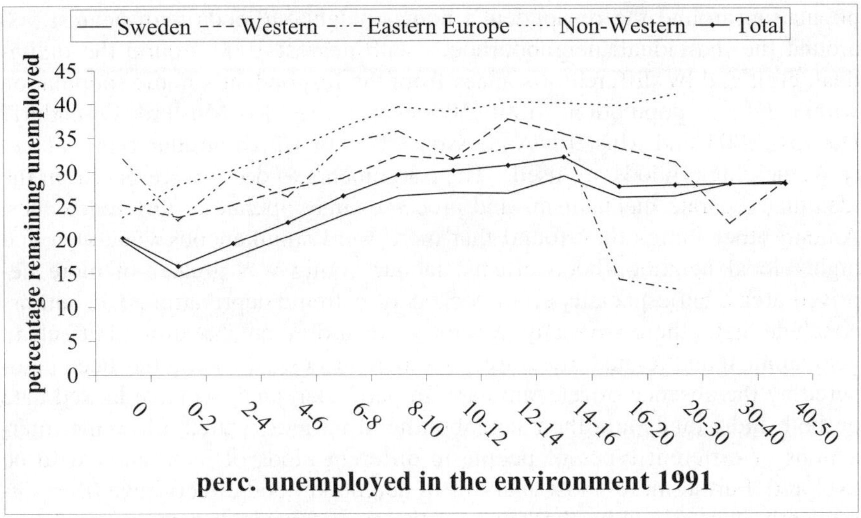

Source: Musterd / Andersson, 2006.

Figure 2: Percentage unemployed staying unemployed in 1995 and 1999, per environment type, per country of birth

5. What Scale Matters?

In the wider literature on the relationship between man and environment some argue that the direct neighbourhood of individuals has lost significance, especially for life chances and social opportunities of the adult population. Fischer (1982), for example, stated that people tend to become socially integrated through differentiated, looser networks at different scales. However, Bridge / Forrest / Holland (2004, 39), who summarised the research evidences on neighbouring, state that "The evidence for the widely held perception that neighbourliness is declining is in fact mixed."

The 'what scale matters' question is highly relevant to the more general 'does neighbourhood matter' question. That is, if the 'wrong scale' is used in neighbourhood effect studies, we easily may arrive at wrong conclusions about neighbourhood effects; we may over- or underestimate them. Then the question should be asked whether that conclusion holds when other scales are applied.

A study carried out by Johnston et al. (2004) is very interesting from this perspective. They focused on scale and neighbourhood effects on voting behaviour and applied the British Household Panel Study. They created 'bespoke' neighbourhoods, local areas defined for each individual separately; these environments were built up with enumeration district data. Two different types of bespoke neighbourhoods were created: by different numbers of nearest population around the respondent's home (neighbourhoods with nearest 500 around the individual; neighbourhoods with nearest 1000 around the individual, etc); and by different distances from the respondent's home (population within 250 m, population within 500m, etc.; see also Musterd / Ostendorf / De Vos, 2003 and Musterd / Andersson, 2006 in which similar types of bespoke neighbourhoods are used). Their arguments to do so were based on the idea that separate mechanisms and processes may operate at different scales. Among other things they found that there were simultaneous wide-area and highly local neighbourhood effects; labour voting was greater in more deprived areas, but especially so in pockets of extreme deprivation. The authors conclude that: "there are many hypotheses regarding neighbourhood effects in geographical and related literatures, but their successful testing has been hampered by the absence of relevant data. In particular, analysts have lacked data on both individuals and their neighbourhood milieus, which allow the interactions of different types of people in different kinds of local context to be explored. Furthermore, most analyses of neighbourhood effects have been significantly constrained by the nature of the areas for which data are available. In many cases these are relatively large and in almost all cases no data are available to explore variations in the nature and strength of the sought-for effects at different scales." (Johnston et al., 2004, 367).

These statements were the drivers behind a recent Andersson / Musterd (2006) paper in which the question is raised:

> *"to what extent individual social mobility of adults is influenced by individual and neighbourhood characteristics, with a special focus on various levels of scale and various definitions of area compositions."*

We assumed *that if endogenous neighbourhood effects are in operation, such effects would be greater in the immediate surrounding of an individual and they would decrease as the size of the unit increases.* However, for correlated effects it is more difficult to hypothesize which level would be the most important and the spatiality can also be expected to vary according to which outcome we decide to study. In our case, focusing on labour market-related outcomes, both the existence of spatial mismatch (number of jobs available nearby, uneven public transportation services etc) and uneven support provided to people who are unemployed or in need of job information services *can be expected to be more influential at the municipal and urban district levels than at the level of the immediate surrounding of individuals.* Or put the other way around: at higher levels of geographical scale we expect endogenous effects to be less strong than they are at the scale of peoples' closest environment. If correlated effects exist at higher levels (municipality, urban district) they would exist also at lower levels, adding up to more strong neighbourhood effects at the lowest geographical scale.

There is, however, one particular aspect of correlated effects that might operate primarily at lower geographical scales, namely spatial stigmatization. Galster (2006) identifies stigmatization both as a type of endogenous effect and as a correlated effect: "Endogenous stigmatization of a place transpires when important institutional, governmental or market actors negatively stereotype all residents of a place and / or reduce the flows of resources flowing into the place because of its household composition. This might occur as the percentage of households in some disadvantaged ethnic group in the neighbourhood exceeds the threshold of where they are perceived by these external actors as "dominant." (...) "External stigma: certain neighbourhoods may be stigmatized regardless of their current population because of their history, environmental or topographical dis-amenities, style, scale and type of dwellings, or condition of their commercial districts and public spaces." (Galster, 2006, 8) It is highly plausible that both types of stigmatization occur at a relatively low geographical scale, such as neighbourhoods and maybe urban districts.

In this study we operationalized 'neighbourhood' at four spatial scales, running from the municipality, over an officially existing neighbourhood definition (SAMS) to coordinate-based bespoke neighbourhoods (environments constructed individual by individual on the basis of coordinate information; 500 meter and 100 meter around each individual, respectively). Using multivariate statistical techniques on employment and income development 1995 – 2002 for all inhabitants residing in Sweden's three largest urban regions, controlling for a wide variety of personal and household characteristics, we were able to confirm our basic hypothesis that contextual effects on labour market performance are strongest at the very local level and non-existent or weak at the municipal level. We were also able to show – indirectly – that stigmatization probably plays a significant role. By analysing a subset of politically targeted poor neighbourhoods we found neighbourhood effects to be much stronger there compared to what we found for non-targeted (presumably much less stigmatized) neighbourhoods. From a policy point of view this result indicates that mixing policies should aim at the micro neighbourhood level.

6. What Time Matters?

There are several types of time issues that so far have not been subject to systematically designed empirical analyses. First of all, some of the theories concerning neighbourhood effects suggest that we should expect instant effects for people residing in particular contexts. Most of the correlated effects (spatial mis-match, external stigmatization etc) would have more or less instant impact on for example labour market performance. The same apply for some of the endogenous effects (social networks, local competition over finite resources, and maybe also relative deprivation). Other effects would probably appear as a result of a longer period of exposure to certain environments (socialisation and other processes affecting behaviour and related to local social interaction). Secondly, effects might also last for shorter or longer periods, so that some would disappear if a person moves out of the specific context while other could last for years and maybe even decades regardless of later trajectories (certainly correlated effects on health due to bad environmental conditions, such as air pollution, water quality or nuclear-related radiation, but maybe also labour market careers as related to educational achievements in younger ages).

Sweden is a welfare state with high ambitions to allocate resources according to needs. I have hypothesized that neighbourhood effects in countries like Sweden are probably less pronounced compared to countries having less high ambitions in this regard (Andersson, 2001). But there is also another aspect of urban Sweden that speaks in favour of this hypothesis. In some countries, I get the impression that moving out of poor neighbourhoods is a difficult thing and that many are stuck in less resourceful environments for longer periods, maybe even for life and across generations. This is certainly not the case in Sweden and I will end this paper by proving further evidence on the dynamic nature of Swedish neighbourhoods (see also Andersson / Bråmå, 2004; Bråmå, 2006). I have chosen two adjacent neighbourhoods in the Stockholm region, located in the north-western part of the capital city. One of these neighbourhoods is a quite typical middle-class area, comprising predominantly home owners in single housing having a medium to high level of income. Consequently, few are unemployed. This area, Spånga, has about 6,600 residents. The adjacent area, Tensta, is one of Sweden's most immigrant-dense housing estates, home for about 17,000 people. Many are unemployed and rely on social allowances. The average level of income is very low. Tensta has been targeted by both state-funded and municipality-funded restructuring programmes since many years.

In figure 3 and 4 I display results from a longitudinal study 1990 – 2004 of the 1990 cohort for respective area. The figures show year by year and per age group how many remain in respective area. The very high mobility among younger people is a very distinct feature; half of the 20 – 29 years old have left after only about three years. After 14 years, less than two out of ten remain. In general, out migration is at a higher level in the poor housing estate compared to the middle-class area. While 50 percent of the original cohort had left Spånga by the year 2000, 50 percent of the 1990 Tensta residents had left already in 1996. By the end of the period, 27 percent still live in Tensta, while 38 percent remain in Spånga.

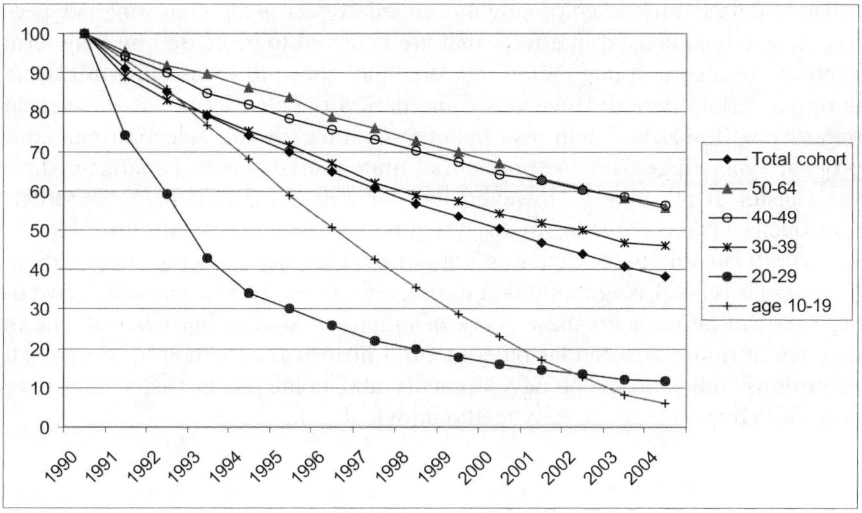

Source: GeoSweden 2004, Institute for Housing & Urban Research, Uppsala university.

Figure 3: Neighbourhood staying frequencies 1990 – 2004 for the 1990 population of Spånga in Stockholm city (area code 1800149; cohort size: $N = 6617$ in 1990; 2537 in 2004)

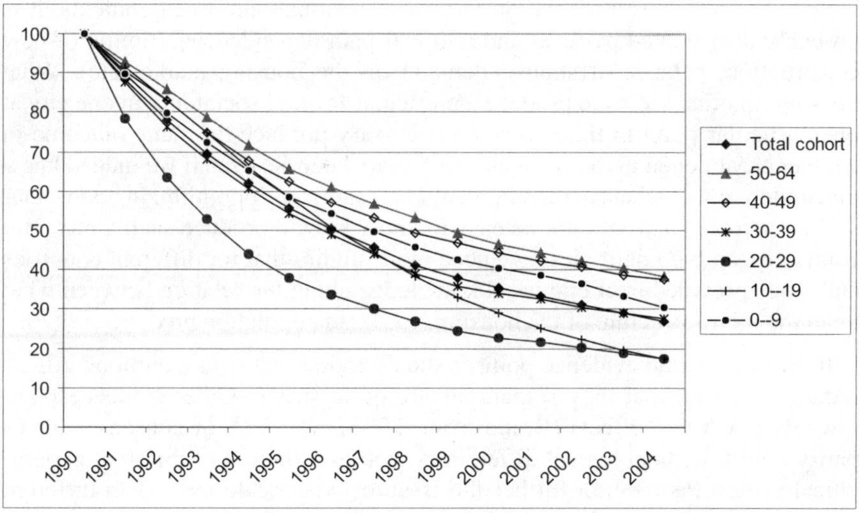

Source: GeoSweden 2004, Institute for Housing & Urban Research, Uppsala university.

Figure 4: Neighbourhood staying frequencies 1990 – 2004 for the 1990 population of Tensta in Stockholm city (area code 1800151; $N = 15567$ in 1990; 4206 in 2004)

These data put the issue of neighbourhood effects in an interesting perspective. If one is interested in effects that are believed to be caused by long term exposure to a certain population mix one may chose to focus only on stayers during a certain period. However if that period is rather long, only a selected minority will qualify. I will also hypothesize that the self selection bias thus probably gets bigger (i.e. the problem of unmeasured personal characteristics, see Galster et al., 2007). However, the dynamic feature of neighbourhoods also opens up possibilities for to systematically study possible time lags in effects attributable to residency. What is the difference of being "exposed" to a particular type of neighbourhood during one, three, five or ten years? Swedish data can be used for these types of empirical studies but whether one in fact can attribute a particular outcome to a historical neighbourhood context, controlling for subsequent developments and contexts, is easier said than done. It is by no means an easy methodological task.

7. Conclusions

This paper summarizes some of the basic questions that appear both in the neighbourhood effect literature and in planning practices and policy discourses. It draws on a series of studies using Swedish data.

Clarifying the relation between housing mix and social mix is one important issue. Not only does this relation vary with national and urban contexts, it is probably also shaped by local and regional path dependencies (timing of new construction, balance of supply / demand on the housing market etc). What housing mix that seems to produce a particular form of social mix in one city at one particular point in time does not necessary produce the same outcome in another city or even in the same city five years later. So even if we indeed knew much more about what social mix would be beneficial for optimizing particular social outcomes it would not be easy to know how to produce such a mix. But from a research point of view, we need more studies that for different countries and cities provide better empirical knowledge about the relation between what I call the micro structure of the housing stock and population mix.

In Sweden, some evidence point in the direction that neighbourhood effects indeed exist and that they sometimes are quite strong. Other evidence point towards much less effects (Brännström, 2006). The lack of consensus arises partly out of methodological differences, not least the use of different geographical scales. Penetrating further the issue of what scale matters in different urban contexts is not only wishful for expanding our knowledge about causalities and how certain mechanisms might operate, it is necessary if research results should be used for informing policy makers (planning for mix). Finally, yet another basic question should be raised in future neighbourhood effects studies, namely the time issue. This also relates to hypotheses about causality:

effects now or later, effects due to instant exposure or cumulative exposure? I have provided some empirical data on neighbourhood population dynamics, data that confirm the need of taking the time issue seriously into consideration.

Not all countries have data resources of the Swedish kind. Realising this, there are still many types of studies that can be conducted without such data. I would in particular welcome more – also international comparative – studies that look into the black box of especially endogenous neighbourhood effects. Such studies would require collecting primary data on the geography of social interaction and how that might differ across social, ethnic and demographic strata and in different urban contexts.

References

Andersson, R. (2000): Etnisk och socioekonomisk segregation i Sverige 1990–1998, in: SOU 2000 (37), Arbetsmarknad, Demografi och Segregation, Stockholm, 223–266.

Andersson, R. (2001): Spaces of Socialization and Social Network Competition: A Study of Neighbourhood Effects in Stockholm, Sweden, in: H. T. Andersen / R. van Kempen (eds.), Governing European Cities: Social Fragmentation and Urban Governance, Aldershot, 149–188.

Andersson, R. (2003): Urban development programmes in a Scandinavian welfare state: a topdown approach to bottom-up planning?, in: K. Decker et al. (eds.), On the origins of urban development programmes in nine European countries, Antwerpen-Apeldoom, 165–195.

Andersson, R. (2007): Ethnic Residential Segregation and Integration Processes in Sweden, in: K. Schönwälder (ed.), Residential Segregation and the Integration of Immigrants: Britain, the Netherlands and Sweden, Discussion Paper Nr. SP IV 2007–602, Berlin: Wissenschaftszentrum Berlin für Sozialforschung, 61–90.

Andersson, R. / *Bråmå,* Å. (2004): Selective Migration in Swedish Distressed Neighbourhoods: Can Area-based Urban Policies Counteract Segregation Processes?, Housing Studies 19, 517–539.

Andersson, R. / *Musterd,* S. (2005): Social mix and social perspectives in post-war housing estates, in: R. van Kempen / K. Dekker / S. Hall / I. Tosics, Restructuring large housing estates in Europe, Bristol, 127–147.

Andersson, R. / *Musterd,* S. (2006): What Scale Matters? Exploring the relationships between individuals' social position, neighbourhood context and the scale of neighbourhood. Paper presented at the Urban Affairs Association's 36th Annual Meeting, Montreal, Canada, April 19–22, 2006.

Andersson, R. / *Musterd,* S. / *Galster,* G. / *Kauppinen,* T. (2007): What Mix Matters? Exploring the relationships between individuals' incomes and different measures of their neighbourhood context, Housing Studies 22 (5), 637–660.

Beaumont, J. / *Burgers,* J. / *Dekker,* K. / *Dukes,* T. / *Musterd,* S. / *Staring,* R. / *van Kempen,* R. (2003): Urban Policy in the Netherlands, in: K. Decker et al. (eds.), On the origins of urban development programmes in nine European countries, Antwerpen-Apeldoom, 119–137.

Borevi, K. (2002): Välfärdsstaten i det mångkulturella samhället. Acta Universitatis Upsaliensis. Skrifter utgivna av Statsvetenskapliga föreningen i Uppsala, 151. Uppsala: Department of Political Science, Uppsala University.

Bråmå, Å. (2006): Studies in the Dynamics of Residential Segregation, Geografiska regionstudier no 67. Uppsala: Department of Social and Economic Geography, Uppsala University.

Brännström, L. (2006): Phantom of the neighbourhood – Studies on area-based conditions and individual outcomes, Stockholm: Swedish Institute for Social Research 67.

Bridge, G. / *Forrest,* R. / *Holland,* E. (2004): Neighbouring: A Review of the Evidence, CNR Paper 24: November. Bristol: ESCR Centre for Neighbourhood Research, Bristol University.

Fischer, C. S. (1982): To dwell among friends. Personal networks in town and city, Chicago.

Galster, G. (2006): Neighbourhood mix, social opportunities, and the policy challenges of an increasingly diverse Amsterdam, Wibaut lecture, Amsterdam Institute for Metropolitan and International Development Studies (AMIDSt), University of Amsterdam.

Galster, G. (2007): Neighbourhood Social Mix as a Goal of Housing Policy: A Theoretical Analysis, European Journal of Housing Policy 7 (1), 19–43.

Galster, G. / *Andersson,* R. / *Musterd,* S. / *Kauppinen,* T. (2007): Does Neighbourhood Income Mix Affect Earnings of Adults? New Evidence from Sweden, Journal of Urban Economics, doi: 10.1016/j.jue.2007.07.002.

Housing Studies (2007): Issue 5 on Neighbourhood Effects.

Johnston, R. J. / *Jones,* K. / *Burgess,* S. / *Propper,* C. / *Sarker,* R. / *Bolster,* A. (2004): Scale, Factor Analyses, and Neighbourhood Effects, Geographical Analysis 36 (4), 350–369.

Manski, C. F. (2000): Economic Analysis of Social Interactions, Journal of Economic Perspectives 14 (3), 115–136.

Musterd, S. / *Ostendorf,* W. / *Vos,* S. de (2003): Environmental Effects and Social Mobility, Housing Studies 18 (6), 877–892.

Musterd, S. / *Andersson,* R. (2005): Housing Mix, Social Mix and Social Opportunities, Urban Affairs Review 40 (6), 761–790.

Musterd, S. / *Andersson,* R. (2006): Employment, Social Mobility and Neighbourhood Effects, International Journal of Urban and Regional Research 30 (1), 120–140.

Musterd, S. / *Andersson,* R. / *Galster,* G. / *Kauppinen,* T. (2007): Are Immigrants' Earnings Influenced by the Characteristics of their Neighbours? Accepted for publication in: Environment and Planning A.

Özüekren, A. S. / *Magnusson,* L. (1997): Housing conditions of Turks in Sweden, in: A. S. Özüekren / van Kempen R. (eds.), Housing conditions of Turks in European Cities, London.

Palander, C. (2006): Områdesbaserad politik för minskad segregation –En studie av den svenska storstadspolitiken, Geografiska regionstudier no 66. Uppsala: Department of Social and Economic Geography, Uppsala university.

van Kempen, R. / *Murie,* A. / *Knorr-Siedow,* T. / *Tosics,* I. (eds.) (2006): Regenerating large housing estates in Europe. A guide to better practice, Restate report, Utrecht: Urban and Regional Research centre, Utrecht university.

Schmollers Jahrbuch 128 (2008), 65 – 73
Duncker & Humblot, Berlin

Which Progress for Poverty Studies can we expect from new large Data Sources?

By Jürgen Friedrichs

Abstract

Large data sources would allow us to test the impact of neighborhood characteristics, such as poverty rates, on the attitudes and behavior ot residents. The article explores the feasibility of existing large data sets for such a purpose. Unfortunately, none of the three sets reviewed, the Microcensus, the ALLBUS and the SOEP, allows for such multi-level analyses, because data cannot be regionalized due to data protection or insufficient sample size. To overcome these problems in a limited sense, it is suggested to pursue a "puzzle strategy" to combine data from different existing data sets.

JEL Classifications: C31, C33, C42, I32

Introduction

Over the last twenty years there has been a rapid development in the research on context effects, e.g, on school composition and educational achievement (e. g., Kristen, 2002; van Tubergen / Maas / Flap, 2004; Vartanian, 1999), on voting patterns (e.g., Brown, 1982; Falter, 1991) or networks (as contexts) on juvenile delinquency (e. g., Haynie, 2001). A significant part of the research has been devoted to neighborhoods effects (Dietz, 2000; Leventhal / Brooks-Gunn, 2000; Sampson / Morenoff / Gannon-Rowley, 2002).

In my view, three developments have contributed to this increasing number of studies. First, the methodological paradigm of micro-macro analysis (Blalock, 1984; Blau, 1994; Hernes, 1989; for urban research: Galster / Quercia / Cortes, 2000), namely the influential work of Coleman (1987, 1990, 2000). Coleman posits that any outcome at the macro level Y_j should not be explained by macro-level variables X_i, instead by a context effect from X_i to a micro-level variable x_i, further, a theory, e.g., rational choice theory, linking x_i to a behavior outcome y_i at the micro-level, and the aggregation of outcomes y_i to the macro-level variable Y_i.

Second, the statistical methods of hierarchical linear modeling (HLM), allowing to determine context from individual effects on individual level outcomes (Hox, 1996; Snijders / Bosker, 1999). Third, an increase in poverty rates in many countries combined with a spatial concentration of poverty in few but growing urban areas or neighborhoods (e.g., Jargowsky, 1996; Wilson, 1987). This, in turn has led to national and regional programs to alleviate the living conditions of residents in deprived of poor urban areas, such as the German program "The Social City" or the U.S. Gautreaux and MTO programs.

Thus, the study of neighborhood effects is not solely a scholarly problem, but has, due to its implications, become an issue of vital interest for national urban policies.

1. The Problem: Data Requirements

Studies of neighborhood contexts effects require data on two levels: neighborhood and residents. Neighborhood data most often come from official statistics or are constructed from individual-level data, such as the poverty quota. Individual data have to come from surveys; among the dependent variables often used in neighborhood studies are deviant behavior, ranging from crime to teenage pregnancy, school achievement, incomes, migration. To make analyses even more complicated, it is advisable to introduce a meso level, for instance schools; we then study the direct impacts of neigborhoods and school characteristics on individuals and the indirect effect on neighborhood on individuals (cf. Friedrichs / Galster / Musterd, 2003).

Typically, such data are not available from official sources, but have to be collected for the purpose of the respective research. Examples are the seminal studies on collective efficacy and violence (Sampson / Raudenbush / Earls, 1997; Sampson / Morenoff / Earls, 1999) or the German study by Oberwittler (2003, 2004). However, there are exceptions, for instance U.S. studies on the impact of neighborhood's share of homeowners on residents have used the General Social Survey, the U.S. Panel Study of Income Dynamics (PSID), or the U.S. Public Use Microsample (PUMS) of the 1980 Census of Population and Housing (Boehm / Schlottmann, 1999, 2002; Harkness / Newman, 2002).

In the following, I will examine research strategies based on three types of sources: large data sets, combined data sets, and new surveys, starting with a basic example of a research design.

2. A Basic Example

In his contribution to "Inner-City Poverty in U.S. Cities" (Lynn / McGeary, 1990), Weicher (1990, 69) supplies some data on the distribution of poor and non-poor persons over urban areas, classifying them as poor (lowest quartile of share of recipients of social assistance) and non-poor. The data encompass the 100 largest central cities in the U.S. in 1980. Inferring the rest of the data yields the distributions presented in Table 1.

Table 1

Persons living in poor or non-poor areas by poverty status of person, U.S. cities, 1980

1A: Absolute numbers, in millions

Residence area	Status Person		Total
	Poor	Non Poor	
Poverty	5,2 A	10,3 B	15,5
Non-poverty	2,9 C	29,1 D	32,0
Total	8,1	39,4	47,5

1B: In percent

Residence area	Status Person		Total
	Poor	Non Poor	
Poverty	10,9 A	21,7 B	32,6
Non-poverty	6,1 C	61,3 D	67,4
Total	17,0	83,0	100,0

Source of data: Weicher 1990: 69.

As a preliminary test whether the distributions are comparable to German conditions, we calculated the distribution for the urban 85 districts of Cologne. The results are reported in Table 2.

Table 2

Persons living in poor or non-poor areas by poverty status of person, Cologne, 2005

2A: Absolute numbers

Residence area	Status Person		Total
	Poor	Non Poor	
Poverty	60,457 A	86,109 B	146,566
Non-poverty	165,064 C	711,471 D	876,535
Total	225,521	797,580	1,03,1201

2B: In percent

Residence area	Status Person		Total
	Poor	Non Poor	
Poverty	5,9 A	8,4 B	14,3
Non-poverty	16,1 C	69,6 D	85,7
Total	22,0	78,0	100,0

Notes: "Poor = Social assistance recipients.

"Poverty area" = All districts of the lowest quartile of percentage of social assistance recipients.

Source: Author's calculations.

Comparing the percentages of the U.S. cities and the Cologne data, Tables 1B and 2B exhibit very similar distributions. Although this is a preliminary replication of the U.S. results (different periods, number of cities), results obtained for Cologne point into the same direction. Of course, the categorization of the two variables can be refined by grouping the variables into three or four categories.

The data reveal some interesting facts: First, more poor live in non-poor areas than in poor areas (cells C vs. A). Second, more non-poor than poor persons are living in poor areas (cells B vs. A). This raises some important research questions:

1. How do persons fare in cell A vs. cell B?
2. How do persons fare in cell B vs. cell D?
3. How do persons fare in cell A vs. cell C?

The first question pertains to the impact of poverty areas on poor and non-poor residents. This problem is addressed in a research project on the living conditions and attitudes toward crime in a study of a deprived area in Cologne, Vingst-Hoehenberg (Blasius / Friedrichs, 2007; Friedrichs / Blasius, 2006).

The second question, again, refers to a neighborhood effect, but now comparing non-poor in poor vs. non-poor neighborhoods. This may compliment studies devoted to the first question. Such comparisons are crucial for programs such as the "Social City" program in Germany, since so far only deprived neighborhoods, to which the policy measures are directed, are analyzed – without comparisons with non-poor areas or correcting for sample bias. Hence, we do not know whether the findings (e.g., correlations, trends) obtained for deprived areas hold true as well for non-poor or not deprived areas. (It is like studying a gentrifying area without controlling for upgrading processes in other areas of the city.)

The third question seems to be of specific interest, since the context hypothesis is that poor will fare better in non-poor than in poor neighborhoods. It is this hypothesis that underlies the northamerican Gautreaux and more specifically the MTO-program of relocating poor residents from poor to non-poor areas. Boldly generalizing the results from the MTO program, the studies suggest more positive than negative effects.

3. Research Strategies

To arrive at a research strategy for the study of neighborhood effects, I will first review the options and restrictions of three major large data sets available in Germany, then discuss the potential of combining existing data sets, finally explore the costs of new surveys and their implications for the methodology of neighborhood study designs.

3.1 Large Data Sources

The major large (or mass) data sets available in Germany are the ALLBUS (General Social Survey), the Microcensus., and the Socio-economic Panel (SOEP). For the purposes of studying neighborhood effects, these data sets have to be regionalized and cumulated. Unfortunately, this is only to a limited extent possible.

A single wave of the ALLBUS is by no means sufficient for the regionalization required. If several waves are combined, as in the Cumulative ALLBUS, due to different sampling we have different residents in the regional units and thus residential change as an error.

The Microcensus can be regionalized, but the Public Use Files comprises only a 70 percent sample of the total sample; further, the spatial units have changed after 1990. From 1990 onwards, each sample unit comprises an average of nine dwellings – which is by far too small for our purposes.

Therefore, the only candidate from the large surveys – except for a new survey – is the Socio-economic Panel. Due to data protection, the SOEP data presently cannot be regionalized, although it would be possible to allocate respondents by their residence to urban districts. However, efforts to regionalize SEOP data are under way, an example being the study of total poverty quotas and those of persons aged 65 and older for the 97 Regional Policy Regions in Germany (Knies / Krause, 2005). Moreover, data are now regionalized down to the level of zip codes (Knies / Spiess 2007), and presently work is under way to link SOEP data with data from microm Micromarketing on a household basis (Goebel et al., 2006).

Such regionalized SOEP datasets would allow to test hypotheses derived from the typology in Tables 1 and 2. If this does not result in a sufficient number of cases, we could then aggregate urban districts for several cities having similar characteristics assumed to be related to the individual outcome, such as GDP, poverty rates or percent ethnic minorities. In both strategies, the individual residences do not have to be disclosed.

Nonetheless, two drawbacks remain: First, the number of cases per urban district is to small (e.g., for each of the 85 Cologne districts) to conduct contextual analyses in the tradition of neighbourhood effect studies; further, zip codes according to our experiences cannot be aggregated to urban districts. Second, this large data set comprises only some of the dependent variables relevant for assessing neighborhood effects, e.g. income and educational achievement, but no variables of deviant behaviour or social capital (collective efficacy), which are crucial for an international cumulative and comparative study.

It should be noted, however, that only panel data allow us to do research truly testing the *causal* effects that most scholars of neighbourhood effects have proposed. In contrast, the majority of the studies which posit effects of the neighbourhood on behaviour of residents use cross-sectional survey data for one point in time. Finally, the SOEP panel data would allow us to examine changes in the composition of urban areas by specifying the socio-economic characteristics of those moving in vs. those moving out.

3.2 Combining Existing Datasets

A second strategy is to combine official statistical data from different sources. In Cologne, for instance, we combined data for the urban districts from the Statistical Office with data from the Department of Health on a survey of children aged 4 to 6 years on their health, physical and mental conditions, these tests serving as a criterion of the ability to enter elementary school. Even at the risk of stating the obvious, I suggest to search for such data "hidden" in urban departments or other institutions.

3.3 New Surveys

An evident third strategy is to conduct new surveys. In the following section, I attempt to give examples for the calculation of costs of fieldwork. They serve to more specify the relationship between methodology of neighborhood effects studies if costs are taken into account.

Which cities? The study cannot compare too many cities, if survey data for all districts or neighborhoods are to be collected. Example 1: Imagine, we wish to draw a probability sample of residents in the 85 Cologne districts with only 150 residents in the final sample, this would require 12,750 completed interviews. If we calculate € 25 Euro per face-to-face interview, the costs amount to € 318,750 – excluding all costs of questionnaire construction, pretesting, data correction and data entry. If total field costs are calculated, a commercial institute will charge € 100 Euro per interview (including a corrected SPSS file), with the total amount rising to € 1,127,000.

Example 2: If, as proposed in Table 1 and 2, we use two neighborhoods per four cells by 150 interviews at € 100 Euro each, costs are 120,000 per city for the field work only.

Example 3: Since we wish to study several cities, selected e.g. by different extents of income inequality or different GDP's, the calculation in example 2 and categorizing the independent variable into three categories (e.g., low – medium – high income) and taking two cities per category, the total costs of fieldwork would be 6 × € 120,000 = 720,000.

It is easy to vary the calculations given in the three examples, for instance by doubling the number of interviews per cell. Of course, a high amount of funding is feasible if project costs are shared by several countries. But under which conditions is such a study justified? We may think of two major legitimate reasons. First, the study is innovative and makes a crucial contribution to our knowledge of neighborhood effects, taking the PISA studies as a model. This given, we arrive at a second reason: The policy implications. Results should allow for programs and the implementation of measures to alleviate living conditions of the poor segment of the population. One of the conclusions may pertain to the question of whether area-based or people-based strategies are advisable.

4. Conclusions: Towards a "Puzzle Strategy"

It is evident, that comparative studies of neighborhood effects require large data sets, with data for the aggregate level of the neighborhood and on the individual level. To cope with the data problems outlined, we have to carefully design a study combining elements from all three strategies, based on the existing theoretical reasoning and empirical evidence on neighborhood effects. I therefore suggest a "puzzle strategy".

The design of a comparative study, encompassing several countries and cities, should include several of those dependent variables listed in the introductory section. Further, large data sets available might lend themselves to different parts of the total design, e.g. the SOEP data of the U.K. data set on wards. We therefore have to specify which effect can be approached by a specific data set. Even further, we have to explore for each city if so far not used individual data from institutional sources exist. Based on this evidence of available data, we can determine those parts of the total design which are not captured. The final step would then require a larger new survey in few cities filling the methodological and data gaps. We assemble the different data a like parts of a puzzle. As stated above, both for scholarly and policy reasons, we need a European study.

If such new surveys are conducted, the data should be available, e.g., at the DIW in Berlin or the Central Archive for Empirical Social Research, Cologne, Germany, to enable scholars from different countries to make use of the data und perform secondary analyses, as the widely used SOEP convincingly demonstrates. Further, the design of the study might as well serve as guideline for additional studies in other cities.

References

Blalock, H. M. (1984): Contextual Effects Models: Theoretical and Methodological Issues, Annual Review of Sociology 10, 353 – 372.

Blasius, J. / *Friedrichs,* J. (2007): Internal Heterogeneity in a Deprived Urban Area and its Impact on Resident's Perceptions of Deviance, Housing Studies 22 (5), 753 – 780.

Blau, P. M. (1994): Structural Contexts of Opportunities. Chicago (IL).

Boehm, Th. P. / *Schlottmann,* A. M. (1999): Does Home Ownership by Parents Have an Economic Impact on Their Children?, Journal of Housing Economics 8, 217 – 232.

Boehm, Th. P. / *Schlottmann,* A. M. (2002): Housing and Wealth Accumulation: Intergenerational Impacts, in: N. P. Retsinas / E. S. Belsky (eds.): Low-Income Homeownership. Examining the Unexamined Goal, Cambridge (MA): Joint Center for Housing Studies und Washington, DC, 407 – 426.

Brown, C. (1982): The Nazi Vote. A National Ecological Study, American Political Science Review 76, 285 – 301.

Coleman, J. S. (1987): Microfoundations and Macrosocial Behavior, in: J. C. Alexander et al. (eds.): The Micro-Macro Link, Berkeley (CA), 153 – 173.

Dietz, R. (2000): Estimation of Neighborhood Effects in the Social Sciences, URAI Working Paper No. 00 – 03, Columbus, OH: Ohio State University, Urban and Regional Analysis Initiative.

DiPasquale, D. / *Glaeser,* E. L. (1999): Incentives and Social Capital: Are Homeowners Better Citizens?, Journal of Urban Economics 45, 354 – 384.

Falter, J. (1991): Hitlers Wähler (Hitler's Voters). München.

Friedrichs, J. / *Blasius,* J. (2006): Attitudes of Owners and Renters in a Deprived Neighborhood, Paper, presented at the ENHR Conference, Workshop "Poverty Neighborhoods", Ljubljana July 10, 2006.

Friedrichs, J. / *Galster,* G. / *Musterd,* S. (2003): Neighborhood Effects on Social Opportunities, The European and American Research and Policy Context, Housing Studies 18, 797 – 806.

Galster, G. (2003): Investigating Behavioral Impacts of Poor Neighborhoods: Towards New Data and Analytic Strategies, Housing Studies 18, 863 – 914.

Galster, G. / *Quercia,* R. G. / *Cortes,* A. (2000): Identifying Neighborhood Thresholds: An Empirical Investigation, Housing Policy Debate 11, 701 – 732.

Goebel, J. / *Knies,* G. / *Krause,* P. / *Spiess,* C. K. / *Scheike,* I. (2006): Verknüpfung des SOEP mit microgeo-graphischen Daten: Neue Möglichkeiten für Wissenschaft und Forschung, Vortrag, gehalten auf der Statistischen Woche 2006 der Deutschen Statistischen Gesellschaft, Dresden.

Green, R. K. / *White,* M. J. (1997): Measuring the Benefits of Homeowning: Effects on Children, Journal of Urban Economics 41, 441 – 461.

Harkness, J. / *Newman,* S. J. (2002): Homeownership for the Poor in Distressed Neighborhoods: Does This Make Sense?, Housing Policy Debate 13, 597 – 630.

Haynie, D. L. (2001): Delinquent Peers Revisited: Does Network Structure Matter?, American Journal of Sociology 106, 1013 – 1057.

Hernes, G. (1989): The Logic of the Protestant Ethic, Rationality and Society 1, 123 – 162.

Hox, J. J. (1996): Applied Multilevel Analysis, www.fss.uu.nl / ms / jh / publist / amaboek.pdf.

Jargowsky, P. A. (1996): Poverty and Place, New York.

Jencks, Ch. / *Mayer,* S. E. (1990): The Social Consequences of Growing up in a Poor Neighborhood, in: L. E. Lynn / M. G. H. McGeary (eds.): Inner-City-Poverty in the United States, Washington (DC.), 111 – 186.

Knies, G. / *Krause,* P. (2005): Armut und Alter, in: Nationalatlas Bundesrepublik Deutschland, Vol. 7: Arbeit und Lebensstandard, Heidelberg / Berlin, 118 – 199.

Knies, G. / *Spiess,* C. K. (2007): Regional Data in the German Socio-Economic Panel Study (SOEP), Data Documentation 17. Berlin: Deutsches Institut für Wirtschaftsforschung.

Kristen, C. (2002): Hauptschule, Realschule oder Gymnasium? Ethnische Unterschiede am ersten Bildungsübergang, Kölner Zeitschrift für Soziologie und Sozialpsychologie 54, 534 – 552.

Leventhal, T. / *Brooks-Gunn,* J. (2000): The Neighborhoods They Live in: The Effects of Neighborhood Residence on Child and Adolescent Outcomes, Psychological Bulletin 126, 309 – 337.

Oberwittler, D. (2003): Die Messung und Qualitätskontrolle kontextbezogener Befragungsdaten mithilfe der Mehrebenenanalyse – am Beispiel des Sozialkapitals von Stadtvierteln, ZA-Information 53, 11 – 41.

Oberwittler, D. (2004): Sozialstruktur, Freundeskreise und Delinquenz. Eine Mehrebenenanalyse zu sozialökologischen Kontexteffekten auf schwere Jugenddelinquenz, in: D. Oberwittler / S. Karstedt (Hg.): Soziologie der Kriminalität, Wiesbaden, 135 – 170. (Sonderheft 43 der Kölner Zeitschrift für Soziologie und Sozialpsychologie).

Sampson, R. J. / *Morenoff,* J. D. / *Gannon-Rowley,* Th. (2002): Assessing "Neighborhood Effects": Social Processes and New Directions in Research, Annual Review of Sociology 28, 443 – 478.

Sampson, R. J. / *Raudenbush,* S. W. / *Earls,* F. J. (1997): Neighborhoods and Violent Crime: A Multilevel Study of Collective Efficacy, Science 277, 918 – 924.

Sampson, R. J. / *Raudenbush,* S. W. / *Earls,* F. J. (1999): Beyond Social Capital: Spatial Dynamics of Collective Efficacy for Children, American Sociological Review 64, 633 – 660.

Snijders, T. A. B. / *Bosker,* R. (1999): Multilevel Analysis. An Introduction to Basic and Advanced Multilevel Modeling. London.

van Tubergen, F. / *Maas,* I. / *Flap,* H. (2004): The Economic Incorporation of Immigrants in 18 Western Societies: Origin, Destination, and Community Effects, American Sociological Review 69, 704 – 727.

Vartanian, Th. P. (1999): Adolescent Neighborhood Effects on Labor Market and Economic Outcomes, Social Service Review 73, 142 – 167.

Weicher, J. C. (1990): How Poverty Neighborhoods are Changing, in: L. E. Lynn / M. G. H. McGeary (eds.): Inner-City Poverty in the United States, Washington (DC.), 68 – 110.

Schmollers Jahrbuch 128 (2008), 75 – 108
Duncker & Humblot, Berlin

Keeping up with the Schmidt's – An Empirical Test of Relative Deprivation Theory in the Neighbourhood Context

By Gundi Knies, Simon Burgess, and Carol Propper

Abstract

We test empirically whether people's life satisfaction depends on their relative income position in the neighbourhood, drawing on a unique dataset, the German Socio-economic Panel Study (SOEP) matched with micro-marketing indicators of population characteristics. Relative deprivation theory suggests that individuals are happier the better their relative income position in the neighbourhood is. To test this theory we estimate micro-economic happiness models for the years 1994 and 1999 with controls for own income and for neighbourhood income at the zip-code level (roughly 9,000 people). There exist no negative and no statistically significant associations between neighbourhood income and life satisfaction, which refutes relative deprivation theory. If anything, we find *positive* associations between neighbourhood income and happiness in all cross-sectional models and this is robust to a number of robustness tests, including adding in more controls for neighbourhood quality, changing the outcome variable, and interacting neighbourhood income with indicators that proxy the extent to which individuals may be assumed to interact with their neighbours. We argue that the scale at which we measure neighbourhood characteristics may be too large still to identify the comparison effect sought after.

JEL Classifications: I31, C23, Z1

1. Introduction

Research in the field of happiness has shown that people are happier the more income they have, and that, more importantly, they care about how this income compares to that of others (Clark / Oswald, 1996; Easterlin, 1974; Frey / Stutzer, 2002; Layard, 2005). On the other hand, social scientists placed growing emphasis on geography as an explanatory factor for social inequalities between individuals (for literature reviews see, e.g., Dietz, 2002; Durlauf, 2003; Jencks / Mayer, 1990; Sampson / Morenoff / Gannon-Rowley, 2002). In this paper we integrate these two strands of research by an empirical investigation of whether levels of and changes in happiness depend on one's financial position within one's neighbourhood. We estimate micro-economic happiness models with controls for the neighbourhood context and systematically test the neighbourhood effects theory of relative deprivation (see Buck, 2001; Dietz, 2002; Jencks / Mayer, 1990).

Neighbourhood effects research is flawed by econometric and conceptual challenges, which we address in as much as is feasible. Using very rich matched individual and neighbourhood level panel data for Germany the research makes controls for the endogeneity of the neighbourhood choice and for unobserved individual and neighbourhood level heterogeneity. Adding in variables that measure the distance to local public infrastructure does not only attenuate possible biases on the effect of neighbourhood income on happiness but it also provides empirical evidence that other aspects of the neighbourhood, which are not usually included in neighbourhood effects studies, affect life satisfaction (and thereby possibly other outcomes). The study is the first using German longitudinal data and uses very immediate scales of the neighbourhood.

1.1 Literature Review

The theory of relative deprivation is distinct among the theories that have been put forward to explain the mechanisms through which neighbourhood context impacts on people's life chances (see Buck, 2001; Dietz, 2002; Jencks / Mayer, 1990) in that it suggests negative outcomes of living in a better-off neighbourhood. Relative deprivation concepts (see Stouffer, 1949) have been employed, for instance, to explain rioting (e.g., Canache, 1996; Gurr, 1970), schooling outcomes (e.g., Davis, 1966; Meyer, 1970), and emotional and behavioural outcomes (Lopez Turley, 2002).

Runciman defines relative deprivation as „a psychological effect deriving from comparison with others who have achieved something that would be feasible to achieve for oneself, that one desires but does not have himself" (Runciman, 1966, 9). Empirically, this effect has been shown to exist with respect to happiness, a heavily researched area in psychology, sociology and more recently in economics (see Diener / Suh / Lucas / Smith, 1999 for a review). Under the umbrella of testing the relative income hypothesis[1] a strand of happiness research looks at how individuals react to objectively existing or perceived differences in their own life circumstances compared to those of others (e.g., Blanchflower / Oswald, 2004; Clark / Oswald, 1996; Ferrer-i-Carbonell, 2005). Popular examples of comparison groups drawn on in the happiness literature are the society as a whole and people from the same profession.

While an impact of neighbourhood and community contexts has been suggested in the happiness literature (e.g., Layard, 2005), few empirical studies

1 This hypothesis states, in brief, that individual utility is derived not so much from one's absolute income position but from one's income position within a relevant group.

have actually considered the neighbourhood context as a relevant variable in the prediction of happiness.[2] In particular, neighbours have not typically been chosen as a comparison group in happiness research that addresses the relative income hypothesis. However, there are good reasons to assume that it also holds for this reference group. In the local housing market, for instance, it may not be some absolute amount of money that will ensure that the richest individual gets the best-quality land and property, but rather that income position of all people with a demand for land and property in the city or town will determine who gets what and how much it costs to get the best spot.[3] The implications for happiness are that if we observe two individuals that are statistically identical apart from living in different neighbourhoods where the incomes of the neighbours in one neighbourhood are higher and lower in the other, the individuals in the richer neighbourhood will be unhappier with their lives (assuming that satisfaction with housing and the home affects life satisfaction, see Sirgy / Cornwell, 2002), because their income will not have allowed them to find as nice a place as would have been possible in the neighbourhood with less affluent competitors.[4] Luttmer (2005) discusses the role which the neighbours' income position plays for overall life satisfaction in this argument. The author uses income as a proxy for consumption and argues that „if utility depends on relative consumption, one person's increase in consumption has a negative externality on others because it lowers the relative consumption of others" (964). Using socio-economic panel data linked with Census data for the US, Luttmer finds a strong negative association between neighbour's earnings and self-reported levels of happiness that is robust to a wide range of model specifications (including controlling for individual fixed effects, individual relocations, and interaction effects).[5]

Our empirical strategy is very similar to Luttmer, however, we use German data and draw on longitudinal neighbourhood data which are measured at the same time as the characteristics of the individual that affect happiness, our neighbourhood units are more immediate and the time interval we look at is shorter and more recent.

---

2 Examples include Sirgy / Cornwell (2002) and Shields / Wooden (2003).

3 This argument builds on the assumption that individuals have a preference for living in some given neighbourhood, say the area of a particular city, for instance, because all their family and friends live there, or their workplace is in this town. Gaarder (2002) argues that it is this mechanism which determines who gets exposed to air pollution.

4 This is true at least if we believe that the type and quality of houses that makes people (dis-)satisfied is the same for everyone.

5 The only analysed case where no effect of neighbour's earnings could be found is when individual- and neighbourhood level fixed-effects were controlled for.

2. Methodology

We undertake an empirical test of the relative deprivation theory in the neighbourhood context applying it to the outcome of self-reported levels of happiness.[6] Veenhoven (1984, 10) defines life satisfaction „as the degree to which an individual judges the overall quality of his life-as-a-whole favourably". A judgement of the overall quality of one's life is the result of a process that involves an assessment of one's objective living conditions but also of interpersonal and intertemporal comparisons. If feelings of relative deprivation are present we expect this to show in lower happiness scores.

However, not all lower happiness scores should be regarded as deriving from not being as well off as people think they deserve to be. In the absence of a dataset that observes objective and subjective deprivations at the same time, we need to operationalise relative deprivation on the basis of some measure of how people match up to others. In our study, this is the relative income position that individuals occupy in their neighbourhood. We define that people who have less income than their average neighbour are relatively deprived and *assume* that relatively deprived people will be unhappier.

Our empirical analyses unfold as follows. We first provide descriptive tables and graphs that show the mean life satisfaction by classes of household and neighbourhood income at two points in time, 1994 and 1999. We proceed to a multivariate model where we predict life satisfaction controlling for other aspects that are regarded to influence how satisfied people are with their lives.

2.1 Multivariate Predictions

We include in our models controls for five domains of life that have been shown to impact on subjective well-being. These spheres are family context, financial situation, work, community and friends (which we proxy with neighbourhood characteristics), and health, respectively.[7] In addition, we include basic characteristics such as age and gender.

6 We use the terms 'happiness', 'subjective well-being' and 'life satisfaction' interchangeably throughout the paper.

7 Layard (2005) refers to two more aspects that have been argued to impact on subjective well-being. These are personal values and personal freedom. There are no direct measures of personal values available in the large-scale dataset we employ. Variables relating to personal freedom are mostly employed in cross-country analyses when the focus is on the impact of living in democratic political systems versus living under dictatorship. In our single country study, this aspect is mostly redundant. We do, however, employ a dummy for German nationality. The citizenship rights tied to the German citizenship might proxy for higher personal freedom and should be positively correlated with happiness.

A source for heterogeneity that is not usually considered in the international research on happiness is regional differences. In the German context, it has been shown that people in East Germany are unhappier with their lives than people living in West Germany (e.g., Ferrer-i-Carbonell, 2005). In addition, average personal incomes in East Germany are lower than in West Germany. This does not necessarily mean that all neighbourhoods in the East are poorer than neighbourhoods in West Germany. In fact, research by Knies / Krause (2006) has shown that some regions within West Germany are on average poorer than regions in East Germany. Also, it has been shown that the levels of happiness in the two regions converged over time and that most of the increase in East German's happiness cannot be attributed to increases in personal income (Frijters / Haisken-DeNew / Shields, 2004).

We estimate the impact of these characteristics on subjective well-being employing a so-called bottom-up approach. The bottom-up approach builds on the philosophical assumption that there are universal needs which have to be met in order for people to be happy.[8] The settlement of needs is thought to be dependent upon external factors, and people who find themselves in a 'good situation' for the fulfilment of needs are happy, while those who find themselves in a 'bad situation' are unhappy (see, e.g., Diener / Suh / Lucas / Smith, 1999). The context in which individuals can be happy is implicitly thought to be the same for everybody, and people will be happier the more happy moments they experience. It follows from this that the independent variables employed in bottom-up models are objective life circumstances.

Our statistical approach is as follows. We start off with a standard microeconomic life satisfaction function (Clark / Oswald, 1996; Frey / Stutzer, 2002)

$$LS_i = \alpha + \beta' X_i + \varepsilon_i \qquad i = 1, \ldots, n$$

where LS_i is a continuous measure of life satisfaction[9] for individual i, X is a vector of objective characteristics that are held to influence the life satisfaction of individual i, and ε is a randomly distributed error term. As our model is

8 An alternative philosophical theory to understanding happiness is the so-called top-down approach. These models assume that subjective well-being is influenced by characteristics that are internal to the individual. Among the factors that these models include are personality traits like determination, optimism and self-confidence. While some characteristics like employment, health and marital status will play a role in these models it is the subjective evaluations of these states that the focus is on rather than the objective states. A third type of models acknowledges the multiple interactions between the internal and external context in which individuals operate. The so-called interactionist models recognise, for instance, that married people are happier than non-married people but also that more optimistic and happier people are more likely to get married. See: Brief / Butcher / George / Link (1993).

9 Empirically, this is often measured on a cardinal scale. Ferrer-i-Carbonell / Frijters (2004) show that the difference is negligible.

after identifying neighbourhood effects on subjective well-being, we rewrite the model as

$$LS_i = \alpha + \beta' X_i + \gamma' Z_i + \varepsilon_i \qquad i = 1, \ldots, n$$

where LS_i denotes life satisfaction for individual i, X is a vector of objective characteristics that are held to influence the life satisfaction of individual i, Z is a vector of neighbourhood characteristics in which individual i lives, and ε is a randomly distributed error term.

We include the own income and neighbourhood income variables in the logged form. Mathematically,

$$LS_i = \beta_1 \log x_{1i} + \gamma_1 \log z_{1i} + \ldots + \varepsilon_i$$

where LS_i denotes life satisfaction for individual i, x_{1i} is the income of individual i, z_{1i} is the income in the neighbourhood of individual i, and ε is a randomly distributed error term. This allows us to look at two different hypotheses about the effect of neighbourhood income on happiness at the same time. The more general relative income hypothesis will be supported if the coefficient on neighbourhood income is negative. In addition, the more specific relative deprivation hypothesis will be supported if γ_1 is negative and its absolute value is greater or equal the coefficient on household income.

2.2 Robustness Tests

2.2.1 Measurement of Relative Deprivation

The first robustness test that we undertake is that we look at the relationship between peoples' income position and a more direct measure of relative deprivation. In our multivariate model we try to identify feelings of relative deprivation in the form of lower life satisfaction. That is, we argue that objectively deprived people feel deprived and will thus report to be not as happy as people who are not relatively deprived, ceteris paribus. However, relative deprivation theory concedes that not all the deprivations that we can objectively identify necessarily imply feelings of relative deprivation.

In this robustness test, we first investigate whether our objective measure of deprivation is associated with the degree to which people feel that they have not achieved what they should have achieved in comparison to others. Our indicator of subjective feelings of deprivation does not directly relate to specific others, but if neighbours are a relevant comparison group we expect a significant relationship between this variable and our objective indicator of relative deprivation in the neighbourhood. We then need to show that if we replace the outcome variable 'self-reported happiness' by our indicator of subjective deprivation, the β_1 and γ_1 coefficients in the models go in the same direction. If our theory is right that feelings of relative deprivation can be measured in the form of reduced happiness, the signs of the coefficients should be significant and in the same direction as in the baseline regressions.

2.2.2 More Neighbourhood Quality Controls

In our baseline models we include a rather limited number of controls for the neighbourhood context within which individuals operate. Apart from controlling for neighbourhood income, we only control for the type of community in which individuals live. The latter variable picks up the effects of living in villages or cities, in residential areas or business districts, in a detached house or in a multiunit property, but the indicator does not tell us anything about the quality of the neighbourhoods.

The quality of the neighbourhood is important, however. If we observe a positive effect of neighbourhood income on happiness, one might argue that it is upward-biased because we do not control for other things that are correlated with on-average higher neighbourhood incomes. Residents in these richer neighbourhoods may have access to institutions to which the residents of poorer neighbourhoods do not have access, or the quality of the institutions may be better. Children may get better education because the teachers are more qualified and use more up-to-date teaching methods. Sick people may get better treatment because the general practitioner in the richer neighbourhood has better medical equipment.

Similarly, if we observe a negative impact of neighbourhood income on happiness, one might argue that this is not due to the neighbours' better financial position but due to some unobserved characteristics of the neighbourhood which reduce happiness. Higher housing prices in the neighbourhood might be one reason to be unhappy with living in richer neighbourhoods (compare our relative consumption example in the literature review).

Our data allows us to include in our regressions a number of indicators of the availability of public facilities in the neighbourhood. The list of facilities includes basic day-to-day infrastructure (i.e., doctors, banks, and public transport), recreational facilities (i.e., parks, gyms, bars), and institutions such as primary schools, kindergartens, and clubs for the youth or the elderly.

If unobserved neighbourhood characteristics are driving our baseline results, we would expect our neighbourhood income effect to change significantly when we control for the presence of the abovementioned facilities. In addition, these controls allow us to investigate whether the availability of local public infrastructure has an impact on people's life satisfaction. They are proxies for neighbourhood quality, however, do not provide us with information about the quality of the particular services and amenities available, which is a drawback.[10] Generally, accessibility might be regarded as something good. However, living next to an amenity of low quality might have an outweighing negative effect on the level of happiness. While in general people may, for instance, be assumed to be happy about having green space right in front of their doorstep, if the public park is cluttered with rubbish they may wish there was no park at all.

2.2.3 People's Interaction with the Neighbourhood

Comparison effects can only be present if neighbours are indeed a relevant group for comparison. This is the case when the particular neighbourhood indicator we employ is socially structured (Merton / Rossi, 1968, 296). The neighbourhood property should also be observed by the individuals – otherwise we can not expect to find significant comparison effects. We have no direct means of testing whether this requirement is met. However, we hypothesise that for some groups of the population the neighbourhood effect is more robust.

Neighbourhood effects should be stronger for individuals that may be assumed to interact on a more regular basis with their neighbourhood because these persons may know their neighbours better. We test for interaction terms of neighbourhood income with whether or not an individual lives in a household with a child below the age of 7 (Interaction 1), with whether or not the individuals have a dog as a pet (Interaction 2), with whether or not individuals interact socially with their neighbours (Interaction 3), and with whether or not individuals work in their town of residence (Interaction 4).[11]

Individuals living in households with young children may be assumed more likely to interact with their neighbourhood and to know people in the neighbourhood because they make use of institutions that are placed in proximity to the place of residence (i.e., playgrounds, kindergartens, and local doctors' practices). They also go for a walk with their youngest and by this means may get to know the neighbourhood and, so we argue, they may get to talk to people they meet in the streets. The same is true for dog owners. Walking the pet, on the one hand, facilitates having a look around the neighbourhood and, so we argue, seeing how much prosperity there is. On the other hand, the pet might attract other people's interest which is why dog owners, we argue, have a higher propensity of getting to talk to their neighbours.

---

10 SOEP also surveys neighbourhood quality by means of asking respondents to the study how much they are affected by noise pollution, atmospheric pollution and lack of accessible green space. Accounts of the quality of personal relationships among the neighbours are also available. However, in our study we want to control only for objective context measures and disregard these qualitative indicators.

11 Not employed individuals are treated like individuals who are working and living in the same neighbourhood.

The relationship between our direct measure of whether or not individuals interact socially with their neighbours, neighbourhood income and happiness is less straightforward. While we may assume that individuals who socialize with their neighbours have a better knowledge of their neighbours' financial circumstances – which should deserve for feelings of relative deprivation if the neighbours are better off – utility maximising individuals may avoid interaction with individuals that cause unhappiness. In other words, whether or not individuals interact with their neighbours is endogenous.

As to the fourth interaction term, we may assume that individuals who work in the town where they live have a better knowledge than others of the financial position of the people in their environment because of interaction with colleagues and knowledge of the local salaries at least in their employment sector.

Finally, the neighbourhood income effect might be driven less by how much individuals may be assumed to interact with their neighbours than by how much pressure is exerted on individuals to keep up with their neighbours' incomes. Young children may want to have the same toys as their peers in the neighbourhood and parents may not want their children to go without them. If this is true, we might be able to see the same effect for individuals in households with teenagers, i.e., individuals aged 12 – 16.[12] Young and financially dependent people may exert pressure on their parent(s) to be able to keep up with their peers in the neighbourhood and this may lead to reduced happiness for all members of households with teenagers. The fifth interaction term captures this effect.

2.2.4 Unobserved Heterogeneity

A common critique on cross-sectional models is that it cannot be controlled for unobserved heterogeneity at the level of observations, which results in biased estimates. In the field of happiness research it is known, for instance, that the genes people have defines their ability to feel happy (e.g., Layard, 2005, 55). Genetic codes, however, are not available in surveys and thus cannot be employed as independent variables. Surveys also do not usually collect information on personality traits that determine how a person establishes how happy she is.

An advantage of the longitudinal structure of our dataset is that we can make some controls for those unobserved characteristics of the individual, and of the neighbourhood (i.e., when we select on individuals that did not relocate) that do not change over time. We expect our neighbourhood and own income

12 The age brackets for this group have been thus defined because children of this age will be in secondary school and will not usually have started vocational training. This implies that the money the children can draw upon must come from within the household.

effects to work in the same direction as in the cross-sectional level models when we isolate from our model those unobserved fixed characteristics. The size of the effects, however, can be expected to be smaller in the change model since biases in the cross-sectional estimates will be lessened due to the inclusion of more controls (i.e., time-invariant individual characteristics). An additional source of bias is measurement error, which can be assumed to be rather high on both our dependent variable life satisfaction and on our key independent variables (i.e., neighbourhood income and household income). If these errors are time-invariant, they will downwardly attenuate the coefficients in the fixed effects model.

3. Data

This research uses data derived from the German Socio-Economic Panel Study (SOEP). SOEP is a longitudinal survey representative of the German population living in private households, and contains data on a wide range of economic and social topics. SOEP provides information on all household members, and covers persons living in the Old and New German States, foreigners, and recent immigrants to Germany. The salient features of the survey include data on household composition and occupational biographies, as well as employment and earnings, health and satisfaction indicators. The panel was started in 1984, and since then the same households, persons and families have been surveyed annually. Our analysis focuses on the 1994 and 1999 waves of the survey. In these years, the special focus of the study is on neighbourhood infrastructure and social networks.

Our key dependent variable is a measure of life satisfaction derived from the following question addressed to SOEP respondents in every wave of the survey: „How satisfied are you at present with your life, all things considered?" There are eleven response categories running from 0 (completely dissatisfied) to 10 (completely satisfied). As controls we employ characteristics that have been shown to impact on happiness in other research on subjective well-being (compare Appendix 1 and 2 for variable descriptions and summary statistics). We divide the controls into six blocks, namely basic characteristics (age, gender, number of years in education and nationality), health (here: disability status), family (marital status and number of children in the household), financial situation (annual per capita household income, change in annual per capita household income from previous year to current year, homeownership), work (employment status), and last but not least neighbourhood context (annual per capita neighbourhood income – as described below – and type of community). All control variables apart from the annual per capita neighbourhood income are derived from SOEP.

A lesser known feature of SOEP, which we explore in this study, is that it contains geographical references that allow matching the study with geocoded data.[13] We linked SOEP data of 1994 and 1999 with context data at the zip-code level. The zip-code level is the smallest entity at which external geographical context variables can be matched with SOEP.[14] Out of 8,256 zip-code areas in Germany[15] 2,256 are represented in SOEP.

To illustrate how sensibly zip-code areas may be used as a proxy for 'neighbourhood', we ordered all German zip-code areas by their population size and created deciles. We report the minimum, the mean and the maximum population size in each of these deciles to get some idea about the number of people living in these zip-code areas (Table 1).

Table 1

Distribution of population size of zip-code areas in Germany 1995 and 1998 (*N* = 8,256)

Deciles of populatio size in zip-code area	1995			1998		
	mean	*min*	*max*	*mean*	*min*	*max*
Bottom decile	967	9	1,370	1,009	10	1,442
2	1,756	1,371	2,169	1,859	1,444	2,297
3	2,638	2,170	3,152	2,778	2,298	3,317
4	3,770	3,153	4,443	3,955	3,320	4,642
5	5,271	4,444	6,235	5,512	4,642	6,506
6	7,579	6,237	9,133	7,843	6,508	9,399
7	11,058	9,140	13,027	11,237	9,408	13,138
8	15,272	13,029	17,455	15,296	13,144	17,637
9	19,869	17,457	22,875	20,071	17,637	22,970
top decile	29,940	22,896	63,005	29,801	22,987	59,852
Mean population size		9,810			9,934	

Source: SOEP 20. Neighbourhood indicator dataset. Authors' calculations.

In 1995, the average population size in German zip-code areas was 9,810 individuals (1998: 9,934). The smallest zip-code area had just 9 inhabitants (1998: 10) and the largest had 63,005 (1998: 59,852). The population size in half of the zip-code areas is less than 6,235 in 1995 (1998: 6,506). This figure

13 See Knies / Spiess (2007) for detailed information.

14 Due to data protection legislation SOEP data at zip-code level can only be matched and analysed with special permission and at DIW Berlin. A special data user contract has to be concluded.

15 This figure refers to only those zip-code areas that existed in both years of observation. We employ population figures for 1995 as a proxy for population figures in 1993.

may be thought of as the population of an average-sized German village. More populated zip-code areas, on the other hand, are most often found in cities and are spatially confined to small areas with a high population density. These zip-code areas may be thought of as representing the geographical scale of a neighbourhood.

Matching SOEP with neighbourhood indicators for 1993 and 1998 resulted in a unique data set that has not been employed before. The neighbourhood data for the years 1993 and 1998 have been purchased by the SOEP Group from a commercial data provider, Infas Geodaten (Infas). They are defined for all zip-code areas that existed in Germany in these years. The indicators are *estimates* of neighbourhood characteristics that the data supplier obtained analysing commercial telephone surveys, local statistics, and mail-order data.

We draw in our analyses on an *estimate* of the average purchasing power of the population in the area in the respective year. The currency is DM (1 DM equals 0.5113 Euro). The term 'purchasing power' relates to „disposable household income“ as used by German Federal Statistical Office (compare Infas Geodaten, 2004). The originally available measure has been re-based in order to make it comparable to annual per capita household incomes derived from the SOEP. This exercise is undertaken to establish whether or not an individual is objectively relatively deprived in his / her neighbourhood.

We have indicators of the total per capita purchasing power and the population count for all German zip-code areas enabling us to calculate Germany's total purchasing power. This total is replaced by a measure of total national annual income yielded from SOEP, and is then proportionally reassigned to the zip-code areas. The neighbourhood income that we use in the analysis is the re-based income divided over the population in the zip-code area. We call this 'annual per capita neighbourhood income'.

We calculated the total national income available to households in Germany on the basis of annual household incomes and household weighting factors provided in the SOEP. The annual household income information is taken from the Cross-National-Equivalent-File (CNEF) instrument of the SOEP.[16] It refers to household income in the previous calendar year. In our multiple regression models, we employ the measure of annual household income divided over the size of the household at the time of the interview. This way the household and neighbourhood incomes are at the same units.

16 Compare http: // www.human.cornell.edu / pam / SOEP / equiv / g-equiv2.pdf, 9 ff.

4. Empirical Results

4.1 Bivariate and Three-dimensional Associations between Household Income, Neighbourhood Income and Happiness

Most empirical research on the association between income and happiness suggests that people are happier the higher their income is. Income does not only make possible the consumption of more goods and services. Having money serves for greater utility than not having it: whereas one is free to give money away if one does not like to have much of it, for the poor, in contrast, it is not realistic to just get money from somewhere. However, „people are really seeking nonmaterial goods such as personal fulfilment or the meaning of life and are disappointed when material things fail to provide them" (Dittmar, 1992 in: Frey / Stutzer, 2002, 81), thus leaving the correlation subject to empirical investigation.

We start our empirical investigation by looking at the average life satisfaction of individuals in different classes of own income and neighbourhood income. We vary the definitions of income bands so as to see whether findings are robust to these definitions. Table 2 presents the results for 1999 (1994: see Appendix 3).

Table 2

Average life satisfaction by classes of income 1999

Class	Household income class definition by			Neighbourhood income class definition		
	household income	*weighted neighbour-hood income*	*neighbour-hood income across Germany*	*weighted neighbour-hood income*	*neighbour-hood income across Ger-many*	*quintiles of household income*
1	6.6	6.6	6.6	6.6	6.5	6.3
2	6.7	7.0	6.8	7.0	6.9	6.7
3	7.0	7.0	6.9	7.0	7.0	7.0
4	7.2	7.1	7.0	7.0	7.0	7.1
5	7.3	7.2	7.2	7.1	7.1	7.0

Source: SOEP 20 and neighbourhood indicator data set. Authors' calculations.

In the first (fourth) column we defined classes of household income drawing on the distribution of annual per capita household incomes (weighted using SOEP individual weighting factors). In the second (fifth) column, we built classes of household income on the distribution of annual per capita neighbourhood incomes that is yielded when the neighbourhood incomes of SOEP respondents are weighted using SOEP individual weighting factors. In the third (sixth) column, income quintiles were built on the basis of the distribution of annual per capita neighbourhood incomes across all zip-code areas in Germany. The income distributions of the two latter would be equal if the neighbourhoods in which respondents to SOEP live were representative of all neighbourhoods in respect to neighbourhood income (compare Appendices 4 and 5 for upper class limits of income classes using different definitions). The happiness measure is on a scale from 0 (very dissatisfied) to 10 (very satisfied).

Table 2 shows that people in Germany are more satisfied with their life the more income they have and that they also are happier if they live in a neighbourhood where the average neighbourhood income is higher. While there is a linear increase in average happiness by classes of household income, average happiness seems to be relatively unaffected by the level of neighbourhood income, however, is markedly higher in the second neighbourhood income class compared to the first neighbourhood income class.

The simple bivariate association between happiness and neighbourhood income class is in line with what most neighbourhood effect theories suggest. If people observe that they are living in a neighbourhood where people, on average, are more affluent they may value this positively, for instance, because they think that they will benefit from affluent neighbours. Another explanation might be that living in a neighbourhood with financially better-off neighbours provides access to better or higher quality services and local amenities. However, as long as we do not control for own income at the same time, we can also not be sure whether those living in the richer neighbourhoods are just happier than those in the poorest neighbourhoods because they are richer.

In a next step we thus focus on individuals' mean life satisfaction broken down by classes of own income and neighbourhood income using the same income bands for both. This way, individuals that are in the same income class on both measures are in a financial situation that is very similar to that or their neighbours. Individuals that are in a higher class of income on any of these measures are either relatively deprived (i.e., if neighbourhood income greater is than household income) or relatively advantaged (i.e., if household income is greater than neighbourhood income). Being relatively advantaged in the neighbourhood should translate into greater happiness, and vice versa.

To illustrate the effect of controlling not only for own income but also for neighbours' income we report – along with mean life satisfaction scores of people in household income classes 1 – 5 differentiated by neighbourhood income classes 1 – 5 (denoted nb y 1- nb y 5) – mean satisfaction scores of people in household income classes 1 – 5 (see Figure 1). If individuals in richer neighbourhoods were only happier because they are richer themselves, all lines would overlap.

Figure 1 shows the empirical results. Reading the lines vertically, we can see that average life satisfaction increases with own income at every level of neighbourhood income. Furthermore, regardless of own income life satisfaction is also higher the higher the level of neighbourhood income is (reading the graphs horizontally).

In line with relative deprivation theory we would expect that the lines representing mean happiness differentiated by neighbourhood income class and household income class cross the bold line, i.e., they should be below the bold line when people are relatively deprived in their neighbourhood and above it when they are relatively advantaged.

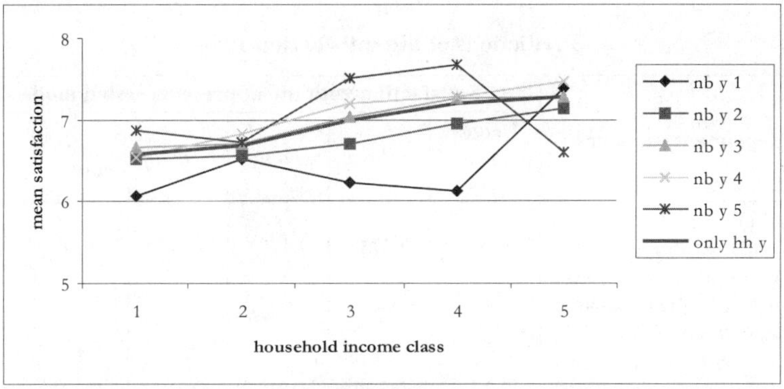

Source: SOEP 20 and neighbourhood indicator data set. Authors' calculations.

Figure 1: Average life satisfaction of individuals in different classes of neighbourhood income by quintiles of household income 1999

The empirical results tell a different story. On average, happiness is lower for people living in neighbourhoods with an income in the bottom two classes irrespective of their own income. Vice versa, it is higher for *all* individuals that live in neighbourhoods with an income in the top three classes of the neighbourhood income distribution. This is first suggestive evidence that relative deprivation theory may not be right.

4.2 Results of Multivariate Regressions

In addition to own income and neighbourhood income a number of other aspects of life have been shown to impact on life satisfaction. We therefore investigate whether the positive relationships we find between own income and happiness, neighbourhood income and happiness and also between household income, neighbourhood income and happiness are also supported when we control for other characteristics at the individual-, household- and neighbourhood-level.

Tables 3 and 4 present the results of a regression of neighbourhood context, basic characteristics, family, health, financial situation, and work characteristics on levels of life satisfaction for 1994 and 1999, respectively.[17] The structure of the regression output is such that we can observe the impact of adding in further (blocks of) controls on the size of the effects of our neighbourhood context variables (i.e., the coefficients reported in the first column apply when only neighbourhood context is controlled and those in the last column when all our dependent variables are controlled for). The sample remains the same across all six models.

Table 3

Predictions of life satisfaction 1994

Independent variables	**Satisfaction with life at present (nested models)**					
	Neighbourhood only	*+ Basic*	*+ Family*	*+ Health*	*+ Finances*	*+ Work*
Annual per capita neighbourhood income (log)	0.48**	0.47**	0.47**	0.43**	0.21	0.16
Type of community (comparison group: single occupancy in village or small town)						
village / small town (not single occupancy)	–0.34**	–0.32**	–0.30**	–0.28**	–0.17*	–0.14*
mid-size town, single occupancy	0.06	0.06	0.05	0.06	0.05	0.05
mid-size town (not single occupancy)	–0.29**	–0.26**	–0.25**	–0.22**	–0.11	–0.1
city, single occupancy	0.06	0.05	0.05	0.07	0.06	0.07
city, old building (not single occupancy)	–0.39**	–0.37**	–0.36**	–0.34**	–0.21**	–0.17*
city, new building (not single occupancy)	–0.38**	–0.36**	–0.35**	–0.32**	–0.20**	–0.19**
city, mixed housing stock, other	–0.31**	–0.31**	–0.29**	–0.28**	–0.18*	–0.17*
West Germany	0.62**	0.66**	0.66**	0.71**	0.62**	0.57**
Female		–0.02	0	–0.03	0	0.01
Age		–0.04**	–0.05**	–0.04**	–0.06**	–0.04**
$Age^2 / 100$		0.04**	0.04**	0.04**	0.06**	0.03**
Number of years of education		0.03**	0.03**	0.03**	0	–0.01
German		0.1	0.11*	0.13*	0.01	–0.02

17 The nature of the dependent variable suggests fitting an ordered logit or probit model. However, the proportional odds and parallel regression assumptions were violated and the general ordered logit, the alternative in this case, did not converge. In line with Oswald (1997) and DiTella / MacCulloch / Oswald (2001) we estimate standard OLS, which is the most parsimonious of imperfect models for our data.

Marital status (comparison group: never married)						
married			0.11	0.1	0.12	0.08
divorced			–0.27**	–0.28**	–0.24*	–0.25**
widowed			–0.07	–0.12	–0.18	–0.21
Number of children in the household			–0.04*	–0.05*	0.09**	0.06*
Disabled				–0.67**	–0.64**	–0.66**
Annual per capita household income (log)					0.56**	0.47**
Change in annual per capita household income (log) $t-t-1$					0	0.01
Homeowner					0.13**	0.14**
Employment status (comparison group: employed)						
registered unemployed						–0.96**
student						–0.27
pensioner						0.30**
not employed (not student or pensioner)						–0.06
not employed / supplementary employed						0
Constant	2.11*	2.69*	2.78**	3.10**	0.53	1.75
Observations	11408	11408	11408	11408	11408	11408
R^2	0.05	0.06	0.06	0.07	0.09	0.11

Notes: * significant at the 0.05 level. ** significant at the 0.01 level.

Source: SOEP 20 and neighbourhood indicator data set. Authors' calculations.

Table 4

Predictions of life satisfaction 1999

Independent variables	**Satisfaction with life at present (nested models)**					
	Neighbourhood only	*+ Basic*	*+ Family*	*+ Health*	*+ Finances*	*+ Work*
Annual per capita neighbourhood income (log)	0.47**	0.44**	0.45**	0.40**	0.23*	0.21*
Type of community (comparison group: single occupancy in village or small town)						
village / small town (not single occupancy)	–0.38**	–0.38**	–0.34**	–0.32**	–0.18**	–0.17**
mid-size town, single occupancy	0.01	0	0	0.02	0.02	0.03
mid-size town (not single occupancy)	–0.31**	–0.29**	–0.27**	–0.25**	–0.11	–0.09

Continued Table 4

Independent variables	Satisfaction with life at present (nested models)					
	Neighbourhood only	*+ Basic*	*+ Family*	*+ Health*	*+ Finances*	*+ Work*
city, single occupancy	0.08	0.06	0.05	0.06	0.05	0.05
city, old building (not single occupancy)	–0.38**	–0.38**	–0.34**	–0.30**	–0.14	–0.13
city, new building (not single occupancy)	–0.32**	–0.32**	–0.29**	–0.25**	–0.1	–0.1
city, mixed housing stock, other	–0.30**	–0.33**	–0.29**	–0.26**	–0.14*	–0.12
West Germany	0.39**	0.44**	0.45**	0.49**	0.44**	0.40**
Female		0.04	0.05	0.03	0.05	0.05
Age		–0.05**	–0.06**	–0.06**	–0.07**	–0.06**
Age^2 / 100		0.04**	0.05**	0.06**	0.07**	0.05**
Number of years of education		0.05**	0.05**	0.05**	0.02**	0.01
German		0.07	0.1	0.13*	0.03	0.01
Marital status (comparison group: never married)						
married			0.25**	0.24**	0.25**	0.23**
divorced			–0.29**	–0.31**	–0.25**	–0.26**
widowed			0.02	-0.04	-0.08	-0.11
Number of children in the household			–0.05*	–0.06**	0.07**	0.05*
Disabled				–0.75**	–0.74**	–0.74**
Annual per capita household income (log)					0.53**	0.47**
Change in annual per capita household income (log) $t - t - 1$					–0.15*	–0.15*
Homeowner					0.12**	0.12**
Employment status (comparison group: employed)						
registered unemployed						–0.84**
student						0.23
pensioner						0.12
not employed (not student or pensioner)						–0.04
not employed / supplementary employed						0
Constant	2.43*	3.20**	3.32**	3.75**	0.96	1.65
Observations	12251	12251	12251	12251	12251	12251
R^2	0.03	0.04	0.05	0.07	0.08	0.1

Notes: * significant at the 0.05 level. ** significant at the 0.01 level.

Source: SOEP 20 and neighbourhood indicator data set. Authors' calculations.

The results in both years are very similar and, in addition, for all controls, they are in line with what has been shown elsewhere in empirical studies on happiness (see Dette, 2005 for an extensive review). The starkest differences in the effects over time are observed for regional differences. In 1994, the coefficient on living in West Germany amounts to 0.57. In 1999 the correlation is 0.4. We focus our discussion on the effects of the personal financial position and of the neighbourhood context.

Financial Situation

One's financial situation, like one's health status, is a very good predictor of life satisfaction. All indicators in this sphere of life show a highly significant impact on happiness. A linear relationship between life satisfaction and own income, as suggested in the bivariate findings, is, however, not supported with the multivariate model. We find a positive relationship between annual household income in log form and happiness, which has been shown in a number of other studies on the economics of happiness. Individuals value gains in income more the less money they start off with (see, e.g., Frey / Stutzer, 2002). The effect of income on happiness is stable over time. It amounts to 0.47 in both years (compare Tables 3 and 4, respectively).

The negative impact of a change in own income from the previous year to the current year is contra-intuitive, but has been found elsewhere (e.g., Burchardt, 2005). We would expect individuals to appreciate positive changes in income. However, as we do not measure incomes in real terms, the income change may not have been a real one, i.e., individuals might not be able to consume more, perhaps even less, despite a nominal increase of income because prices have increased more. Another possible reason might be that the change in income is triggered by a change in the household composition that is perceived as negative by the individuals. The negative impact of a change in income on happiness would then in fact be due to a confound correlation between household composition change and happiness. If, for instance, a child has just moved out of the household this technically implies that the household-size adjusted income measure increases from $year_{t-1}$ to $year_t$ since the income is divided over a smaller adult equivalent. But the moving-out of a child might also leave parents behind threatened because they now have to define the relationship to each family member new ('fill the gap'). To investigate in which direction these muddled-up effects go we run an alternative version of the happiness model where we split up the change in annual per capita household income from $year_{t-1}$ to $year_t$ into the log of change in household income and the log of change in household size. This showed that there is a strong positive association between increases in the number of members of the household and happiness in both years of observation. Though the association between changes in household income and happiness remains negative, it gets less significant which lends some support for our argument (results not reported).

Neighbourhood Effects

In contrast to most neighbourhood effects studies, the neighbourhood effects we identify are sizeable even when other individual and family characteristics are controlled for. For instance, Table 3 and Table 4 show that the inclusion of further controls in the model halves the independent impact of neighbourhood income on happiness (1994: 0.48 to 0.16; 1999: 0.47 to 0.21), but the effect remains statistically significant in 1999. In 1994, the neighbourhood income effect becomes statistically insignificant when controls for own economic circumstances are being added into the regression equation. However, in this year, other neighbourhood characteristics – which are mostly statistically insignificant in 1999 – show an effect on life satisfaction: most of the community type controls are statistically significant.

Our hypothesis that individuals are unhappier than otherwise would be the case when they are financially relatively deprived in their neighbourhood is not supported by the multivariate models. In both years of observation the value of the coefficient on neighbourhood income is positive (and statistically significant in 1999).

4.2.1 Results of Robustness Tests

Table 5 reports the effects of neighbourhood income and personal income on life satisfaction for both years and for all robustness tests.

Table 5

Effects of neighbourhood income and personal income on happiness, robustness tests

	Neighbourhood income (in log form)		**Household income (in log form)**		Adj. R^2	*N*
	Coeff.	*S.E.*	*Coeff.*	*S.E.*		
Baseline model 1994	0.16	1.41	0.47**	9.96	0.11	11408
relatively deprived individuals	0.22	0.16	0.59	0.08	0.12	6412
relatively advantaged individuals	0.15	0.19	0.26	0.10	0.10	4996
Baseline model 1999	0.21*	1.97	0.47**	10.15	0.1	12251
relatively deprived individuals	0.36	0.15	0.53	0.08	0.10	6596
relatively advantaged individuals	0.00	0.17	0.39	0.09	0.09	5671

Robustness tests 1994						
Full set of neighbourhood controls	0.06	0.52	0.45**	8.92	0.12	9340
Interactions						
young children in household	0.1	0.21	0.46**	10.71	0.11	11562
dogowners	0.08	0.6	0.51**	10.85	0.11	10282
socialising with neighbours	0.29	1.28	0.48**	10.92	0.11	11399
work in the neighbourhood	0.01	1.17	0.37**	6.3	0.07	6595
teenager in the household	0.58	2.68	0.47**	10.74	0.11	11432
Robustness tests 1999						
Feelings of relative deprivation	0.02	0.05	0.28	0.02	0.09	12123
Full set of neighbourhood controls	0.08	0.68	0.51**	9.94	0.11	10113
Interactions						
young children in household	–0.07	1.73	0.46**	11.40	0.10	12438
dogowners	0.46	1.82	0.47**	10.63	0.10	10868
socialising with neighbours	0.27	0.48	0.47**	11.31	0.10	12224
work in the neighbourhood	–0.01	1.45	0.43**	7.74	0.06	7173
teenager in the household	0.09	0.76	0.47**	11.34	0.10	12280
Fixed effect model	0.42	1.84	0.33**	5.77	0.03	8491
movers	0.52	1.62	0.11	0.89	0.04	1340
non-movers	0.39	1.07	0.40**	6.21	0.03	7151

Notes: * significant at the 0.05 level. ** significant at the 0.01 level.
Source: SOEP 20 and neighbourhood indicator data set. Authors' calculations.

Relatively Deprived versus Relatively Advantaged Individuals

Estimation of our happiness model separately for relatively deprived and relatively advantaged persons does not change the size and direction of the neighbourhood effect, and it remains statistically insignificant. This differentiation by deprivation status does also not alter markedly any of the coefficients in the model (results not reported). This suggests that both groups of the population react to their local environment and to external circumstances in the same way. If anything, people who have a lower personal income than their neighbours are happier than relatively advantaged people with their lives the richer the neighbours are.

Changing the Measurement of Relative Deprivation

Individuals' subjective account of whether or not they feel they deserve better compared to others is related to the income position they have within their neighbourhood: a higher share of people who are relatively deprived in their neighbourhood report to 'totally agree' or 'agree slightly', 'disagree slightly' and 'totally disagree' with the statement „Compared to others I did not achieve what I deserve" (Table 6).

Table 6

Feelings of relative deprivation broken down by the financial position in the neighbourhood 1999

Compared to others, I did not achieve what I deserve	All		
	Not deprived	*Deprived*	*Total*
totally agree	5.4	9.3	7.4
agree slightly	20.6	28.0	24.4
disagree slightly	46.1	40.4	43.2
totally disagree	27.9	22.3	25.0
Total	100	100	100

Source: SOEP 20. Authors' calculations.

If we further differentiate between individuals that are poor and those that are not, the former are more inclined to feeling deprived than the latter regardless of the financial position in the neighbourhood (Table 7). Feelings of relative deprivation are most marked among poor and relatively deprived people. All associations are statistically significant.

Table 7

Feelings of relative deprivation broken down by the financial position in the neighbourhood and poverty status 1999

Compared to others, I did not achieve what I deserve	Non-poor			Poor		
	Not deprived	*Deprived*	*Total*	*Not deprived*	*Deprived*	*Total*
totally agree	4.7	7.6	6.1	8.9	(11.4)	10.9
agree slightly	21.9	26.7	24.2	20.9	32.8	30.3
disagree slightly	47.0	43.3	45.2	43.1	37.5	38.7
totally disagree	26.5	22.5	24.5	27.2	18.2	20.1
Total	100	100	100	100	100	100

Note: (–) less than 50 cases.
Source: SOEP 20. Authors' calculations.

This suggests that our rather technical definition of who is deprived and who is not bears some credibility. The actual correlation between life satisfaction and our direct measure of relative deprivation (i.e., being more in disagreement with the statement) is 0.29, which is rather low. In other words, though there is a tendency that people who report lower levels of feeling deprived are more satisfied with their life, low happiness and feeling relatively deprived are not identical things. When we substitute self-reported happiness by the direct measure of subjectively felt deprivation the direction of the income effects is in the same direction as in the happiness model, but the estimated coefficients are not statistically significant. This suggests that feelings of relative deprivation are not related to one's own income and neighbours' income.

Taken together this is evidence that our approach to measure feelings of relative deprivation as reduced life satisfaction is tolerable. Our hypothesis that better-off neighbours present a negative externality, however, remains not supported. The results suggest that the income effects are positive, but the estimated coefficients are not statistically significant.

Inclusion of More Neighbourhood Characteristics

We can see that inclusion of more neighbourhood controls does not significantly increase the prediction power of the model and that it also does not change the sign of the neighbourhood income effect. The neighbourhood income effect reduces to less than 0.1 and becomes statistically insignificant in both years. This suggests that access to local public facilities is correlated with neighbourhood income. Most of the effects of distance to local facilities are negative but not statistically significant (results reported in Appendix 6). There only exists a negative association between living further away from sports grounds, gyms and the like, which is in line with what we would expect in a society that enjoys physical activities.

People's Interaction with the Neighbourhood

We hypothesised that neighbourhood is more important for individuals that may be assumed to be more in touch with their neighbours. On the dimensions that we measure, the empirical findings do not lend much support for our hypothesis. The interactions are statistically insignificant and there is an inconsistency of the effects over time.

Effects of Unobserved Heterogeneity

The explained variance for the prediction of changes in life satisfaction from 1994 to 1999 controlling for unobserved heterogeneity (fixed effects models) is only three percent, which is low. However, it is difficult to predict changes in such variables. In addition, we have to bear in mind that some of the changes that we observe may only affect happiness at the time the change occurred. It is known, for instance, that marital transitions have a tendency to have a measurable impact on happiness in the short run, but that effects disappear in the longer run since individuals' happiness returns to baseline levels (see Lucas / Clark / Georgellis / Diener, 2003). The changes we pick up are those that occurred at any time between the 1994 and the 1999 surveys of the SOEP.[18] We thus expect effects to be smaller than would be the case if we looked at changes that occurred in adjacent years. As a consequence, the effects we do identify in our model – though in line with what we would expect – are often not significant. However, despite the identification difficulties in the prediction of changes, we find a number of variables significant. Among these are the life events becoming disabled or unemployed that are associated with changes in life satisfaction to the negative (see Appendix 7). We furthermore find changes in own income positively and highly significantly associated with changes in life satisfaction. The association between changes in the annual change of household income is also negative (and insignificant) in the panel model. Splitting-up the sample into movers and non-movers so as to reduce the extent to which neighbourhood selection effects and unobserved fixed neighbourhood characteristics might be driving the results, does not offer any more insights either – the effect of neighbourhood income is also positive and insignificant for those individuals that have not moved.

These findings back up the results of our cross-sectional baseline models. In those models we also found individuals unhappier when they were in rather undesirable states like unemployment, or disability, or when their income was low. We still find a positive coefficient on neighbourhood income when we control for unobserved individual characteristics, but this effect is highly insignificant. This suggests that the relationship between neighbours' income and happiness that we identified in the level model for 1999 is to some extent indeed picking up things to do with living in a better-off neighbourhood that we do not control for.

5. Conclusions

Relative deprivation theory suggests that people are unhappier than otherwise would be if they are living in a neighbourhood where the average neighbour is financially better off than they are.

Our empirical results suggest that this is not the case. We find a strong positive correlation between both neighbourhood incomes and household incomes

---

18 For a number of respondents more than one change might have occurred on one indicator in the five year period, for instance a divorce might have been followed by a new marriage, or, in terms of neighbourhood changes, individuals might have moved away from their 1994 neighbourhood to take up an apprenticeship but have moved back by 1999. In both cases the change would be confound.

with levels of subjective well-being in our two-and three-dimensional analyses. In particular, people living in the poorest neighbourhoods are much unhappier than others. However, our more detailed multivariate analyses suggest that this effect is driven by living in East Germany where, on average, people are unhappier, and neighbourhoods are poorer.

In the multivariate predictions of life satisfaction we find that people living in Germany are happier the more income they have but also the better off their average neighbour is. But the associations between neighbours' income and personal happiness are very weak and not statistically significant (only at the 5 percent level in 1999 – this might be due to a convergence of levels of happiness and neighbourhood incomes in West and East Germany).

Overall, given the robustness of the positive sign of the neighbourhood income effect in all models that we estimated, we conclude that if neighbourhood income effects exist they are positive. In other words, the empirical evidence lends no support for the relative deprivation hypothesis in the context of German neighbourhoods, when neighbourhoods are operationalised as zip-code areas.

There are a number of reasons why we might expect that there might be positive effects of living in better-off neighbourhoods. One of these is that people may expect to benefit from their neighbourhood at some point in the near future. The fact that the average neighbour has a high(er) income is, at least in parts, a reflection of favourable employment prospects in the area. It certainly signals to business people where the demand for their goods and services is: it is not a coincidence that the neighbourhood data we employ are purchased by companies to help them make their decision on where to start a business. Residents in the poorest neighbourhoods may also suffer from stigmatisation and discrimination in the labour market and in the educational sector, which is why living in a better- off neighbourhood is favourable despite of a low own income. On top of the economic prospect-aspects of having richer neighbours there are social and psychological aspects that may make living among richer people a better experience. Richer neighbours may use parts of their resources to maintain their property at a higher standard, which will make people feel better than living in a neighbourhood with run-down houses. In general people will feel less threatened in a neighbourhood that signals that people care about their social and physical environment.

Most of these effect mechanisms may be expected to operate at the level of the rather great scale of zip-code areas. On average, 9000 people live in German zip-code areas. One of the reasons why we do not find a negative comparison effect of neighbours' income on happiness may be that people do not compare themselves to that many people. There is a lack of data at more immediate neighbourhood scales for the 1994 and 1999 periods, so we cannot investigate this empirically.

6. References

Blanchflower, D. G. / *Oswald,* A. J. (2004): Well-being over time in Britain and the USA, Journal of Public Economics 88, 1359–1386.

Brief, A. P. / *Butcher,* A. H. / *George,* J M. / *Link,* K. E. (1993): Integrating bottom-up and top-down theories of subjective well-being: The case of health, Journal of Personality and Social Psychology 64, 646–653.

Buck, N. (2001): Identifying neighbourhood effects on social exclusion, Urban Studies 38, 2251–2275.

Canache, D. (1996): Looking out my back door: The neighborhood context and perceptions of relative deprivation, Political Research Quarterly 49, 547–571.

Clark, A E. / *Oswald,* A. J. (1996): Satisfaction and Comparison Income, Journal of Public Economics 61, 359–381.

Diener, E. / *Suh,* E. M. / *Lucas,* R. E. / *Smith,* H. L. (1999): Subjective well-being: Three decades of progress, Psychological Bulletin 125, 276–302.

Dietz, R. D. (2002): The estimation of neighborhood effects in the social sciences: An interdisciplinary approach, Social Science Research 31, 539–575.

DiTella, R. / *MacCulloch,* R. J. / *Oswald,* A. J. (2001): Preferences over Inflation and Unemployment: Evidence from Surveys of Happiness, The American Economic Review 91, 335–341.

Durlauf, S. N. (2003): Neighbourhood effects, in: J.-F. Thisse (ed.), Handbook of Regional and Urban Economics, Vol.4.

Easterlin, R. A. (1974): Does economic growth improve the human lot? Some empirical evidence, in: W. R. Levin (ed.), Nations and households in economic growth, Stanford, CA.

Ferrer-i-Carbonell, A. (2005): Income and well-being: an empirical analysis of the comparison income effect, Journal of Public Economics 89, 997–1019.

Ferrer-i-Carbonell, A. / *Frijters,* P. (2004): How important is methodology for the estimates of the determinants of happiness?, Economic Journal 114, 641–659.

Frey, B. S. / *Stutzer,* A. (2002): What Can Economists Learn from Happiness Research?, Journal of Economic Literature 40, 402–435.

Frey, B. S. / *Stutzer,* A. (2002): Happiness and Economics, Oxfordshire.

Frijters, P. / *Haisken-DeNew,* J. P. / *Shields,* M. A. (2004): Money does matter! Evidence from increasing real income and life satisfaction in East Germany after re-unification, American Economic Review 94, 730–740.

Gaarder, B. M. M. (2002): Can population characteristics account for the variation in health impacts of air pollution? A meta-analysis of PM10-mortality studies., University College of London, CSERGE-Economics.

Gurr, T. R. (1970): Why men rebel, Princeton.

Infas Geodaten (2004): http://www.infas-geodaten.de/3000/3200.html, date consulted 02. 04. 2004.

Jencks, C. / *Mayer,* S. E. (1990): The social consequences of growing up in a poor neighborhood, in: M. G. H. McGeary (ed.), Inner-city poverty in the United States, Washington (DC)

Knies, G. / *Krause,* P. (2006): Armut und Alter ('Poverty and Age'), in: Arbeit und Lebensstandard, Munich.

Knies, G. / *Spiess,* C. K. (2007): Regional data in the German Socio-Economic Panel Study (SOEP), DIW Berlin Data Documentation 17.

Layard, R. (2005), Happiness: Lessons from a New Science.

Lopez Turley, R. N. (2002): Is relative deprivation beneficial? The effects of richer and poorer neighbours on children's outcomes, Journal of Community Psychology 30, 671 – 686.

Lucas, R. E. / *Clark,* A. E. / *Georgellis,* Y. / *Diener,* E. (2003): Reexamining adaptation and set point model of happiness: Reactions to changes in marital status, Journal of Personality and Social Psychology 84, 527 – 539.

Luttmer, E. F. P. (2005): Neighbours as negatives: Relative earnings and well-being, Quarterly Journal of Economics 120, 963 – 1002.

Merton, R. K. / *Rossi,* A. S. (1968): Contributions to the theory of reference group behaviour, in,Social Theory and social structure, London.

Meyer, J. W. (1970): High school effects on college institutions, American Journal of Sociology 1970, 59 – 70.

Oswald, A. J. (1997): Happiness and Economic Performance, The Economic Journal 107, 1815 – 1831.

Runciman, W. G. (1966): Relative deprivation and social justice: a study of attitudes to social inequality in twentieth-century England, London.

Sampson, R. J. / *Morenoff,* J. D. / *Gannon-Rowley,* T. (2002): Assessing „neighborhood effects": Social processes and new directions in research, Annual Review of Sociology 28, 443 – 478.

Shields, M. / *Wooden,* M. (2003): Investigating the Role of Neighbourhood Characteristics in Determining Life Satisfaction, Melbourne Institute Working Paper Series 24, The University of Melbourne.

Sirgy, M. J. / *Cornwell,* T. (2002): How Neighborhood Features Affect Quality of Life, Social Indicators Research 59, 79 – 114.

Stouffer, S. A. (1949): Studies in Social Psychology in World War II: The American Soldier, Princeton, New York.

Veenhoven, R. (1984): Conditions of Happiness, Boston.

7. Appendix

Appendix 1

Description of variables used in the multivariate models 1994 and 1999

Variable Name	Description
Life satisfaction	The response to the question „How satisfied are you at present with your life, all things considered?" There are eleven response categories running from 0 (completely dissatisfied) to 10 (completely satisfied).
Feeling less relatively deprived	Respondent's agreement with the statement: „In comparison with others, I have not achieved what I deserve". The categories are coded from 1 (totally agree) to 4 (totally disagree).
Annual per capita neighbourhood income (log)	See detailed description in the data section.
Community typology	
village or small town (1 – 2 family home) *village / small town (not single occupancy)* *mid-size town, single occupancy* *mid-size town (not single occupancy)* *city, single occupancy* *city, old building (not single occupancy)* *city, new building (not single occupancy)* *city, mixed housing stock, other*	This typology that has been developed by researchers at Gesellschaft für wissenschaftliche Datenverarbeitung (GWGD).[19] It is informed by theoretical considerations by urban sociologists, regarding the built and social composite of (inner-city) areas in Germany and the impact thereof on neighbouring (in terms of facilitating interactions between neighbours and attracting people to live in these areas). It builds on the assumptions that (a) differentiation between old and new building stock is redundant in villages and small towns (i.e., settlements with less than 20,000 inhabitants), and also in mid-sized towns (i.e., settlements with 20,000 to 100,000 inhabitants), and (b) that – in cities with more than 100,000 inhabitants – subsections of the city are relatively homogenous in their housing stock. Note that the term 'single occupancy' used in the typology refers to detached houses that are occupied by just one or two households (*1 – 2 Familienhaus*).
West Germany	Dummy that is one if respondent lives in one of the old Federal States
Distance to local public institutions	
shopsbank / ATM *doctors* *public transport* *kindergarten* *primary school* *youth club* *club for elderly people* *pubs, bars, restaurants* *park, green area* *sports ground, gym*	The head of household is asked to give information on how long it takes to get on foot to a number of public facilities. The list of amenities includes (a) day-to-day infrastructure (shops for every day needs, doctors, banking facilities, station / stop for public transport), (b) institutions that serve particular age groups (kindergarten, primary school, youth club, day centre for elderly people), and (c) recreational facilities (pubs / bars / restaurants, public park / green space, sports and other leisure facilities). The answer categories are [under 10 minutes], [10 – 20 minutes], [more than 20 minutes], [not available / not accessible on foot].

19 The authors owe credit to Peter Bartelheimer of the GWGD for sharing syntax files and background information.

Annual per capita household income (log)	See detailed description in the data section.
Homeowner	Dummy that takes the value one if respondent lives in owner-occupied accommodation. Generated by the SOEP team. Provided in the wave-specific household-level generated-variables component of the SOEP data base (i.e., $hgen).
Number of years in education	Taken from the CNEF instrument of SOEP, internationally standardised definition. Inconsistencies over time 'corrected'. Time-inconsistent accounts were replaced with the most frequent, and if this did not exist, with the highest value provided in the 1994 – 1999 period.
German	Dummy that is one if respondent has the German nationality
Marital Status	
married *divorced* *widowed* *never married*	Compressed version of a typology generated by the SOEP team which is provided in the wave-specific household-level generated-variables component of the SOEP data base (i.e., $hgen).
Number of children in the household	Number of persons below the age of 18 in the household.
Employment typology	
employed *registered unemployed* *student* *pensioner* *not employed* *(not student or pensioner)*	The employment status typology has been generated for the purpose of this study drawing on wave-specific individual-level SOEP data sets. Assignment of the employment status was ordered. Priority was given to classifying pensioners (persons older than 64 in receipt of a pension). The group of individuals attending university classes is exclusive of pensioners who may attend university for the purpose of lifelong learning. The 'registered unemployed'-category is exclusive of pensioners and students and contains all individuals that report to be registered unemployed. Individuals are classified as 'employed' or 'not employed', respectively, when they claim to be just that and are in neither of the aforementioned categories. Finally, the 'not employed / supplementary employed'- category picks up not employed individuals who claim to have some sort of job they are getting paid for, if on a very irregular basis.
Disabled	A person is classified as disabled if his / her ability to work is limited and if this is legally recognised by means of a degree of disability of 30 percent or more. Taken from CNEF component of SOEP. We treat individuals reporting being legally disabled in 1994 and having a degree of disability of greater or equal 30 as disabled in 1999, irrespective of their account in 1999.
Movers	Dummy that takes the value one for individuals who live in another zip-code area in 1999 than in 1994.

Source: SOEP 20. Authors' calculations.

Appendix 2

Summary statistics of variables used in the multivariate analysis 1994 and 1999

	1994				1999			
	Mean / percent	*S.D.*	*Min*	*Max*	*Mean / percent*	*S.D.*	*Min*	*Max*
Life satisfaction	6.82	1.84	0	10	6.95	1.78	0	10
Feeling relatively deprived					2.84	0.86	1	4
Female	0.51	0.50	0	1	0.52	0.50	0	1
Age	45.33	16.48	18	98	46.94	16.21	19	96
Number of years in education	11.21	2.43	7	18	11.47	2.47	7	18
German	0.83	0.38	0	1	0.88	0.33	0	1
West Germany	0.70	0.46	0	1	0.72	0.45	0	1
Married	0.69	0.46	0	1	0.67	0.47	0	1
Divorced	0.06	0.23	0	1	0.07	0.26	0	1
Widowed	0.06	0.23	0	1	0.06	0.24	0	1
Never married	0.06	0.24	0	1	0.20	0.40	0	1
Number of children in the household	0.63	0.93	0	6	0.57	0.91	0	9
Employed	0.62	0.49	0	1	0.60	0.49	0	1
Registered unemployed	0.09	0.28	0	1	0.07	0.26	0	1
Student	0.01	0.10	0	1	0.01	0.09	0	1
Pensioner	0.12	0.32	0	1	0.15	0.36	0	1
Not employed (not student or pensioner)	0.17	0.37	0	1	0.17	0.37	0	1
Annual per capita household income (log)	9.13	0.51	3.65	11.77	9.27	0.51	3.81	11.75
Change in annual per capita household income (log) $t - t - 1$	0.06	0.30	–3.04	8.01	0.03	0.28	–4.66	5.63
Homeowner	0.40	0.49	0	1	0.45	0.50	0	1
Disabled	0.09	0.29	0	1	0.11	0.32	0	1
Annual per capita neighbourhood income (log)	9.22	0.22	8.69	10.14	9.34	0.22	8.81	10.08
Village or small town (1 – 2 family home)	0.31	0.46	0	1	0.33	0.47	0	1
Village / small town (not single occupancy)	0.11	0.32	0	1	0.12	0.32	0	1
Mid-size town, single occupancy	0.12	0.32	0	1	0.12	0.33	0	1

Mid-size town (not single occupancy)	0.15	0.35	0	1	0.14	0.34	0	1
City, single occupancy	0.05	0.21	0	1	0.05	0.23	0	1
City, old building (not single occupancy)	0.08	0.27	0	1	0.07	0.25	0	1
City, new building (not single occupancy)	0.09	0.28	0	1	0.08	0.28	0	1
City, mixed housing stock, other	0.10	0.30	0	1	0.09	0.28	0	1
Movers					0.16	0.36	0	1

Source: SOEP 20. Authors' calculations.

Appendix 3

Average life satisfaction by classes of income 1994

Class	Household income class definition by			Neighbourhood income class definition by		
	household income	*weighted neighbour-hood income*	*neighbour-hood income across Germany*	*weighted neighbour-hood income*	*neighbour-hood income across Germany*	*quintiles of household income*
1	6.4	6.6	6.5	6.4	6.3	6.2
2	6.7	6.8	6.7	7.0	6.8	6.4
3	6.9	7.0	7.0	6.9	6.9	7.0
4	7.2	6.9	7.0	7.0	7.0	7.0
5	7.2	7.2	7.2	7.1	7.0	7.0

Source: SOEP 20 and neighbourhood indicator data set. Authors' calculations.

Appendix 4

Upper class limits of neighbourhood income and household income quintiles 1994, in DM

Income Class Definition	Class			
	1	*2*	*3*	*4*
household income (weighted)	6,731	8,833	11,542	15,514
neighbourhood income (weighted)	8,826	10,036	11,003	12,183
neighbourhood income (all areas)	8,091	9,290	10,381	11,672

Notes: Incomes are at the same scales and refer to annual incomes.

Source: SOEP 20. Authors' calculations.

Appendix 5

Upper class limits of neighbourhood income and household income quintiles 1999, in DM

Income Class Definition	Class			
	1	*2*	*3*	*4*
household income (weighted)	7,665	10,196	13,049	17,489
neighbourhood income (weighted)	9,903	11,216	12,400	14,014
neighbourhood income (all areas)	9,235	10,500	11,694	13,295

Notes: Incomes are at the same scales and refer to annual incomes.
Source: SOEP 20. Authors' calculations.

Appendix 6

Controlling for neighbourhood infrastructure 1994 and 1999

Control variable	**Life Satisfaction**	
	1994	***1999***
Annual per capita neighbourhood income (log)	0.06	0.08
Type of community (comparison group: single occupancy in village or small town)		
village / small town (not single occupancy)	–0.12	–0.19**
mid-size town, single occupancy	–0.02	0.02
mid-size town (not single occupancy)	–0.08	–0.15*
city, single occupancy	0.08	–0.02
city, old build., (not single occupancy)	–0.18*	–0.07
city, new build., (not single occupancy)	–0.1	–0.14
city, mixed housing stock, other	–0.15	–0.08
Distance to the next bigger city	0.01	0.03*
... Day-to-day infrastructure		
shops	–0.04	–0.02
bank / ATM	–0.02	–0.03
doctors	–0.02	—0.03
public transport	0	–0.06
... Institutions for different age groups		
kindergarten	0.02	0.04
primary school	–0.04	0.05*
youth club	–0.01	–0.03
club for elderly people	0.01	–0.02
... Recreational facilities		
pubs, bars, restaurants	0.04	–0.01
park, green area	–0.01	–0.04*
sports ground, gym	–0.11**	–0.07**

West Germany	0.57**	0.42**
Annual per capita household income (log)	0.45**	0.51**
Change in annual per capita household income (log) $t - t - 1$	0	–0.20**
Homeowner	0.19**	0.12**
Constant	3.15**	2.80*
Observations	9340	10113
R^2	0.12	0.11

Notes: Models also control for financial situation, health, family, work and basic characteristics. * significant at the 0.05 level. ** significant at the 0.01 level.

Source: SOEP 20 and neighbourhood indicator data set. Authors' calculations.

Appendix 7

Panel estimations of life satisfaction differentiated by moving status

Control variable	**all**	**non-movers**	**movers**
Annual per capita neighbourhood income (log)	0.42	0.39	0.52
Type of community (comparison group: single occupancy in village or small town)			
village / small town (not single occupancy)	–0.05	–0.11	0.07
mid-size town, single occupancy	0.05	0	0.26
mid-size town (not single occupancy)	0.16	0.34*	0.06
city, single occupancy	0.18	0.38	0.05
city, old build., (not single occupancy)	0.11	0.01	0.25
city, new build., (not single occupancy)	–0.07	0.25	–0.09
city, mixed housing stock, other	0.14	0.34	0.13
West Germany	0.11	0	0.08
Year	–0.02**	–0.03*	0
Marital status (comparison group: never married)			
married	0.12	0.1	0.08
divorced	0.13	0.03	0.18
widowed	–0.21	–0.26	–0.03
Number of children in the household	0.08**	0.08*	0.05
Disabled	–0.40**	–0.44**	–0.08
Annual per capita household income (log)	0.33**	0.40**	0.11
Change in annual per capita household income (log) $t - t - 1$	–0.07	–0.08	–0.05
Homeowner	0.15*	0.15	0.16
Employment status (comparison group: employed)			
registered unemployed	–0.74**	–0.68**	–0.94**
student	0.11	0.12	0.06
pensioner	–0.14	–0.1	–0.27
not employed (not student or pensioner)	–0.12*	–0.08	–0.22
not employed / supplementary employed	–0.46*	–0.29	–1.40*

Continued Appendix 7

Control variable	**all**	**non-movers**	**movers**
Constant	40.20**	50.16**	1.92
Observations	16982	14302	2680
Number never changing person id	8491	7151	1340
R^2	0.03	0.03	0.04

Notes: *significant at the 0.05 level. ** significant at the 0.01 level.

Source: SOEP 20 and neighbourhood indicator data set. Authors' calculations.

Schmollers Jahrbuch 128 (2008), 109 – 120
Duncker & Humblot, Berlin

Neighbourhood Effects on Health: A Structural Equation Modelling Approach

By Mai Stafford, Amanda Sacker, Anne Ellaway, Steven Cummins, Dick Wiggins, and Sally Macintyre

Abstract

Many studies document associations between area deprivation and health but the explanatory pathways linking deprivation to health are not clear. Potential neighbourhood determinants of health include socio-relational characteristics, the built environment and neighbourhood amenities. Using obesity as an example, we theorised a model of the potential causal pathways linking neighbourhood characteristics, through diet and physical activity, to obesity. A structural equation modelling approach was used to test the model empirically using health data from national surveys in England and Scotland. The advantages and limitations of structural equation modelling are discussed and we contend that the approach provides a useful way of combining data from several sources to test theorised explanatory models linking the neighbourhood to health.

JEL Classifications: C3, I18

1. Background

Several recent studies have shown that morbidity and mortality varies across different kinds of neighbourhoods (Duncan et al., 1995; Wiggins et al., 1998). Neighbourhood deprivation is one exposure that has been strongly and consistently related to several health outcomes (Diez-Roux et al., 1997; Brooks-Gunn et al., 1998; Galea et al., 2007; Winkleby et al., 2007). Many of the more recent studies are based on multilevel data and analysis combining information on individual and area level determinants of health. These are able to test for contextual explanations (due to something about the neighbourhood itself) versus compositional explanations (due to the characteristics of the resident population) for neighbourhood inequalities. Reviews of these multilevel studies generally indicate that area deprivation is related to health, although the relationship is weaker and smaller in magnitude than the relationships between well-established *individual* socioeconomic factors and health (Pickett / Pearl, 2001; Riva et al., 2007).

Area deprivation is typically captured using summary indicators of multiple deprivation based on census characteristics (Townsend et al., 1988; Carstairs / Morris, 1991). Multiple deprivation is a marker for features of the local area that are plausibly causally related to health. However, neighbourhood effects largely remain a "black box of somewhat mystical influences on health" (Macintyre et al., 2002). These studies have contributed to a rediscovery of the importance of the (local) social environment for health (Krieger, 1994; Diez Roux, 1998) but they leave unanswered questions about precisely what it is about neighbourhoods that are important and where efforts to improve neighbourhoods should be focused. Recently, researchers have proposed theoretical frameworks (Macintyre et al., 2002; Bernard et al., 2007; Franzini et al., 2005) and empirical work has begun to explore neighbourhood socio-relational characteristics, urban design and services as potential explanatory factors linking neighbourhood deprivation to health outcomes. However, a number of limitations remain. Firstly, empirical research has tended to use only a small number of indicators to characterise neighbourhoods. Secondly, studies have sometimes used summary indices whereby different neighbourhood problems and / or resources are counted and combined into a single score. This limits the ability to distinguish the particular neighbourhood characteristics that are salient for a given health outcome. A more detailed understanding of the specific neighbourhood determinants is required before suitable interventions can be devised. Thirdly, an alternative approach has been to estimate the effect of one neighbourhood exposure whilst statistically controlling for others using multiple regression methods. This can be problematic when neighbourhood characteristics are highly correlated with each other, as is often the case.

2. Structural Equation Modelling Approach

Accordingly, we know very little about how the various contextual domains relate to each other and how they jointly influence health. A structural equation modelling approach is a useful tool to overcome some of these limitations and has several advantages. It goes beyond simple description of the association between a given contextual characteristic and health in that it allows the researcher to develop a theoretical pathway from a given characteristic, through other contextual characteristics and individual responses, to health status. The method forces the researcher to be explicit about their theoretical model. It can be used to test alternative pathways so that a researcher can discount those which do not accord with the data. This allows an iterative refinement towards a final working model. It may also help the researcher and reader to identify important variables which have so far been omitted from the model.

A structural equation modelling approach with latent variables is an efficient way of combining data from several sources. Structural equation modelling is based on the conception that the measured variables are indicators of an underlying unobserved (latent) construct. Rather than estimating the relationships between the measured variables, the relationships between the underlying constructs are estimated. The extent to which the observed indicators capture this underlying construct is assessed using confirmatory factor analysis in a measurement model (Lawley / Maxwell, 1971). Structural equation modeling improves upon simply combining variables into a summary index as it allows measurement error to be taken into account and for data from different sources to be weighted for importance as indicators of the underlying factor.

Developments in statistical software mean that path models incorporating categorical outcomes, continuous outcomes or a mixture of the two can be estimated. Of particular relevance for neighbourhood effects studies is the ability to model complex variation arising from the geographical clustering of the data. This is now possible using standard structural equation modelling software.

Structural equation modelling proceeds in stages. The first stage tests the measurement properties of the underlying latent variables in the model using confirmatory factor analysis. At the second stage, the researcher states how they think the constructs of interest are related to each other. The constructs may all be measured by latent variables, by observed variables or by a combination of the two. A path diagram can help here (Figure 1). Based on these theorized inter-relationships, the expected variances and covariances implied by the model can be calculated. These are then compared with the population variances and covariances estimated from the empirical data. The goodness of fit of the empirical data to the theorized model is then assessed. Several goodness of fit indices can be used (Bollen, 1989). Here we use the Chi-squared test of model fit and the Root Mean Square Error of Approximation (RMSEA). As a guideline, a Chi-squared statistic of the same order of magnitude as the degrees of freedom indicates a well-fitting model and an RMSEA < 0.05 indicates a model with a good approximation to the data.

3. An Example: Neighbourhood Effects on Obesity

Here we illustrate the use of structural equation modelling in studying the relationships between a range of neighbourhood characteristics and obesity. Physical activity level and dietary intake are two key determinants of obesity. There is growing interest in the importance of the local residential (and wider) context for physical activity and diet. Although individual factors play a part, the recent and rapid increase in obesity in many developed and developing countries (Hedley et al., 2004) may also be attributed to “obesogenic environments" (Swinburn et al., 1999; Hill & Peters, 1998; Poston & Foreyt, 1999). This includes the availability of energy-dense food, food marketing, increasing car use and car-friendly street layouts (Egger & Swinburn, 1997).

This work is based on research published elsewhere and the reader is referred there for a full discussion of the literature linking features of the neighbourhood environment to obesity (Stafford et al., 2007). To summarise, based on a review of the literature, we developed a theoretical causal model linking socio-relational characteristics, the built environment and local services / amenities to obesity (Figure 1). This provides the theoretical model for the analyses presented here. Such a model can be drawn for any given health outcome although the relevant neighbourhood determinants and their relative importance are likely to vary according to the outcome under study.

4. Study Areas and Study Participants

Individual level data for the study come from the Health Survey for England (HSE) and the Scottish Health Survey (SHS). These are on-going cross-sectional surveys which provide a sample that is representative of the general population of England and Scotland. A multi-stage selection procedure is used to select a random sample of postcode sectors (average population about 5000) and, within each postcode sector, a random sample of approximately 19 households (Erens / Primatesta, 1998; Shaw et al., 2000). Data from 1994–1999 were combined to maximize sample size and provide health data on 438 postcode sectors for the present study. Postcode sectors were used to define neighbourhood boundaries.

The HSE and SHS surveys provide information on obesity and important individual level determinants of health. Data on height and weight were measured by a trained nurse in the participant's home. Body mass index (BMI) captures overall obesity and was calculated as weight (kg) divided by the square of the height (metres). Data on physical activity and diet were unfortunately not available from the HSE and SHS. Instead, we used neighbourhood average sports participation as a proxy for individual level sports participation. Sex, age and social class based on occupation were obtained by face-to-face interview. Social class was classified into 6 groups according to the Registrar General's classification.

A total of 6848 participants had complete data on neighbourhood characteristics, BMI, age, sex and social class. Analyses based on cases with some missing data did not differ substantially from those with complete cases so, for brevity, only the latter are presented. The sample comprised adults aged 16 plus, 14 % of whom were 65 and over. There were similar proportions of women and men and 48 % were classed as manual workers. Mean BMI was 26.3 kg / m^2.

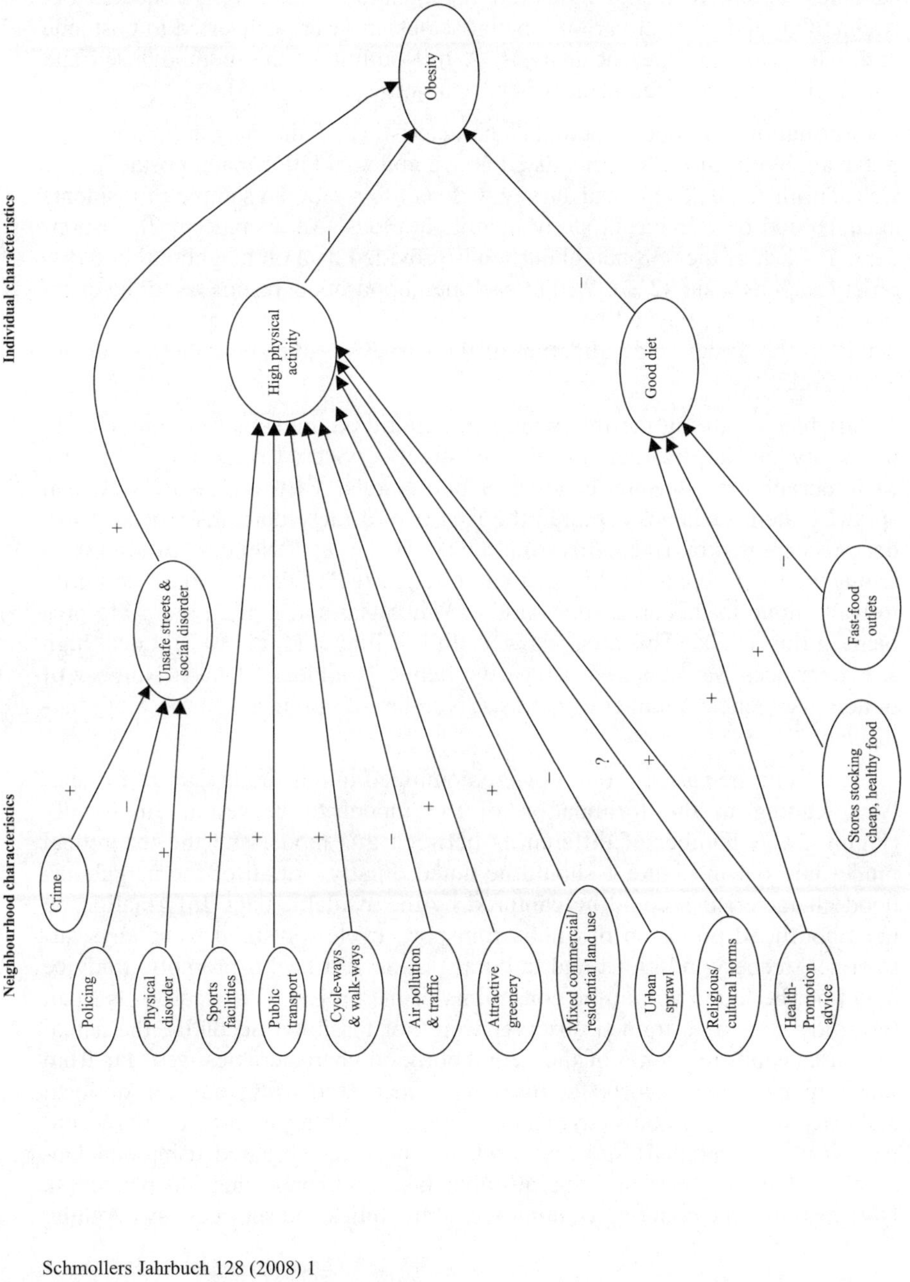

Figure 1: Theoretical model linking the neighbourhood environment to diet, physical activity and obesity

5. Neighbourhood Level Data

Information on local services and the built environment was obtained from central government departments, local authorities, voluntary and public sector agencies, commercial and industrial organizations. Data were collected between 2000 and 2001 at various spatial scales and were converted to postcode sector level for the present analysis. A full outline of the methods used and data collected can be found elsewhere (Cummins et al., 2005).

Information on socio-relational characteristics of the neighbourhood was not available from the sources listed above and so a tailor-made postal survey was administered. The postal survey was sent to a random sample of residents aged 16 and over living in study neighbourhoods. An average of 28 respondents in each of the 438 neighbourhoods provided data on neighbourhood disorder (response rate 42 %). Within each neighbourhood, responses to the questionnaire were aggregated by taking the mean score for all respondents. More detail on the design and validation of the survey is given elsewhere (Stafford et al., 2003).

Variables capturing the following neighbourhood domains were included in this study: Social disorder; Local high street services; Crime; Policing; Physical dereliction; Leisure centres; Supermarkets; Fast-food outlets; Urban sprawl. Latent variables captured the first two of these domains. Social disorder was captured by five items from the postal survey ("Neighbours are threatening"; "Most people in this area can't be trusted"; "People would be afraid to walk alone in this area after dark"; "Vandalism and graffiti are a big problem in this area"; "This area is always full of litter and rubbish"). Local high street services was captured using five items (Number of banks; Number of building societies; Number of dentists; Number of opticians; Number of pharmacies).

Data from the various sources were combined into a single dataset for analysis leading to the formulation of the model to be tested empirically (Figure 2). A number of differences between this model and the theoretical model laid out in Figure 1 should be noted. Firstly, not all of the neighbourhood characteristics could be captured by the available data. Information on neighbourhood provision of public transport, cycle-ways and walk-ways, attractive greenery, religious and cultural norms and health promotion advice could not be found within the constraints of the project. (Physical visits to all the study sites by a trained observer were not feasible.) Secondly, the actual measures capturing some of the neighbourhood characteristics were far from ideal. In particular, sports facilities were measured using number of local authority swimming pools (so that other types of public and private sports centres were not included) and fast-food outlets were measured using MacDonald's restaurants (thus omitting all other fast-food chains and independents). Note also that the counting of numbers of amenities and services says nothing

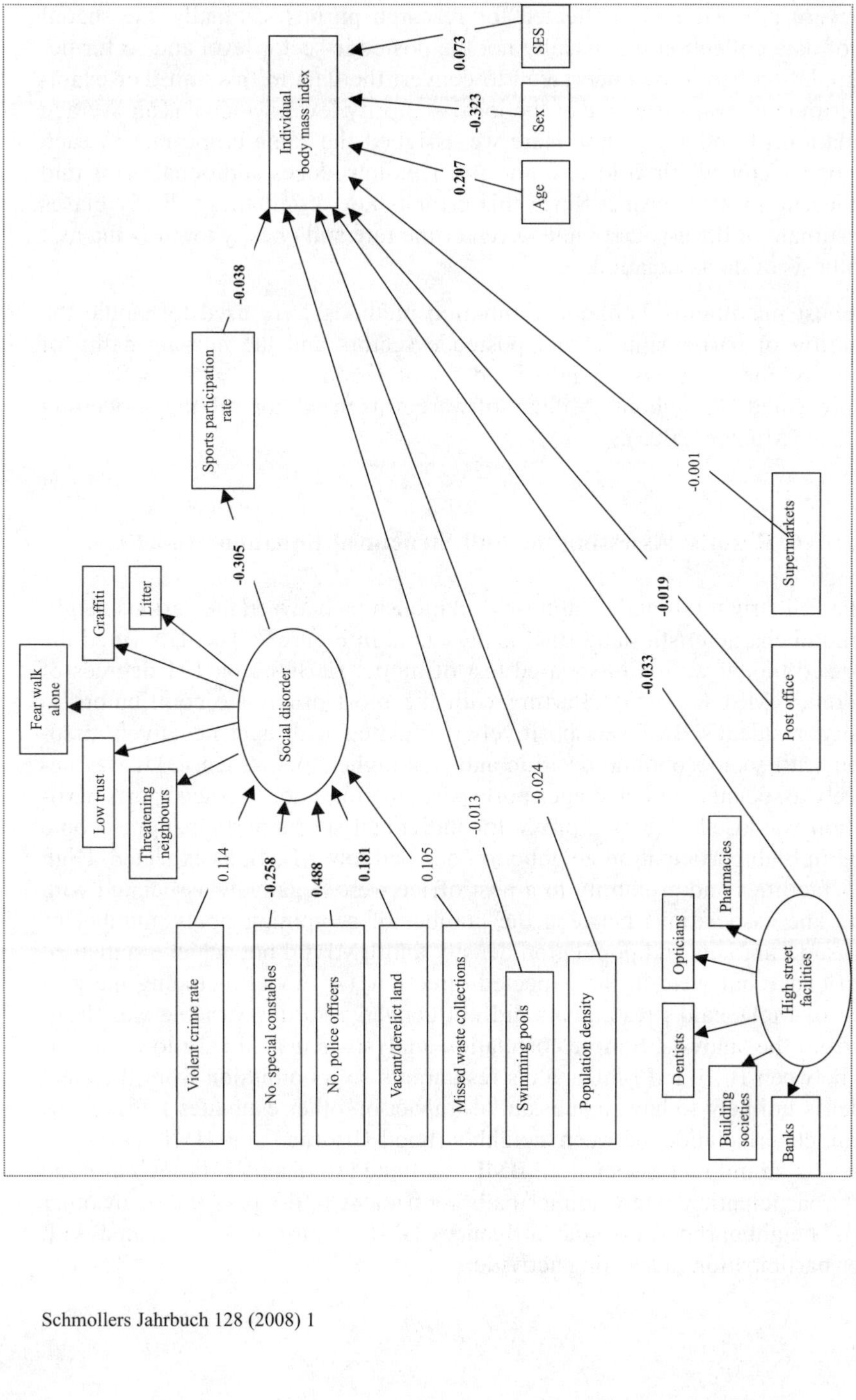

Numbers on each arrow are standardised path coefficients. **Bold** indicates statistical significance at the 5 % level.

Figure 2: Structural model linking neighbourhood characteristics to body mass index about their quality or appropriateness for the needs of the local community. Even where data were a reasonable approximation to the theorized characteristic, questions over its accuracy across all the study sites remain since the data were not originally collected for research purposes. Finally, the spatial unit of data collection was usually not the postcode sector level and so further manipulation had to be undertaken to convert the data to this unit. For example, crime rate was measured at the local authority level, which has an average population of about 125,000. Here we assigned the same crime rate to each postcode sector within a local authority. This introduces additional error into the measurement of crime. Since this error is not systematic, it likely biases the estimate of the association between crime rate and obesity towards the null hypothesis of no association.

Robust maximum likelihood estimation methods were used to handle the clustering of participants within postcode sectors and the non-normality of several of the variables. Standardised factor loadings and path coefficients are presented throughout. Mplus software was used for all the modelling (Muthen / Muthen, 2005).

6. Results: Assessing the Full Structural Equation Model

The full structural model capturing relationships between the various neighbourhood characteristics and BMI is presented in Figure 2. The data fitted the theorized model well (Chi-squared test of model fit 360.7 on 171 degrees of freedom, RMSEA 0.013). Starting with the most proximate contributors to obesity, resident's BMI was positively associated with age, negatively associated with socioeconomic position and was higher for women. BMI was negatively associated with average sports participation rate. Average sports participation was used here as a proxy for individual sports participation: people living in high participation neighbourhoods had lower BMI, as expected. High street facilities and proximity to a post office were negatively associated with BMI. The associations between the number of swimming pools, number of local supermarkets and population density and BMI did not achieve statistical significance but were in the expected direction. (A model including the presence of McDonald's restaurants did not converge so this variable was dropped from the analysis. Simple correlation analysis indicated very low correlation between BMI and McDonald's restaurants so its omission from the final model is unlikely to have a substantial impact on other estimates.) There was no direct association between neighbourhood disorder and BMI. However, there was an indirect association. BMI was linked to disorder through average sports participation rate (indirect path coefficient 0.013 $p < 0.05$). In other words, neighbourhood disorder influences BMI because it is associated with lower participation in sporting activities.

Moving along the explanatory pathway, higher levels of neighbourhood disorder were seen in places with higher crime rates. Neighbourhoods with greater numbers of special constables had lower levels of social disorder. Number of regular police officers was also associated with disorder although the direction of the association was counterintuitive. A positive association between signs of physical dereliction (viz vacant and derelict land) and neighbourhood disorder was found.

7. Strengths and Limitations of the Study

A primary limitation is the mismatch between the idealized and available dataset, as discussed earlier. Despite these data limitations, we were able to gather a large amount of data relating to the neighbourhood from several sources. We used a latent variable approach to combine data from these disparate sources where they were thought to capture one underlying factor. This improves upon simply combining them into a summary index as it allows measurement error to be taken into account and for data from different sources to be weighted for importance as indicators of the underlying factor.

A structural equation modeling approach was then used to test theorized pathways linking the latent variables, directly measured variables and obesity. We cannot make claims about causality based on observational, cross-sectional data. However, we contend that this approach takes us a step forward in understanding the complex interplay between different facets of the neighbourhood and health.

Nevertheless, some limitations with structural equation modeling must be acknowledged. Structural equation modeling compares the empirical data with a given theorised model but it is possible that two or more different formulations of a model can be supported by the data. In other words, the solution is not necessarily a unique one. The choice of model specification should be guided as much by theory, plausibility and expert knowledge of the subject as by statistical considerations. Secondly, structural equation modeling usually proceeds in an iterative way whereby the researcher sets out their initial model, tests this against the data, refines the model and tests against the data again. Most structural equation modeling software packages produce modification indices which guide the researcher in how to modify the model to ensure a better fit to the data. In principle, the refinements should be tested on a different dataset. In practice, the researcher often uses the same set of data to test the first and subsequent formulations of the model, thus generating a potentially spuriously well-fitting model.

In common with most other studies in the field, other limitations include the use of administrative boundaries to approximate neighbourhoods, the lack of longitudinal data and the endogeneity problem. The latter problem of self-selection of obese people into certain types of neighbourhood could invoke a spurious relationship between neighbourhood characteristics and BMI. However, we have adjusted for personal socioeconomic position and this is a key determinant of a person's ability to choose where to live. In our view, it seems implausible that a large section (the overweight and obese section) of the sample would be choosing to live in places characterised by social disorder, less green space and fewer supermarkets / other places to buy healthy food. Unfortunately, longitudinal data that would allow us to investigate the extent of this problem and to assess the temporality of the association between neighbourhood environment and health and the obesity levels of movers and non-movers were not available. Future studies should aim to incorporate longitudinal data to discount the possibility that the observed relationship between neighbourhood environment and BMI is due to obese people having recently moved to obesogenic neighbourhoods.

8. Concluding Remarks

In summary, the study highlights the importance of the neighbourhood environment, including socio-relational characteristics, the built environment and amenities, for health. Efforts to tackle obesity should incorporate strategies which are cognizant of its wider, contextual determinants. Structural equation modeling is a useful approach for studying neighbourhood effects. Whilst it cannot be used to attribute causality, we contend that it is one step on the way to understanding the causal, multilevel processes between neighbourhood environments and individual's health.

References

Bernard, P. / *Charafeddine,* R. / Frohlich, K. L. / *Daniel,* M. / *Kestens,* Y. / *Potvin,* L. (2007): Health inequalities and place: a theoretical conception of neighbourhood, Social Science & Medicine 65 (9), 1839–52.

Bollen, K. A. (1989): Structural equations with latent variables, New York.

Brooks-Gunn, J. / *McCormick,* M. C. / *Klebanov,* P. K. / *McCarton,* C. (1998): Health care use of 3-year-old low birth weight premature children: effects of family and neighborhood poverty, Journal of Pediatrics 132 (6), 971–5.

Carstairs, V. / *Morris*, R. (1991): Deprivation and Health in Scotland, Aberdeen.

Cummins, S. / *Macintyre,* S. / *Davidson,* S. / *Ellaway,* A. (2005): Measuring neighbourhood social and material context: generation and interpretation of ecological data from routine and non-routine sources, Health & Place 11 (3), 249–60.

Diez-Roux, A. V. (1998): Bringing context back into epidemiology: variables and fallacies in multilevel analysis, American Journal of Public Health 88, 216 – 22.

Diez-Roux, A. V. / *Nieto,* F. J. / *Muntaner,* C. / *Tyroler,* H. A. / *Comstock,* G. W. / *Shahar,* E. / *Cooper,* L. S. / *Watson,* R. L. / *Szklo,* M. (1997): Neighborhood environments and coronary heart disease: a multilevel analysis, American Journal of Epidemiology 146 (1), 48 – 63.

Duncan, C. / *Jones,* K. / *Moon,* G. (1995): Psychiatric morbidity: a multilevel approach to regional variations in the UK, Journal of Epidemiology & Community Health 49 (3), 290 – 5.

Egger, G. / *Swinburn,* B. (1997): An "ecological" approach to the obesity pandemic, BMJ, 315 (7106), 477 – 80.

Erens, B. / *Primatesta,* P. (1998): Health Survey for England: Cardiovascular Disease 1998, London.

Franzini, L. / *Caughy,* M. / *Spears,* W. / *Esquer,* M. E. F. (2005): Neighborhood economic conditions, social processes, and self-rated health in low-income neighborhoods in Texas: a multilevel latent variables model, Social Science & Medicine 61 (6), 1135 – 50.

Galea, S. / *Ahern,* J. / *Nandi,* A. / *Tracy,* M. / *Beard,* J. / *Vlahov,* D. (2007): Urban neighborhood poverty and the incidence of depression in a population-based cohort study, Ann Epidemiol 17 (3), 171 – 9.

Hedley, A. A. / *Ogden,* C. L. / *Johnson,* C. L. / *Carroll,* M. D. / *Curtin,* L. R. / *Flegal,* K. M. (2004): Prevalence of overweight and obesity among US children, adolescents, and adults, 1999 – 2002, Journal of the American Medical Association 291 (23), 2847 – 50.

Hill, J. O. / *Peters,* J. C. (1998): Environmental contributions to the obesity epidemic, Science 280 (5368), 1371 – 74.

Krieger, N. (1994): Epidemiology and the web of causation: has anyone seen the spider? Social Science & Medicine 39, 887 – 903.

Lawley, D. N. / *Maxwell,* A. E. (1971): Factor analysis as a statistical method – 2nd edition, London.

Macintyre, S. / *Ellaway,* A. / *Cummins,* S. (2002): Place effects on health: how can we conceptualise, operationalise and measure them? Social Science & Medicine 55 (1), 125 – 39.

Muthen, L. K. / *Muthen,* B. O. (2005): MPlus user's guide – 3rd edition. Los Angeles.

Pickett, K. E. / *Pearl,* M. (2001): Multilevel analyses of neighbourhood socioeconomic context and health outcomes: a critical review, Journal of Epidemiology & Community Health 55 (2), 111 – 22.

Poston, W. S. 2nd / *Foreyt,* J. P. (1999): Obesity is an environmental issue, Atherosclerosis, 146 (2), 201 – 9.

Riva, M. / *Gauvin,* L. / *Barnett,* T. (2007): Toward the next generation of research into small area effects on health: a synthesis of multilevel investigations published since July 1998, Journal of Epidemiology and Community Health, 61 (10), 853 – 61.

Shaw, A. / *McMunn,* A. / *Field,* J. (2000): The Scottish Health Survey 1998. Volume 1. A survey carried out on behalf of The Scottish Executive Department of Health, UK.

Stafford, M. / *Bartley,* M. / *Wilkinson,* R. / *Boreham,* R. / *Thomas,* R. / *Sacker,* A. / *Marmot,* M. (2003): Measuring the social environment: social cohesion and material deprivation in English and Scottish neighbourhoods, Environment & Planning A 35 (8), 1459 – 75.

Stafford, M. / *Cummins,* S. / *Ellaway,* A. / *Sacker,* A. / *Wiggins,* D. / *Macintyre,* S. (2007): Pathways to obesity: identifying local, modifiable determinants of physical activity and diet, Social Science & Medicine 65 (9), 1882 – 97.

Swinburn, B. / *Egger,* G. / *Raza,* F. (1999): Dissecting obesogenic environments: the development and application of a framework for identifying and prioritizing environmental interventions for obesity, Preventative Medicine 29, 563 – 70.

Townsend, P. / *Phillimore,* P. / *Beattie,* A. (1988): Health and Deprivation: Inequality and the North, London.

Wiggins, R. D. / *Bartley,* M. / *Gleave,* S. / *Joshi,* H. / *Lynch,* K. (1998): Limiting long-term illness: a question of where you live or who you are? A multilevel analysis of the 1971 – 1991 ONS longitudinal study, Risk Decision & Policy 3, 181 – 98.

Winkleby, M. / *Sundquist,* K. / *Cubbin,* C. (2007): Inequities in CHD incidence and case fatality by neighborhood deprivation, American Journal of Preventative Medicine 32 (2), 97 – 106.

Schmollers Jahrbuch 128 (2008), 121 – 152
Duncker & Humblot, Berlin

Economic and Ethnic Polarisation among Children in Sweden's Three Metropolitan Areas

By Danuta Biterman, Björn Gustafsson, and Torun Österberg*

Abstract

This paper investigates certain issues of economic and ethnic segregation from the perspective of children in the three metropolitan regions of Sweden by using a relative new operationalization of the neighbourhood concept. Neighbourhoods are clustered by population share of visible immigrants in proportion to share of native born residents. The target variable under study is child income based on income of parents. Inequality in child income 1990, 1996 and 2002 is studied by decomposing additively decomposable inequality indexes. Based on this, measures of residential economic polarisation and residential ethnic polarisation are obtained. Of major significance is that residential polarisation increased for all three regions and for both sub-periods 1990 – 1996 and 1996 – 2002. For example, while in the Stockholm region 7 percent of inequality in child income in 1990 was due to differences in mean income across neighbourhoods, the proportion had increased to as much as 22 percent in 2002. Ethnic residential polarisation increased as well and we report a relatively large overlap between economic and ethnic polarisation. Based on estimated regression models, we conclude that increased returns to parental education have forcefully contributed to larger economic polarisation among children in Swedish metropolitan regions.

JEL Classifications: D31, J13, J15

1. Introduction

In many European countries, a high proportion of immigrants from low and middle income countries and their dependent children reside in less-privileged neighbourhoods of the larger cities. Such a spatial concentration – where the physical distance between neighbourhoods functions as a barrier – is often seen as obstacle in the integration process into the host society. For children,

* Earlier versions of this paper were presented at the Second Migrant Ethnicity Meeting (MEM), IZA, Bonn, Germany May 2006 and a seminar at The Stockholm University Linnaeus Center for Integration Studies (SULCIS), March 2007. We thank for comments received at those occasions as well as at the conference "Neighbourhood Effects Studies on the Basis of European Micro-data". A special thanks to Eva Franzén for help with the data and to the referee of this journal for constructive suggetions.

residential segregation signifies socialisation into certain social settings which probably yield long-run consequences. As the consequence of residential segregation between recently arrived immigrants (and other deprived groups) and the majority, a polarisation of living conditions can arise, a polarisation that can foster social tensions and unrest.

In this paper we present an empirical study of the extent and changes of residential economic polarisation and ethnic polarisation in the country of Sweden. Sweden has long been known for its equal distribution of income and its ambitious social programs. However, the large economic downturn which took place in the beginning of the 90s led to widespread joblessness from which the labour force participation rate has not fully recovered. The trend of increasing earnings and income inequality that started during the first part of the 80s has continued. Housing policies have been dismantled. Together, these processes have increased residential polarisation. Concurrently, the fact, that the immigrants have been concentrated to metropolitan regions – especially to their less attractive areas, has begun to draw the public attention. Residential segregation, economic as well as ethnic, has been placed on the political agenda. For the first time ever, a metropolitan policy for Sweden was formalised in 1998 (Ministry of Finance, 1998). This policy consists of programs aimed at supporting disadvantaged areas. (Andersson, 2006)

Although there have been attempts to counteract residential segregation in Sweden, relatively few systematic efforts (in contrast to the US, for instance) have been made to measure the changes in and reasons for residential segregation.[1] This paper is an attempt to shed new light on these issues. We apply a

1 Janson (1987) studied residential segregation (defined as the difference in residential patterns between Social Democratic party voters, i.e. the working class, and the total population) in the three metropolitan areas of Stockholm, Göteborg and Malmö from 1936 to 1976. The probably first study on ethnic segregation in Greater Stockholm showed that that residential segregation varies in scale among different immigrant groups (Andersson-Brolin, 1984). Biterman (1994) examined economic segregation between low and high income earners and ethnic segregation between native born residents, immigrants from European countries and immigrants from non-European countries in the Stockholm region during 1970 – 1990; the first residential group included native born residents as well as immigrants from other Scandinavian countries, West Europe and North America; the second included immigrants from East Europe and Finland, and the third – immigrants from South European and from non-European countries. Such a rank order of immigrant groups after degree of segregation has been confirmed by other studies (Andersen, 2001; Bevelander / Carlssson / Rojas, 1997; Ministry of Health and Social Affairs, 1997). Some studies have noted a decline in segregation in certain respects. A study by the Swedish National Integration Office of ethnic residential segregation in the three metropolitan areas and in six medium-sized Swedish municipalities during the period 1997 – 2003 showed that the segregation trend is not uniform. Segregation has declined in Malmö, for instance, but has remained largely unchanged in Stockholm and Göteborg in latest years (National Integration Office, 2004, 2005). Biterman / Franzén (2007) showed significant increase in ethnic but not in economic segregation since 1990.

division of metropolitan regions into neighbourhoods which are used as a building block when investigating residential polarisation in each of Sweden's three metropolitan areas. We derive results for 1990, 1996 and 2002, making it possible to show changes over time. Further, we link mean income at the neighbourhood level to education and other household characteristics in order to understand reasons for the changes.

According to various explanatory models for why segregation arises (see Huttman / Blaw / Saltman, 1991), residential segregation can be seen both as an outcome of individual decisions – voluntary and involuntary – as well as decisions at the policy level. Most often, residential segregation between population groups is defined as their respectively uneven distribution across subunits (here neighbourhoods) of the city, see for example Allison (1978) or White (1986), which results in various groups within society not sharing physical and / or social space. People in urban areas tend to arrange themselves in accordance with their particular characteristics in terms of socioeconomic or ethnic status, religion, lifestyle or other cultural properties. The income gaps between population groups are especially important in this process. In our societies, segregation is associated with such negative phenomena as dissimilarities, fragmentation, distance and conflict, for individual households as for the whole society.

This discussion addressing segregation issues deals primarily with adults' preferences, choices and decisions. The perspective of children is often not present, though the strongest argument concerning residential segregation should take their situation into account. Children are typically not the primary decision-makers regarding household choice of residency though one could argue that the location where they grow up is a significant aspect of their childhood and might affect their future life. In the political tradition of Western countries, equality in opportunities for children – included small differences in residential pattern – is considered desirable. However, the segregation studies where children are primary target are few. That motivates us to study residential segregation from the perspective of children, concentrating on income gap across neighbourhoods, which we name "polarisation".

Our target variable is "child income", a variable based on the disposable income and the expenditure needs of the child's family. Applying an additively decomposable income index to income tax data, we define economic polarisation as the proportion of inequality in child income in a particular region that can be attributed to differences in mean income across neighbourhoods. That is, in the operationalization use of the concept "polarization" we follow Zhang / Kanbur (2001), remembering that there are also other measures of the concept (see for example Estaban / Rao, 1994 and Wolfson, 1994). As a first research question we examine how large a part of the inequality in child income in each of the three regions is due to inequality across neighbourhoods and how this spatial polarisation has changed.

Our second research task is to investigate ethnic polarisation and the link between spatial polarisation and ethnic segregation. We claim that it is relevant to cluster neighbourhoods according to level of concentration of visible minorities.[2] Our question is: How large proportion of inequality in child income can be attributed to the level of concentration of visible minorities in the diverse clusters of neighbourhoods and how has such a proportion changed? Related to this, we ask for the overlap between economic and ethic polarisation. Finally, we aim to better understand why differences in neighbourhoods' mean child income are so much greater in 2002 than in 1990. Using regressions we investigate the roles played by parental education and other household characteristics and their payoffs.

In the paper we confirm that mean child income changed little between 1990 and 1996, while larger increases took place from 1996 to 2002. During the period studied, inequality in child income increased profoundly. At the neighbourhood level there is considerable mobility across years in average child income, which means that while some neighbourhoods had gained positions in the ranking of neighbourhoods, others lost. A major finding is that in all regions and between all years of investigation, residential economic polarisation has increased. For example, using the Mean Logarithmic Deviation we find that while in the Stockholm region 7 percent of inequality in child income in 1990 was due to differences in average income across neighbourhoods, the corresponding proportion (of a higher inequality value) had increased to 16 percent in 1995 and to as much as 22 percent in 2002.

We also show that ethnic polarisation has increased in all three metropolitan regions. Most remarkably, while mean child income in neighbourhoods with few or no visible minorities was much higher in 2002 than in 1990, mean income remained more or less constant in neighbourhoods where a high share of residents are visible minorities. We report a relatively large overlap between economic and ethnic polarisation. Finally we find that increased returns to parental education are a major factor leading to larger economic polarisation among children in Swedish metropolitan regions.

The rest of the paper is laid out as follows: In the next section we introduce the building block of neighbourhood used in this study, while the central concepts of child income, its inequality and polarisation are defined in Section 3. Results on the extent of spatial polarisation and its change are reported in Section 4 while Section 5 contains results on ethnic polarisation. In Section 6 we investigate the changed relation between parental education and other household characteristics and mean child income at the neighbourhood level. The paper ends with a concluding section.

---

2 I.e. those whose appearance / or behaviour is perceived as foreign by the majority of the population.

2. Neighbourhoods in the Three Major Urban Regions of Sweden

In all empirical studies of residential segregation, the choice of primary spatial unit is central (the issue of scale). In many cases, researchers by necessity have to work with administrative units as other alternatives are not available. However, a choice of for example municipalities as subunits is in the Swedish context not well motivated since municipalities are hardly comparable because of large differences in population size. Most municipalities have created their own systems of area classification for planning purposes. Such planning areas are not very suitable either, since they may differ significantly in population size and their borders usually change relatively often. Here, however, we are able to use a classification based on sociological considerations.[3] A "neighbourhood" is an area smaller than a municipality, but larger than a city block and normally larger then a planning area (it often aggregates few planning areas), and as such it represents a convenient intermediate level. Residential segregation affects basic conditions for social interaction between the city's inhabitants. Since the neighbourhood represents a natural social arena for its residents, it is an understandable choice of a sub-area. Furthermore, the division into neighbourhoods is not dependent on administrative changes, which means the borders do not change during the period under review – a great advantage while studying segregation processes (see Biterman / Franzén, 2007).

The neighbourhood is defined as a built-up area that:

- is demarcated by "natural borders" (larger streets, green areas, etc).
- corresponds to a city district or a residential area.
- possesses a number of inhabitants large enough to provide a basis for certain private or public services.
- can be considered as an "area of identification" by its inhabitants.

A geographical division into neighbourhoods in accordance with these criteria has only been established for the metropolitan regions, i.e. municipalities of Stockholm, Göteborg and Malmö with neighbouring, suburb municipalities[4], see Table 1.

---

3 Other units used for Sweden include the municipality (Grönqvist, 2006) and a circle of 250 meters around each individual, see Musterd / Andersson (2006) who studied the three metropolitan areas.

4 For technical reasons, the area under review should be limited to neighbourhoods with more than 500 inhabitants. This excludes neighbourhoods with very few inhabitants, usually industrial areas. A neighbourhood commonly houses between four thousand and ten thousand inhabitants, except in a few odd cases. Given that segregation is an urban phenomenon, the focus is on urban neighbourhoods, which means that sparsely populated and rural areas on the outskirts of suburban municipalities have been excluded from the analyses. Note that the number of sparsely populated neighbourhoods changes over time as new housing is built and new inhabitants move in.

Table 1

The three Swedish metropolitan regions, number of neighbourhoods, population size and country of origin composition, 2002

Region	*Stockholm*	*Göteborg*	*Malmö*
Municipalities	Stockholm, Solna, Sundbyberg, Danderyd, Ekerö, Järfälla, Lidingö, Sigtuna, Sollentuna, Täby, Upplands-Bro, Upplands Väsby, Vallentuna, Österåker, Botkyrka, Haninge, Huddinge, Nacka, Salem, Tyresö, Värmdö, Norrtälje, Nynäshamn and Södertälje	Göteborg, Kungälv, Ale, Lerum, Partille, Härryda, Mölndal and Kungsbacka	Malmö, Burlöv, Kävlinge, Lomma, Lund, Staffanstorp, Svedala, Vellinge and Trelleborg
Number of neighbourhoods	337	205	154
Number of urban neighbourhoods with a population larger than 500 persons	271	138	92
Total population as of 2002 (number)	1 0830 600	769 900	528 300
Foreign-born population (number)	324 400	116 400	90 700
Foreign-born population (percent of the total population in the region)	18	15	17

Source: Biterman / Franzén (2007).

Of Sweden's 9 million inhabitants, 3.3 million or 37 percent live in the three metropotitan ares. The region around Stockholm, the capital, in the mid-eastern part of the country is the largest, and consists of not less than 24 municipalities (city level units) and 337 neighbourhoods. Eight municipalities make up the Göteborg region on the west coast, which is the second largest region by population and which has 205 neighbourhoods. As is usually the case for these types of studies, we treat Malmö in the south together with the eight municipalities surrounding it as a separate region, although if the national border to Denmark is disregarded, it can be considered to be the eastern (and smaller) part of the Copenhagen-Malmö region. The Malmö region has 154 neighbourhoods.

Immigrants (defined here as foreign-born persons) make up 12 percent of the population in Sweden, but as many as half of them live in the three metropotitan areas a profound concentration. In 2002 the foreign born in the Stockholm region made up 18 percent of the population, and the corresponding proportion is only slightly lower in the Göteborg and Malmö regions, see Table 1.

There are more differences across regions regarding country of origin, a variation that to some extent mirrors the varying geographic distance to sender countries. Finland is the largest sender country of immigrants living in the Stockholm region and ranks number two among sender countries to the Göteborg region, but has a much lower ranking in the Malmö region. In contrast, Poland is the second largest sender country for immigrants living in the Malmö region, but ranks much lower in the other two regions. If Yugoslavia and its successor states are considered to be one unit, it is the single largest sender of immigrants living in the Göteborg and Malmö regions. Iraq ranks high as a sender country for all three regions (number two in the Stockholm region, number four in the Göteborg region and number three in the Malmö region). Other highly ranked sender countries are Iran (particularly in the Göteborg region) and Turkey (particularly in the Stockholm region). In the Swedish context it is generally perceived that various forms of discrimination and social exclusion are social problems for some, but not all, foreign born. For reasons discussed in Section 5 we will therefore distinguish between visible immigrants and other immigrants.

3. Defining Child Income; its Inequality and Polarisation

From the various perspectives of residential segregation possible to analyse, this paper uses the economic situation of children, and we make comparisons within the population of children.[5] We define a child as a person under age 18 and measure his or her economic situation based on the disposable income of the parents. An important component of a household's disposable income is wages subject to income tax. In addition, there can be income from capital received as dividends and interest as well as income from capital gains from selling stocks and property. Tax files provide this information delivered to Statistics Sweden. We work with data on all children, not a sample.

Other income components we add to receive "gross income" are receipt of social insurance benefits (sickness benefits and unemployment compensation,

---

[5] The alternative of making income comparisons among all individuals, and not only children, as reference would probably not have much affected the picture here reported. This, as mean disposable equivalent income for children in Sweden typically is found to bee relatively close to mean disposable income for the entire population. For example Gustafsson / Johansson / Palmer (2003) report, based on the Household Income Survey, and a chosen equivalence scale, that during the period 1991 to 1998 average disposable child income was around 10 percent lower than average disposable income for the entire population.

for example) and transfers such as child allowances, housing benefits and social assistance. Statistics Sweden obtains this information from various registers kept by the authorities paying the transfers. Statistics Sweden also obtains information from the tax authority on income taxes paid by the households and after subtracting this component from gross income, the disposable income is obtained. We derive our target variable "child income" by adjusting the disposable income of each household with children with an equivalence scale used by Statistics Sweden.[6] In a final step, each person under 18 is assigned this income and we perform the analysis of child income using individuals (children) as the unit of analysis.[7]

Some measurement problems make our measure of child income somewhat noisy. As is the case for all studies based on tax data, undeclared earnings and capital income are not covered in the data; it is difficult to have a well-based view of how important such underreporting is. While there are thus reasons to expect child income to be underestimated in some cases, there are reasons to expect it to have been overestimated in others. The latter occurs as we work with a narrow income pooling and need unit. In any particular case we do not know whether the real income-sharing unit also includes one or more persons over 18 years of age; a person that is not the father or mother of the child. Probably the largest category of such persons consists of older siblings living with the parents. Typically such persons are non-workers signifying low personal income while adding to the real expenditure needs of the family.

In order to quantify economic polarisation we decompose inequality in child income across neighbourhoods. We use two additively decomposable inequality indices, namely the Theil index defined as:

$$I(y) = \frac{1}{n}\sum_{i}^{N}\left(\frac{y_i}{\mu}\right)\log\left(\frac{y_i}{\mu}\right)$$

and the Mean Logarithmic Deviation (MLD) defined as:

6 In order to be able to compare different families' or households' economic standards, it is advisable to relate income to the dependency burden. It is usually done by an equivalence scale. A simple such is the number of persons in the family. However, it is possible to refine such a scale by giving each person a weighting depending on age and number of family members and various equivalence scales have been constructed. In this study we use an equivalence scale recommended by the National Boards of Health and Welfare, which starts at 1.16 for the first adult person in the household, 1.92 for two adults, and adds weight of 0.56, 0.66 and 0.76 for each child aged 0 – 3 years, 4 – 10 years and 11 – 17 years respectively. Ministery of Justice (2002, 89 – 132) discusses the issue of choice of equivalence scale from the perspective of Swedish experiences.

7 This means we follow a now common practice, used in, for example, contributions to Vleminckx / Smeeding (2001), and when studying child poverty, see Bradbury / Jenkins / Micklewright (2001).

$$I(y) = \frac{1}{n}\sum_{i}^{N} \log\left(\frac{y_i}{\mu}\right)$$

where μ is the mean income, y_i income of i:th individual and N the total number of individuals. Of the two indices, is the MLD index more sensitive to inequality at the bottom of the income distribution. If the sample is divided into k groups (here neighbourhoods), the Theil-index can be decomposed as:

$$I(y) = \sum_{g}^{k} \frac{n_g}{n}\left(\frac{\mu_g}{\mu}\right) I_g + I(\mu_1 e_1, \ldots, \mu_k e_k)$$

and the MLD can be decomposed as:

$$I(y) = \sum_{g}^{k} \frac{n_g}{n} I_g + I(\mu_1 e_1, \ldots, \mu_k e_k)$$

where n_g is the number of individuals in the gth group (neighbourhoods), I_g inequality within the gth group, μ_g the mean of the gth group income, and e_g the n_g vector of ones.

Within this framework we define *residential economic polarisation* as the ratio between between-group income inequality and total income inequality, a measure which by definition ranges from 0 to 1.[8] The "between-group" part represents the inequality that would vanish if mean income of all neighbourhoods were to be equally large. In a similar manner we define *residential ethnic polarisation* based on a classification of clusters of neighbourhoods formed after ethnic composition. Details on this classification are provided in Section 5.

The measures of residential and ethnic polarisation (for each metropolitan region) are related which can be seen from the following identities:

Total income inequality =
Within neighbourhood inequality + Between neighbourhood inequality (1)

Between neighbourhood inequality =
Between ethnic cluster inequality + Within ethnic cluster inequality (2)

Substituting (1) into (2) we arrive at:

Total income inequality = Within neighbourhood inequality +
Between cluster inequality + Within ethnic cluster inequality (3)

8 Thus the index is similar, but not identical, to the Neighbourhood Sorting Index (NSI) introduced by Jargovsky (1996). NSI is defined as the ratio between the standard deviation of neighbourhood mean income and the standard deviation of the income among units in the entire territory studied.

The relative sizes of the two sign terms on the right provide an indication of the overlap between residential segregation and economic segregation. We can for example define a measure of overlap as:

$$\text{Between ethnic cluster inequality / Between neighbourhood inequality} \quad (4)$$

By definition the ratio defined in equation (4) assumes values from 0, as is the case if there is no ethnic segregation, up to 1.0 (or 100 percent) which is the case if economic and ethnic segregation strictly follow each other.

To repeat: The tax data we work with contain all individuals and households living in the three regions studied. Thus there are no sample errors in our numbers. The database at our disposal, the Social Medicine Database from Centre for Epidemiology at The National Board of Health and Welfare, contains annual data from 1990 to 2002. We chose to make computations for the first and last years and also include computations for 1996 which makes it possible to investigate changes across two six-year sub-periods. Of the two, the first is characterised by some economic growth initially followed by a deep downturn of the economy, while the latter sub-period was a period of rapid recovery.

4. The Extent of Spatial Polarisation and its Change

Table A1 in the Appendix provides an overview of development of child income in 2002 for the three regions combined and which refers to the 652 000 children living there. It can be seen that mean child income in 1996 was only 4 percent higher than in 1990, but between 1996 and 2002 it had increased by as much as 28 percent. Further, inequality in child income increased between both pairs of years according to all inequality measures computed. Table 2 shows example of neighbourhoods as we present the six neighbourhoods with lowest and highest average child income in 2002, as well as some neighbourhoods at the centre of the distribution. Mean child income is actually lower 2002 than in 1990 for most neighbourhoods at the bottom of the distribution, while neighbourhoods at the top have experienced rapid increase. Most parents in the poorest neighbourhoods have a short education, but the share where both parents only have a compulsory education or less has decreased substantially between 1990 and 2002. More than two third of children living in the poorest neighbourhoods have a foreign background from middle and low income countries in 1990, while the corresponding is the case among less than six percent of children living in the richest neighbourhoods. In 2002 more than 4 / 5 of the parents in the low income neighbourhoods are born in middle in low income countries. Different from high income neighbourhoods many parents in the poorest neighbourhoods have low or no labour market attachment, and the fraction has increased between the two years studied. Further it can bee noted that poor neighbourhoods are located in all three metropolitan

Table 2: **Characteristics of neighbourhoods at the bottom, in the middle and at the top of the distribution of average child income in 2002 (roportions, if not other stated)**

	City-region	Dis-posable income in 1990 (hundreds of SEK, in 2000 prices)	Dis-posable income in 2002 (hundreds of SEK, in 2000 prices)	Children from MLIC 1990	Children from MLIC 2002	Mother's age when child born 1990	Mother's age when child born 2002	Both parents compul-sory education 1990	Both parents compul-sory education 2002	Both parents with long university educations (3 years or more) 1990	Both parents with long university educations (3 years or more) 2002	Single parents 1990	Single parents 2002	Both parents strong labour market attache-ment 1990	Both parents strong labour market attache-ment 2002
S Rosengård	M	776	604	0.61	0.93	25.8	26.8	0.37	0.17	0.00	0.02	0.31	0.22	0.16	0.03
Fittja	S	694	687	0.67	0.86	26.6	27.7	0.39	0.24	0.01	0.02	0.19	0.21	0.24	0.13
Hjällbo	G	793	738	0.58	0.93	27.0	27.5	0.34	0.18	0.01	0.01	0.32	0.36	0.20	0.05
N Biskopsgåden	G	827	738	0.48	0.81	25.2	27.0	0.42	0.17	0.00	0.02	0.26	0.28	0.23	0.08
Holma	M	734	751	0.46	0.77	25.8	26.7	0.36	0.12	0.01	0.02	0.31	0.30	0.16	0.07
Södra Rinkeby	S	801	755	0.58	0.83	26.1	27.1	0.40	0.18	0.01	0.02	0.30	0.33	0.24	0.09
Middle-6															
Glesb N Sigtuna	S	992	1261	0.00	0.01	28.1	30.0	0.10	0.04	0.06	0.04	0.13	0.16	0.48	0.62
Fjärås tätor	G	978	1261	0.01	0.01	28.0	28.6	0.07	0.03	0.08	0.06	0.09	0.23	0.44	0.56
Furuskog-Furulund	G	983	1261	0.02	0.04	28.8	30.1	0.07	0.02	0.06	0.10	0.12	0.18	0.51	0.61
Tygelsjö by	M	917	1262	0.01	0.01	28.3	29.3	0.09	0.03	0.04	0.06	0.05	0.13	0.54	0.62
Bandhagen	S	1085	1262	0.06	0.18	27.2	29.1	0.12	0.04	0.03	0.07	0.33	0.37	0.48	0.47
Västergård	S	967	1263	0.10	0.17	26.6	27.8	0.18	0.06	0.02	0.02	0.20	0.34	0.51	0.57
Top-6															
Södra Ängby	S	1299	2049	0.01	0.01	31.9	33.9	0.01	0.00	0.40	0.49	0.09	0.08	0.62	0.78
Ålsten-Äpplev	S	1288	2072	0.00	0.00	31.7	33.0	0.01	0.00	0.35	0.41	0.09	0.11	0.64	0.67
Stocksund-Tranh	S	1357	2088	0.02	0.01	31.3	32.8	0.01	0.00	0.34	0.41	0.11	0.12	0.62	0.61
Karlapl-Strandv	S	1347	2185	0.02	0.02	31.6	33.1	0.02	0.00	0.29	0.29	0.22	0.24	0.53	0.51
Lärkstaden	S	1379	2214	0.02	0.02	31.9	33.2	0.03	0.00	0.33	0.32	0.23	0.20	0.49	0.52
Djursholm	S	1365	2302	0.02	0.02	31.6	32.8	0.02	0.00	0.32	0.39	0.11	0.12	0.53	0.53

Source: Authors calculations from the Social Medicine Database, Centre for Epidemiology at the National Board of Health and Welfare.

Note: G = Göteborg Metropolitan Region, M = Malmö Metropolitan Region and S = Stockholm Metropolitan Region.

For a definition of the variables used see Table A2 in the Appendix.

regions while in contrast data shows that all of the six richest neighbourhoods are located in the Stockholm region.

Table 3

Mean child income and income inequality in the metropolitan areas of Stockholm, Göteborg and Malmö 1990, 1996 and 2002

	Mean disposable income 100s SEK in 2000 prices	MLD	Theil	Gini	*N*	Between group inequality as a percent of total inequality (MLD) Percent	Between group inequality as a percent of total inequality (Theil) Percent
Stockholm							
1990	1052	0.1075	0.1049	0.2392	341 780		
1996	1098	0.1563	0.1858	0.2867	370 272		
2002	1442	0.1957	0.2968	0.3174	386 448		
Göteborg							
1990	987	0.0929	0.0948	0.2220	145 286		
1996	1010	0.1192	0.1403	0.2538	156 608		
2002	1253	0.1267	0.1344	0.2590	160 539		
Malmö							
1990	974	0.0960	0.0949	0.2231	98 880		
1996	988	0.1293	0.1538	0.2625	103 283		
2002	1205	0.1487	0.1477	0.2745	104 572		
Within group (region) inequality							
1990		0.1020	0.1009				
1996		0.1426	0.1701				
2002		0.1711	0.2386				
Between group (region) inequality							
1990		0.0006	0.0006			0.6	0.6
1996		0.0010	0.0010			0.7	0.6
2002		0.0030	0.0029			1.7	1.2

Source: Authors calculations from the Social Medicine Database, Centre for Epidemiology at the National Board of Health and Welfare.

Table 3 reports mean child income and income inequality using the additively decomposable indices and for comparison, the Gini coefficient for each of the three regions. We also decompose inequality in child income for the combined three regions by metropolitan region (the lower part of the table).

Stockholm has the highest mean child income and the gap to the other two regions has widened slightly. This development becomes visible when we decompose inequality in the combined three regions by region (the lower rows of Table 3), as larger fractions can be attributed to the between region part. Still very little of the inequality in child income in the three regions combined is due to differences in mean income across regions; for 2002 less than 2 percent.

Table 3 also shows that by all indices used, child income is most unequally distributed in the Stockholm region in 1996 and 2002, and less unequal in the Göteborg region with the difference to the Malmö region being slight. The pattern of increased inequality in child income is found to prevail in all regions during the first sub-period, but for the second sub-period increases are recorded according to all three indices in the Stockholm region only.

With this background we now look at mean income at the level of neighbourhood. Figure 1 shows that the distribution of mean child neighbourhood income in 2002 has moved to the right and is more unequal than that of 1990. Figure 2 shows a close relation between mean child income in 1990 and 2002 and the fitted regression line is fairly steep. However, there is also a variation across the regression line.

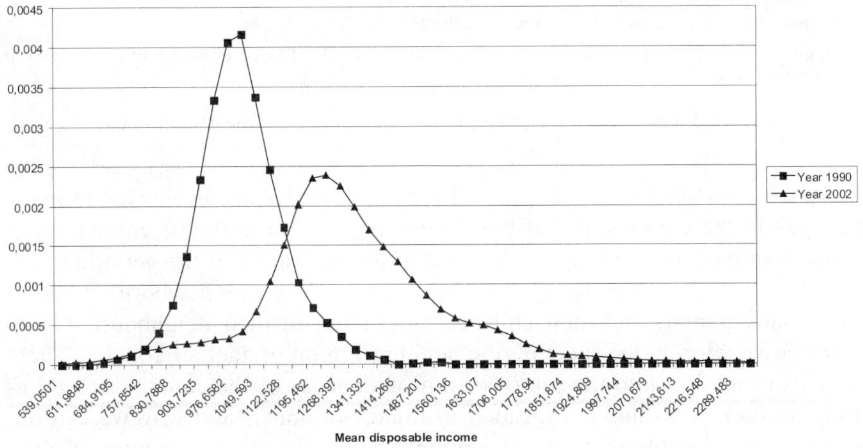

Source: Authors estimations from the Social Medicine Database, Centre or Epidemiology at the National Board of Health and Welfare.

Figure 1: Kernel Density estimate (Epanechnikov) for mean disposable income (in year 2000 prices) in neighbourhoods for year 1990 and 2002

During the 12 year period studied here, few dwellings were constructed or renovated and changes in the physical structure of the neighbourhoods were relatively minor, particularly during the first part of the period as the construc-

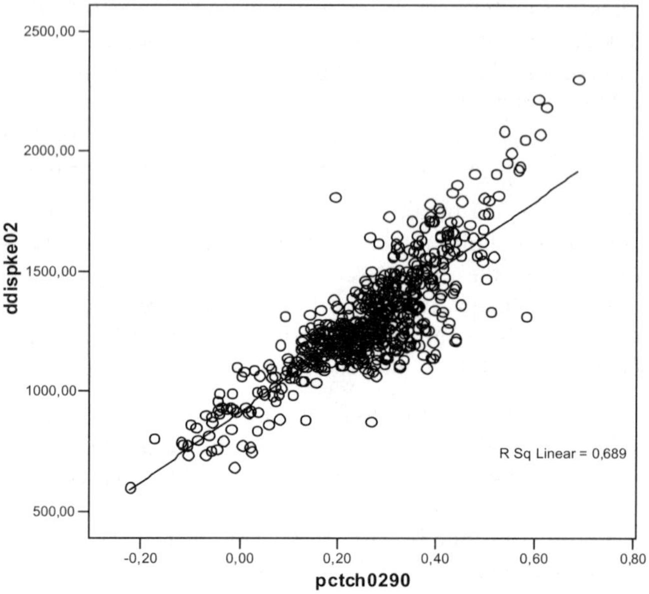

Pctch0290 = percentage change between 2002 and 1990.
Ddispke02 = mean disposable income in each neighbourhood in 2002.

Source: Authors calculations from the Social Medicine Database, Centre for Epidemiology at the National Board of Health and Welfare.

Figure 2: Changes in mean neighbourhood child income 1990 to 2002

tion industry had almost collapsed. However, demographic events led to many changes in the composition of the studied population in the neighbourhoods. More than half of the children observed at the beginning of the period left the population as they became adults. They were replaced by newborns. In addition, many parents and their children moved out of their neighbourhoods to other destination in the same region, another region or another country. There was also mobility into the regions from other parts of the country as well as from abroad. With this background in mind, we understand why we can observe a considerable mobility of neighbourhoods in the distribution of child income across the years.

Table 4 shows the extent of mobility of neighbourhoods in the distribution of child income in the Stockholm region as a matrix. We have classified neighbourhoods into deciles for each year and show the association as percentages of units observed the first year. We see that slightly more than half of the neighbourhoods located in the bottom decile in 1990 remained in the same decile in 2002. Mobility is even larger in the middle of the distribution where a relatively small change in mean child income can cause the neighbourhood to change deciles. Most stability is found at the top of the distribution, although actually one-third of the neighbourhoods that were at the top in 1990 had moved down one or two deciles. While clearly neighbourhood mobility most often is short, Table 3 reports a few cases with long distance mobility. For example, one neighbourhood moved from the first decile in 1990 to the ninth in 2002 while another moved from the ninth decile down to the first.

Table 4

Neighbourhood mobility in the distribution of child income 1990 – 2002, the Stockholm metropolitan area

(Row percent)

	Decile in 1990									
Decile in 2002	1	2	3	4	5	6	7	8	9	10
1	53.3	20.0	13.3	3.3	3.3	3.3	0.0	0.0	3.3	0.0
2	24.2	21.2	21.2	21.2	3.0	3.0	3.0	3.0	0.0	0.0
3	9.1	36.4	21.2	21.2	3.0	3.0	3.0	3.0	0.0	0.0
4	6.3	12.5	9.4	28.1	28.1	6.3	3.1	0.0	3.1	3.1
5	0.0	9.1	15.2	9.1	18.2	24.2	12.1	12.1	0.0	0.0
6	3.1	0.0	9.4	21.9	21.9	18.8	18.8	6.3	0.0	0.0
7	0.0	0.0	3.2	3.2	9.7	25.8	29.0	16.1	9.7	3.2
8	0.0	0.0	6.1	0.0	6.1	12.1	21.2	39.4	9.1	6.1
9	3.0	3.0	0.0	3.0	0.0	3.0	9.1	12.1	45.5	21.1
10	0.0	0.0	0.0	0.0	0.0	0.0	0.0	6.1	27.3	66.7

Source: Authors calculations from the Social Medicine Database, Centre for Epidemiology at the National Board of Health and Welfare.

We are now in a position to answer the first research question, that of the extent and changes in residential economic polarisation. Table 5 reports the within and between terms for all three regions and all three years computed for the two inequality indices. First we compare the three regions. Residential economic polarisation is found to be largest in the Stockholm region for both measures and for all years investigated. In 1996 and 2002, residential polarisation was smaller in the Göteborg region than in the Malmö region.

Now let us compare changes over time. Most profoundly, residential polarisation is found to have increased between each pair of years, in each region and according to both inequality indices. The increase is rapid. While for example the MLD index indicated that in the Stockholm region, 7 percent of inequality in child income could be attributed to differences in mean income across neighbourhoods, the corresponding proportion had increased to 16 percent in 1996 and as much as 22 percent in 2002.

Table 5

Inequality in child income and its decomposition by neighbourhood (polarisation) in the Stockholm, Göteborg and Malmö metropolitan areas 1990, 1996 and 2002

	MLD	Theil	Between group inequality as a percent of total inequality (MLD)	Between group inequality as a percent of total inequality (Theil)
Within group inequality				
Stockholm				
1990	0.1005	0.0980		
1996	0.1350	0.1635		
2002	0.1598	0.2580		
Göteborg				
1990	0.0888	0.0971		
1996	0.1090	0.1300		
2002	0.1131	0.1212		
Malmö				
1990	0.0920	0.0910		
1996	0.1159	0.1404		
2002	0.1287	0.1290		
Between group inequality				
Stockholm				
1990	0.0070	0.0069	7.0 %	7.1 %
1996	0.0212	0.0223	15.7 %	13.6 %
2002	0.0359	0.0388	22.4 %	15.0 %
Göteborg				
1990	0.0041	0.0041	4.6 %	4.2 %
1996	0.0102	0.0103	9.4 %	7.9 %
2002	0.0136	0.0131	12.1%	10.8%
Malmö				
1990	0.0040	0.0039	4.3 %	4.3 %
1996	0.0134	0.0134	11.5 %	9.6 %
2002	0.0201	0.0187	15.6 %	14.5 %

Source: Authors calculations from the Social Medicine Database, Centre for Epidemiology at the National Board of Health and Welfare.

Looking more closely at our data (and not reported in a table), and dividing neighbourhoods into deciles, a comparison of the first and last details in this development are worth mentioning. Mean child income for the first decile increased by as little as 7 percent, while for the tenth it increased by 43 percent. Even more revealing is to examine income components in the data. In the first decile, average mother income decreased by 19 percent and average father income by as much as 29 percent. Counteracting the decreased reliance on parental market income, those in the first decile became more relying on social assistance; the rate of social assistance receipt went up from 18 to 26 percent. In contrast, in the top decile, average mother earnings rose by 42 percent and average father earnings by as much as 48 percent; here the rate of social assistance receipt fell from 6 to 2 percent.

5. Ethnicity and Polarisation

In order to study the degree of ethnic polarisation we classify neighbourhoods by the ethnic composition of its population. Such a classification can obviously be made using various criteria. Here we apply a criterion based on the rate between the number of visible immigrants born (of all ages) and the number of native born (of all ages). In the Swedish context it is generally perceived that various forms of discrimination and social exclusion are social problems for some, but not all foreign born persons. People from distant countries with low or medium-high GDPs are easy to recognise by the colour of their skin or by their names and they are treated unfavourably in many cases. Many such immigrants have entered Sweden as refugees during recent few decades and these minority groups often have only a short history of residing in Sweden. In contrast, people from neighbouring countries, mainly from Scandinavian countries and from countries in Western and Eastern Europe (with high GDP) are most often difficult to distinguish from natives by looks, colour of skin or by given name, and are usually not discriminated by majority population. These – non-visible – immigrant groups commenced their residence in Sweden relatively earlier. The majority among them came to Sweden as labour immigrants and are now well integrated into Swedish society.

A more detailed description of the classification is as follows: For each of the three large city regions the average rate of visible foreign born residents to native born population is computed and put equal to 1.0, and for each neighbourhood the corresponding ratio is computed.[9] According to this definition

[9] See Biterman / Franzén (2007) for the exact definition. It is to some extent arbitrary where to place the dividing line between visible and non-visible immigrants. Here people born in Hungary, Russia and Romania (together with those from for example Finland, Norway, Germany and United States) for example, are not considered visible immigrants. This in contrast to persons born in Yugoslavia (and its successor countries), Bulgaria, Greece, Spain and Italy who are considered visible immigrants (together with people from Africa, Africa and Latin America). Nevertheless, we can argue that all immigrants from countries in dispute comprise no more than 6–7 per cent of all non-visible immigrants, according to this categorisation. If we categorised them as "visible"

the number of non-visible foreign-born persons in a particular neighbourhood does not affect the ethnic classification of a neighbourhood. Based on the value for this variable, the neighbourhood is classified into one of eight different categories. Neighbourhoods with populations of less than 500 individuals are not classified. There are three categories of neighbourhoods with varying degrees of homogenous native-born population (values less than 0.25, 0.25 – 0.49, 0.50 – 0.79), two categories of integrated neighbourhoods (values 0.80 – 1.24, 1.25 – 1.99) and three categories with a concentration of visible minorities (2.0 – 3.99, 4.00 – 9.99, 10 and higher). From 594 neighbourhoods classified, 416 are homogenous with predominantly native born population, 104 integrated and 74 have a large concentration of visible minorities.

For each of the eight clusters of neighbourhoods defined in this manner as well as for the category of unclassified, we compute mean child income and inequality in child income. Based on these numbers we decompose child inequality to show the extent of ethnic polarisation and its changes. The results are presented in the Appendix Table A2. While there is not much of a pattern of differences in child income inequality across ethnic categories, more is found regarding mean income as well as changes in mean income. Not surprisingly, the highest mean incomes are found in neighbourhoods with few visible foreign born residents while the mean incomes are slightly lower in the clusters of neighbourhoods with more mixed compositions of the population. The lowest means are found in clusters with a dominant composition of visible minorities. This gap in mean income across ethic clusters has increased; an increase which has been rapid and has occurred during both sub-periods.

An example from the Stockholm region can illustrate how differently mean income has developed in clusters with varying ethnic composition (see Figure 3). Observe first cluster 2 where 120 000 children lived and where rather few had larger concentration of visible minorities. With the second lowest concentration of visible immigrants, average child income was the highest among the clusters in 1990. Its mean income had increased by 9 percent in 1996, and between 1996 and 2002 by another 36 percent; in 2002 mean income was as much as 48 percent higher than in 1990. Now observe cluster 8 with 11 000 children and the highest concentration of visible minorities. From 1990 to 1996 child mean income decreased by 10 percent, and the recovery from 1996 to 2002 was as little as 11 percent, thus mean income in 2002 was almost exactly the same as in 1990. The gap in mean child income between cluster 2 and cluster 8 increased from 1:1.5 to 1:1.8 and then up to 1:2.2. The development in the two other regions are rather similar.

---

instead, it would not change the clustering of neighbourhoods in some profound way, nor have some impact on the final results and conclusions. Another potential limitation of the definition is that it is based only on people who are born outside Sweden. Thus it does not take into consideration that some second generation immigrants are visible different from the majority.

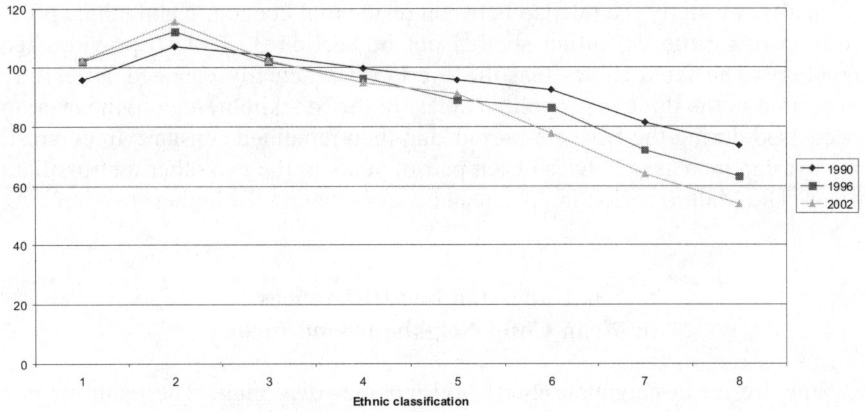

Source: Authors calculations from the Social Medicine Database, Centre for Epidemiology at the National Board of Health and Welfare.

Figure 3: Mean disposable child income in clusters of neighbourhoods with different ethnic compositions 1990, 1996 and 2002 for the Stockholm metropolitan area

From this report of enlarged differences in mean income between clusters of neighbourhoods formed according to ethnicity, it comes as no surprise that our measure of ethnic polarisation shows increases in all regions and for both sub-periods. In 1990 the ethnic polarisation was largest in the Stockholm region, but the increase was most rapid in the Malmö region and in 2002 this region had the largest ethnic polarisation. While less than 2 percent of inequality in child income in the Malmö region could be attributed to differences in mean income across the clusters in 1990, this proportion had increased to 10 percent (when MLD is applied) in 2002.

Table 6

Overlap between economic and ethnic polarisation in the Stockholm, Göteborg and Malmö metropolitan areas 1990, 1996 and 2002 in percent

Year	Measures based on MLD			Measures based on the Theil index		
	Stockholm region	Göteborg region	Malmö region	Stockholm Region	Göteborg region	Malmö region
1990	55	27	41	53	26	40
1996	45	44	60	40	40	54
2002	46	63	76	38	59	72

Source: Authors calculations from the Social Medicine Database, Centre for Epidemiology at the National Board of Health and Welfare.

For definition of overlap see the text.

Finally, we study the overlap between residential economic and ethnic polarisation using the definition spelled out in Section 3. Table 6 provides the numbers. The table shows that the overlap has actually changed differently over time in the three metropolitan areas. In the Stockholm region, the overlap decreased during the first sub-period, and then remained constant. In contrast, the overlap increased between each pair of years in the two other metropolitan areas. The Malmö region in 2002 stands out as having the highest overlap.

6. Understanding Differences in Mean Child Neighbourhood Income

Why are mean neighbourhood child incomes diverging? The main income source for parents is earnings and earnings are in turn related to level of education. Increased rates of return to (parental) education therefore provide one potential factor behind increased spatial polarisation, while a changed educational composition of neighbourhoods could provide another. We investigate the explanatory power of the alternatives by estimating income functions for 1990 and 2002 at the neighbourhood level. The omitted category is both parents having long university educations. There are five variables measuring the proportion of parents with particular education levels. In the specification we also include one variable for the proportion of single parents, four for the proportion of children with various foreign region of birth and period of residency, three for indicating parent's labour market attachment and two dummy variables for metropolitan region. We use the coefficient estimates as well as the variable values to analyse possible causes for polarisation to increase over time. Are the main reasons changed parental education, family structure and labour market involvement by parents? Or are the main causes changed payoffs of the variables that affect child income?

The intercept in Table 7 indicates the mean child income of a neighbourhood in the Stockholm metropolitan region where all children have two parents with strong labour market attachments and long university educations; no child is foreign born. The two models predict that (in case mother's average age at child birth is 30 and the child lives in Stockholm), mean child income in 2002 to be as much as 49 percent higher than in 1990. In contrast, if both parents have educations not higher than at the compulsory level, mean child income is predicted to have decreased by 11 percent.

In addition to the strongly changed effects of parental education, the estimates show positive coefficients for mothers age at first child birth as well as negative coefficients estimated with high t-values for both years analysed for the proportion children from low- and middle-income countries. There are negative coefficients for the metropolitan region dummies, and positive coefficients for the proportion single parents and for certain coefficients for labour

Table 7

Regression models explaining mean child income (neighbourhoods are unit of analysis) 1990 and 2002

	Coef.	*t*	$P > \|t\|$	Coef.	*t*	$P > \|t\|$
	1990			**2002**		
Intercept	652.51	4.35	<.0001	652.23	2.13	0.0339
Reference: Greater Stockholm						
Greater Goteborg	–26.14	–4.84	<.0001	–94.96	–9.48	<.0001
Greater Malmö	–31.60	–5.22	<.0001	–112.36	–8.18	<.0001
Age of mother when child was born	24.13	5.54	<.0001	46.47	5.39	<.0001
Reference: Child with Swedish background						
Child MLIC 0–9 years in the country	67.79	0.82	0.4150	–454.69	–3.11	0.0020
Child MLIC mt 9 years in the country	–129.97	–2.38	0.0176	–204.32	–2.58	0.0101
Child HIC 0–9 years in the country	16.60	0.08	0.9378	3561.01	6.04	<.0001
Child HIC mt .9 years in the country	–174.37	–2.25	0.0247	–769.14	–3.27	0.0011
Reference: Both parents have long university educations						
One parent with a long university education	–160.37	–1.73	0.0849	–562.37	–2.81	0.0052
At least one parent with short university education	–282.12	–4.05	<.0001	–743.15	–5.70	<.0001
At least one parent with secondary education	–290.45	–4.26	<.0001	–584.88	–4.61	<.0001
Both parents compulsory education	–194.34	–2.09	0.0368	–990.24	–3.30	0.001
One parent compulsory education	–349.54	–5.26	<.0001	–750.48	–4.38	<.0001
Single parents	613.47	23.33	<.0001	494.33	8.38	<.0001
Both parents with strong labour market attachements						
One parent with strong labour market attachment	–214.05	–4.85	<.0001	–397.09	–4.05	<.0001
Both parents with low labour market attachement	–652.33	–11.06	<.0001	–558.99	–3.92	0.0001
Both parents with no working or unemployment income	–552.78	–5.13	<.0001	–96.78	–0.55	0.5804
Adjusted R^2	0.84			0.86		

Source: Authors estimations from the Social Medicine Database, Centre for Epidemiology at the National Board of Health and Welfare.

For a definition of the variables used see Table A2 in the Appendix.

market attachment. Some of the coefficients for labour market attachment are lower in 2002 than in 1990.[10]

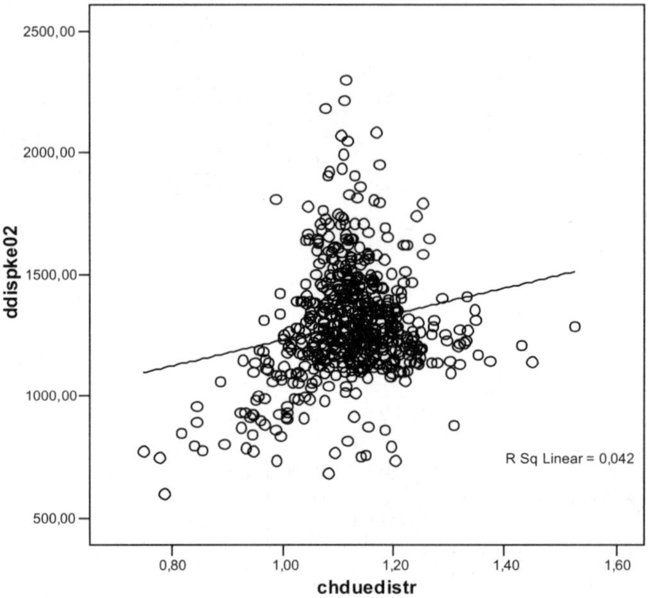

Chduedistr = predicted disposable income from the 2002 model with the 2002 distribution of the independent variables / predicted disposable income from the 2002 model with the 1990 distribution of the independent variables (Changes due to changes in distribution).

Ddispke02 = Mean disposable income in each neighbourhood in year 2002.

Source: Table 7 and authors calculations from the Social Medicine Database, Centre for Epidemiology at the National Board of Health and Welfare.

Figure 4: Predicted changes in mean child neighbourhood incom from 1990 to 2002 due to changes in distribution of variables

We use the parameter estimates for 1990 and 2002 to illustrate the importance of changes in coefficient versus changes in variables for the increased dispersion of mean child neighbourhood income. To construct Figure 4 we start from the 2002 coefficient estimates and predict mean child neighbourhood income using variables as observed for 1990 and 2002. Then we relate the 2002 prediction to the 1990 predictions. On the *x*-axis we display the change in income due to changes in variables and on the *y*-axis we display the mean disposable income in the neighbourhood. For each neighbourhood, there

10 When analysing residuals we notice that the model significantly underpredicts mean neighbourhood income for the three neighbourhoods with the highest mean incomes in both year 1990 and year 2002.

is one point showing change at the income level of income in 2002. We find that in most, but not all cases, changes in variables have caused mean child neighbourhood income to increase. However, increases are almost always lower than the 33 percent observed in the aggregate. Further, there is no linear relation between initial income level and change.

When we use changes in parameter estimates between 1990 and 2002, and variables in 2002 to predict changes in mean child neighbourhood income in Figure 5, the picture becomes rather different. Almost without exception, neighbourhood child income is predicted to have increased; for a substantial proportion of neighbourhoods, the increase is more than 33 percent. Further, there is a strong positive linear relation between initial income level and income change. Changes in coefficients are thus the major driving force behind the increase in spatial polarisation in child income across neighbourhoods in Swedish metropolitan areas.

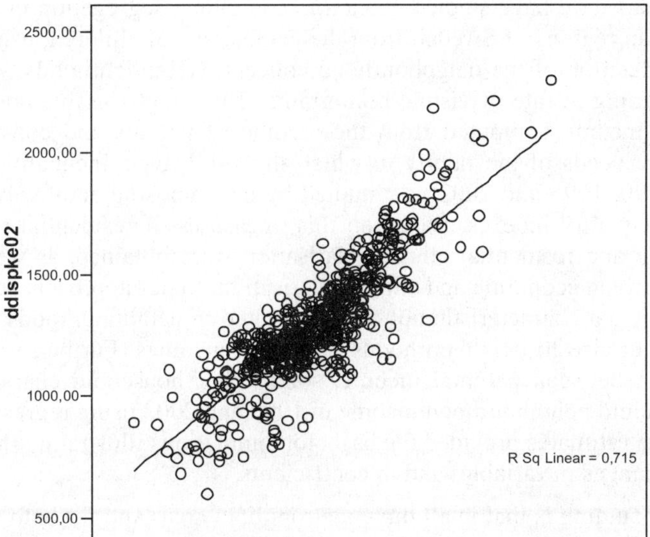

Chdueretur = predicted income from the 2002 model with the 2002 distribution of the independent varaibles / predicted income from the 1990 model with the 2002 distribution of the independent variables. (changes due to changes in returns).

Ddispke02 = Mean disposable income in each neighbourhood in year 2002.

Source: Table 7 and authors calculations from the Social Medicine Database, Centre for Epidemiology at the National Board of Health and Welfare.

Figure 5: Predicted changes in mean child neighbourhood income from 1990 to 2002 due to changes in coefficients in model estimations

When understanding these results it is useful to remember that child income is the sum of several income components: Wages of parents received during a full year, dividends, interests, capital gains as well as various transfers and with income taxes enter with a negative sign. Increased coefficients are thus most likely the outcome of several changes. One possible channel is increased rates to return to education in the labour market that has previously been documented.[11] In addition Sweden experienced a tax reform during the period studied. Its components were decreased marginal tax rates as well as the introduction of two tax bases, not as previously one. As a consequence capital gains and interests are now subject to a proportional tax rate of 30 percent. In the old system such incomes were added to earnings and when earned by an average or higher paid person taxed at a high rate. The tax reform is thus an additional possible reason why coefficients have increased.

7. Conclusions

In this paper we have studied economic and ethnic segregation in the three metropolitan regions of Sweden from the perspective of children, using a new operationalization of the neighbourhood concept. Neighbourhoods were clustered according to rate of visible immigrants. The target variable under study was child income computed from the income of parents and considers the expenditure needs of the family in which the child lives. Inequality in child income 1990, 1996 and 2002 was studied by decomposing additively decomposable inequality indexes. Based on this, measures of residential economic polarisation and residential ethnic polarisation were obtained, as well as the overlap between economic and ethnic polarisation. In our approach, residential polarisation is a characteristic not only attributed to neighbourhoods with low incomes, but also to neighbourhoods with high incomes. Further, we studied the relation between parental income, some other household characteristics and mean child neighbourhood income in 1990 and 2002 using regression analysis. These estimates provided the basis for simulations illustrating the importance of changes in variables and in coefficients.

A major finding is that in all three metropolitan areas and for both sub-periods studied, residential polarisation increased. For example, while in the Stockholm region 7 percent of inequality (measured by the MLD index) in child income in 1990 was due to differences in mean income across neighbourhoods, the corresponding proportion of the now larger inequality had increased to 16 percent in 1996 and to as much as 22 percent in 2002.

The study has found that ethnic residential polarisation increased as well across both sub-periods studied in all three cities. Most strikingly we found

[11] See Gustavsson (2006) who analysed wages in Sweden 1992 to 2001 by estimating wage functions.

that mean real income had increased rapidly from 1990 to 2002 in clusters with predominantly Swedish born population. In contrast, mean child income in clusters where many visible foreign born live had not grown. We report a relatively large overlap between economic and ethnic polarisation.

Finally, based on analysing data for neighbourhoods we have found that increased returns to parental variables, probably most prominently education, are a major factor leading to larger economic segregation among children in Swedish metropolitan regions. Changes in parental variables contributed less. For example we found that children having two parents with long university educations have a much higher income in 2002 than in 1990. In contrast, during the same twelve years, children with two parents who possess only compulsory educations experienced a slight decrease in child income.

While the overall picture for the three metropolitan areas studied is the same, some differences should be noted. While inequality in child income continued to increase during the second sub-period in the Stockholm region, this was not the case in the other two regions. Further, at the end of the period, the overlap between economic and ethnic polarisation was larger in the Malmö region than in the other two regions studied.

References

Allison, P. D. (1978): Measures of Inequality, American Sociological Review 43 (6), 865–880.

Andersen, E. (2001): Från Sorgedalen till Glädjehöjden – omgivningens betydelse för socioekonomisk karriär [From Valley of Sorrows to Happy Heights: the importance of environment for socioenomic careers], Geografiska regionstudier nr. 44 [Geographical regional studies no. 44]. Uppsala, Kulturgeografiska institutionen, Uppsala Universitet.

Anderson, R. (2006): 'Breaking Segregation' – Rhetorical Construction or Effective Policy? The Case of the Metropolitan Development Initiative in Sweden, Urban Studies 43 (4), 787–799.

Andersson-Brolin, L. (1984): Etnisk bostadssegregation [Ethnic residential segregation], Doctoral dissertation, Stockholm, Sociologiska institutionen, Stockholms universitet (Byggforskningsrådet).

Bevelander, P. / *Carlssson,* B. / *Rojas,* M. (1997): I krusbärslandets storstäder: om invandrare i Stockholm, Göteborg och Malmö [Metropolitan areas in the Land of Innocence: immigrants in Stockholm, Göteborg and Malmö]. Stockholm, SNS.

Biterman, D. (1994): Boendesegregationsutveckling in Stockholms län 1970–1990. Underlags PM utförd på uppdrag av Stockholms län landsting, Regionplane- och trafikkontoret [Residential segregation trends in the Stockholm County 1970–1990. Background PM commissioned by the Regional Planning & Urban Transport Office, Stockholm County Council], Stockholm, Inregia AB.

Biterman, D. / *Franzén,* E. (2007): Residential Segregation (Chapter 6), in: Social report 2006. The National Report on Social Conditions in Sweden, International Journal of Social Welfare 16, July Supplement S127 – S162.

Bradbury, B / *Jenkins,* S. / *Micklewright,* J. (2001): The Dynamics of Child Poverty in Industrialised Countries, Cambridge.

Esteban, J. / *Ray,* D. (1994): On the Measurement of Polarization, Econometrica 62 (4), 819–851.

Gustafsson, B. / *Johansson,* M. / *Palmer,* E. (2003): Economic Well-being of Children in the Deep Swedish Recession of the 1990s, in: Bradshaw, J. (ed.), Children and Social Security, Aldershot, International Studies on Social Security 8, 37–62.

Gustavsson, M. (2006): The Evolution of the Swedish Wage Structure: New Evidence for 1992–2001, Applied Economic Letters 13, 279–286.

Grönqvist, H. (2006): Ethnic Enclaves and the Attainment of Immigrant Children, European Sociological Review 22, 396–382.

Huttman, E. / *Blaw,* W. / *Saltman,* J. (eds.) (1991): Urban Housing Segregation of Minorities in Western Europe and the United States, London.

National Integration Office (2004): Rapport Integration 2003 [Integration Report 2003], Norrköping.

National Integration Office (2005): Statistikrapport 2004 – statistisk uppföljning av Rapport Integration 2003 [Statistical Report 2004. Statistical follow-up of Integraton Report 2003], Norrköping.

Janson, C.-G. (1987) : Working Class Segregation in Stockholm and Some Other Swedish Cities, in: U. Bergryd / C.G. Janson (eds.), Sociological Miscellany, Department of Sociology, University of Stockholm, 161–195.

Jargowsky, P. A. (1996): Take the Money and Run: Economic Segregation in U.S. Metropolitan Areas, American Sociological Review 61, 984–998.

Ministry of Finance (1998): Utveckling och rättvisa – en politik för storstaden på 2000-talet [Development and justice: A policy for metropolitan areas in the 21st century], Prop 1997 / 98:165.

Ministry of Health and Social Affairs (1997): Delade städer [Divided cities], Underlagsrapport från Storstadskommittén [Background report from the National Committee on Metropolitan Areas], SOU 1997, 118, Stockholm.

Ministry of Justice (2002): Förbättrad statistik om hushållens inkomster. Utredningen om översyn av den ekonomiska statistiken [Improved statistics on household income], Stockholm: Statens Offentliga Utredningar 2002, 73.

Musterd, S. / *Andersson,* R. (2006): Employment, Social Mobility and Neighbourhood Effects in Sweden, International Journal of Urban and Regional Research 30, 120–140

Vleminickx, K. / *Smeeding,* T. (eds) (2000): Child Well-being, Child Poverty and Child Policies in Modern Nations, Bristol.

White, M. J. (1986): Segregation and Diversity Measures in Population Distribution, Population Index 52 (2), 198–221.

Wolfson, M. C. (1994): When Inequalities Diverge, American Economic Review 84 (2), 353 – 358.

Zhang, X. B. / *Kanbur,* R. (2001): What difference do Polarisation Measures Make? An Application to China, Journal of Development Studies 37, 85 – 98.

Appendix

Table A1

Mean child income and inequality in the three metropolitan areas combined 1990, 1996, 2002

Year	**MLD**	**Theil**	**Gini**	**Mean disposable income 100s SEK in 2000 prices**	***Number of observations***
1990	0.1025	0.1014	0.2334	1022	585 946
1996	0.1437	0.1711	0.2761	1058	630 163
2002	0.1741	0.2415	0.2998	1358	651 559

Source: Authors calculations from the Social Medicine Database, Centre for Epidemiology at the National Board of Health and Welfare.

Table A 2

Definition of variables used in Table 2 and Table 7

Variables:	
Strong labour market attachement	Annual income from work > 128 000 SEK (in constant prices of year 2000)
Neither income from work nor unemployement benefit	Annual income from work = 0 and unemployment benefit = 0
Low labour market attachment	Does not belong to neither of the above mentioned categories
Children with background in:	
Sweden	Two parents born in Sweden
HIC – High Income Countries	Two parents from HIC countries or one Swedish born parent. HIC countries are defined as the member countries of the European Union and the European Economic Area as well as Japan, the countries of Oceania, and the North American countries of the United States and Canada
MLIC – Middle and Low Income countries	Two parents born in all other countries apart from HIC countries and Sweden

Table A3

Decomposing inequality in child income by clusters of neighbourhoods having different ethnic compositions in the Stockholm, Göteborg and Malmö metropolitan areas 1990, 1996 and 2002

a) The Stockholm region

	Mean disposable income 100s SEK in 2000 years prices	**MLD**	**Theil**	**Gini**	***N***	**Between group inequality as a percent of total inequality (MLD)**	**Between group inequality as a percent of total inequality (Theil)**
1990 all:	1052	0.1075	0.1049	0.2392	341 780		
After ethnic status							
0	980	0.1247	0.1208	0.2604	1 217		
1	1009	0.0984	0.0975	0.2295	38 877		
2	1128	0.0982	0.1017	0.2264	119 797		
3	1095	0.1066	0.1039	0.2374	62 019		
4	1050	0.1004	0.0923	0.2309	29 820		
5	1009	0.0990	0.0941	0.2346	39199		
6	971	0.1048	0.0971	0.2400	21 857		
7	855	0.1359	0.1234	0.2762	17 622		
8	775	0.1347	0.1227	0.2730	11 368		
1996 all:	1098	0.1563	0.1858	0.2867	370 272		
After ethnic status							
0	1464	0.4357	0.8902	0.4735	718		
1	1122	0.1549	0.2170	0.2869	51 209		
2	1232	0.1573	0.2102	0.2867	127 540		
3	1120	0.1288	0.1427	0.2617	67 845		
4	1059	0.1239	0.1183	0.2583	34 443		
5	978	0.1228	0.1156	0.2596	27 508		
6	947	0.1399	0.1261	0.2738	29 559		
7	792	0.1750	0.1566	0.3090	17 358		
8	695	0.1731	0.1553	0.3088	14 093		
2002	1442	0.1957	0.2968	0.3174	386 448		
After ethnic status							
0	1604	0.2535	0.3406	0.3772	522		
1	1480	0.1668	0.2265	0.2986	60 638		
2	1668	0.1989	0.3281	0.3219	131 593		
3	1478	0.1488	0.1886	0.2769	67 284		
4	1369	0.1445	0.1459	0.2733	29 270		
5	1314	0.2124	0.5952	0.3235	40 260		
6	1121	0.1585	0.1401	0.2866	22 619		
7	920	0.1853	0.1636	0.3168	20 366		
8	777	0.1944	0.1719	0.3252	13 889		

Within group inequality							
1990		0.1037	0.1012				
1996		0.1467	0.1767				
2002		0.1792	0.2820				
Between group inequality							
1990		0.0038	0.0037			3.57 %	3.48 %
1996		0.0096	0.0089			6.14 %	4.80 %
2002		0.0164	0.0148			8.38 %	4.97 %

Note: Ethnic status is defined based on the average rate visible immigrants to the native born population in the region computed and put equal to 1.0. Status 1 means a rate less than 0.25, status 2 a rate 0.25 to 0.49, status 3 a rate 0.50 to 0.79, status 4 a rate 0.80 – 1.24, status 5 a rate 1.25 to 1.99, status 6 a rate 2.0 to 3.99, status 7 a rate 4.00 to 9.99 and status 10 and higher.

b) The Göteborg region

	Mean disposable income 100s SEK in 2000 years prices	**MLD**	**Theil**	**Gini**	***N***	**Between group inequality as a percent of total inequality (MLD)**	**Between group inequality as a percent of total inequality (Theil)**
1990 all:	987	0.0929	0.0948	0.2220	145 286		
After ethnic status							
0	845	0.0825	0.0771	0.2066	1 621		
1	994	0.0902	0.1069	0.2154	38 825		
2	1010	0.0777	0.0786	0.2036	36 624		
3	1026	0.0968	0.0960	0.2251	21 356		
4	1005	0.0937	0.0874	0.2250	15 347		
5	973	0.0962	0.0916	0.2257	9 861		
6	932	0.1105	0.1015	0.2479	10 272		
7	888	0.1080	0.0986	0.2468	9 266		
8	797	0.1243	0.1150	0.2654	2 114		
1996 all:	1010	0.1192	0.1403	0.2538	156 608		
After ethnic status							
0	910	0.0835	0.0816	0.2103	1 478		
1	1052	0.1220	0.1655	0.2547	41 994		
2	1062	0.1061	0.1412	0.2393	43 059		
3	1061	0.1099	0.1230	0.2463	23 472		
4	996	0.1018	0.09920	0.2386	12 915		
5	956	0.1134	0.1012	0.2455	11 948		
6	899	0.1251	0.1156	0.2661	9 487		
7	833	0.1269	0.1194	0.2712	4 726		
8	713	0.1481	0.1365	0.2901	7 525		

Continued Table A3

	Mean disposable income 100s SEK in 2000 years prices	**MLD**	**Theil**	**Gini**	***N***	**Between group inequality as a percent of total inequality (MLD)**	**Between group inequality as a percent of total inequality (Theil)**
2002	1253	0.1267	0.1344	0.2590	160 539		
After ethnic status							
0	1155	0.0895	0.0882	0.2247	963		
1	1329	0.1135	0.1364	0.2484	46 373		
2	1345	0.1092	0.1183	0.2434	47 924		
3	1284	0.1132	0.1192	0.2444	20 690		
4	1236	0.1259	0.1456	0.2556	13 121		
5	1154	0.1181	0.1048	0.2485	8 984		
6	1056	0.1347	0.1206	0.2693	9 693		
7	929	0.1472	0.1344	0.2871	5 439		
8	759	0.1643	0.1476	0.3021	7 351		
Within group inequality							
1990		0.0918	0.0938				
1996		0.1147	0.1362				
2002		0.1181	0.1266				
Between group inequality							
1990		0.0011	0.0011			1.18 %	1.12 %
1996		0.0045	0.0041			3.73 %	2.94 %
2002		0.0086	0.0077			6.81 %	5.75 %

Note: Ethnic status is defined based on the average rate visible immigrants to the native born population in the region computed and put equal to 1.0. Status 1 means a rate less than 0.25, status 2 a rate 0.25 to 0.49, status 3 a rate 0.50 to 0.79, status 4 a rate 0.80 – 1.24, status 5 a rate 1.25 to 1.99, status 6 a rate 2.0 to 3.99, status 7 a rate 4.00 to 9.99 and status 10 and higher.

c) The Malmö region

	Mean disposable income 100s SEK in 2000 years prices	MLD	Theil	Gini	*N*	Between group inequality as a percent of total inequality (MLD)	Between group inequality as a percent of total inequality (Theil)
1990 all:	974	0.09609	0.09497	0.2231	98 880		
After ethnic status							
0	930	0.1165	0.1094	0.2371	1 650		
1	990	0.0803	0.08706	0.2049	30 582		
2	1026	0.0866	0.0904	0.2129	17 093		
3	978	0.0816	0.08258	0.2095	14 156		
4	1008	0.1060	0.10676	0.2329	10 191		
5	946	0.0995	0.09276	0.2341	10 496		
6	921	0.1253	0.10916	0.2527	9 928		
7	815	0.1819	0.13067	0.2696	1 750		
8	767	0.1188	0.10776	0.2544	3 034		
1996 all:	988	0.12935	0.15381	0.2625	103 283		
After ethnic status							
0	997	0.1330	0.15233	0.2580	1 603		
1	1046	0.1043	0.11746	0.2375	33 372		
2	1105	0.1503	0.26552	0.2780	17 741		
3	975	0.1030	0.10365	0.2383	13 865		
4	1027	0.1276	0.13410	0.2578	9 574		
5	923	0.1131	0.10655	0.2506	9 886		
6	847	0.1429	0.12701	0.2793	11708		
7	763	0.1406	0.13291	0.2806	2 155		
8	573	0.1262	0.12758	0.2692	3 377		
2002	1205	0.1487	0.14772	0.2745	104 572		
After ethnic status							
0	1222	0.1145	0.10773	0.2449	1271		
1	1334	0.1173	0.13054	0.2486	36 602		
2	1354	0.1346	0.15729	0.2608	16 442		
3	1208	0.1218	0.12058	0.2504	15 732		
4	1221	0.1429	0.12751	0.2665	7 332		
5	1098	0.1441	0.12182	0.2691	9 806		
6	933	0.1719	0.14604	0.2992	9 680		
7	845	0.1757	0.14810	0.2998	4 201		
8	591	0.1514	0.14195	0.2922	3 506		
Within group in-equality							
1990		0.0944	0.09332				
1996		0.1213	0.14661				
2002		0.1335	0.13432				

Continued Table A3

	Mean disposable income 100s SEK in 2000 years prices	**MLD**	**Theil**	**Gini**	***N***	**Between group inequality as a percent of total inequality (MLD)**	**Between group inequality as a percent of total inequality (Theil)**
Between group inequality							
1990		0.0016	0.00155			1.70 %	1.63 %
1996		0.0079	0.00720			6.14 %	4.68 %
2002		0.0152	0.01341			10.23 %	9.08 %

Source: Authors calculations from the Social Medicine Database, Centre for Epidemiology at the National Board of Health and Welfare.

Note: Ethnic status is defined based on the average rate visible immigrants to the native born population in the region computed and put equal to 1.0. Status 1 means a rate less than 0.25, status 2 a rate 0.25 to 0.49, status 3 a rate 0.50 to 0.79, status 4 a rate 0.80 – 1.24, status 5 a rate 1.25 to 1.99, status 6 a rate 2.0 to 3.99, status 7 a rate 4.00 to 9.99 and status 10 and higher.

Schmollers Jahrbuch 128 (2008), 153 – 173
Duncker & Humblot, Berlin

Concentrating on Participation: Ethnic Concentration and Labour Market Participation of Four Ethnic Groups

By Wenda van der Laan Bouma-Doff*

Abstract

Urban scholars have exhaustively studied the relationship between place of residence on the one hand and social achievements, health, exposure to crime etcetera on the other. This paper wants to contribute to this field of research by exploring statistical associations between ethnic concentration and labour market participation. It utilizes extensive survey data on the four largest ethnic groups in the Netherlands, matched with postcode-level information on the ethnic composition of the neighbourhood. The research question of the paper is whether ethnic minorities living in ethnically concentrated neighbourhoods participate less in the labour force, and if so, which mechanisms underlie this relationship. The results show that, after controlling for various individual characteristics, Moroccans living in these neighbourhoods show a lower participation rate. Neither the lack of contact with native Dutch nor having traditional values, popular explanations of negative neighbourhood effects, appear to be the social mechanisms underlying this ‘neighbourhood effect’, however. On the contrary, I argue that this statistical relationship exists because Moroccans are a highly marginalized, stigmatized and discriminated ethnic category. As a result of which they are confronted with barriers on both the housing *and* the labour market, resulting in less access to and a weak position in both of these core institutions of Dutch society.

JEL Classifications: J15 J61 R31

1. Researching Neighbourhood Effects

Especially over the last ten years, many studies have investigated the effects of living in poor or ethnically concentrated areas on individual outcomes: the so-called neighbourhood effects. The primary question in these neighbourhood effect studies is whether a concentration of advantaged or disadvantaged

* The author wishes to thank the participants of the conference ‘Neighbourhood Effects Studies on the Basis of European Micro-data’ (Berlin, March 29 – 30, 2007). Marco van der Land and the anonymous referees for their helpful comments on the earlier drafts of the paper, and Stefan van der Laan Bouma for his essential assistance, on both text and content.

groups in certain areas has an additional effect on the well-being of (some or all of) the local population (Buck, 2001). In the western-European debate, it often concerns the issue whether living in ethnically concentrated neighbourhoods impedes the integration and assimilation process of immigrants and their children. In the Netherlands, lack of contact with native Dutch is put forth as the most important cause of the negative effects of living in ethnically concentrated areas (Bolt et al., 1998). The line of reasoning is that, as a consequence of limited contact with native Dutch, ethnic minorities preserve their own language and culture, resulting in limited possibilities on education attainment and labour market success. I referred to this way of reasoning as the isolation thesis, in which it is assumed that living in ethnically concentrated neighbourhoods hampers the formation of 'ethnic bridges' (Briggs, 2007) between ethnic minorities and native Dutch, which, in turn, hinders integration into Dutch society (Van der Laan Bouma-Doff, 2007a). In this last article the following policy text was quoted:

> "There are reasons to believe that (...) living in multi-ethnic neighbourhoods hampers integration. In many multi-ethnic neighbourhoods an ethnic infrastructure has come into existence, which makes the orientation on Dutch society, the use of the Dutch language and the establishment of contacts with indigenous Dutch to a great extent redundant. (...) The question of ethnic concentration can no longer be ignored in integration policy" (House of Representatives, 2003–2004, 28689, 17, pp. 26, Cabinet Balkenende II).

Striking in the current Cabinet (Cabinet Balkenende IV) is the instatement of a new minister, a minister of "Living, Neighbourhoods and Integration" (Wonen, Wijken en Integratie), within the Ministry of Housing, Spatial Planning and the Environment. This Minister is in charge of the 'offensive' in forty selected neighbourhoods with the highest concentration of problems. On the Ministry's website it states: "The connection between integration and the community approach: Integration begins close to home, in your own neighbourhood. (...) The cabinet wishes to encourage people from all ethnic groups – young and old, rich and poor – to integrate into their community and into society. There are neighbourhoods in our country that are in a poor state. *The cabinet is launching a large-scale offensive to give these neighbourhoods a new outlook, which will encourage integration.*" (http://international.vrom.nl, my italics).

Thus, to a certain extent, policymakers assume that spatial isolation implies social isolation, and by changing the neighbourhood integration can be stimulated. It is expected that due to spatial concentration, ethnic groups are less inclined to blend into Dutch society, with regard to behaviour (contacts) as well as orientation (values). Less attention is given to the fact that ethnic minorities in such neighbourhoods have less opportunities and might live there against their own wishes. This does not mean that the Dutch government does not invest in those neighbourhoods extensively, but the rationale for doing so often seems to have more to do with creating social order, civilising and controlling these neighbourhoods, than with emancipating its residents (Uitermark / Duyvendak / Kleinhans, 2007). The motivation of this study is however, primarily based on the question whether the place where one lives affects one's chances in life, in this case residents' economic outcomes. Individuals behave and make choices within a given environment, for example a neighbourhood, formed through interactions and characterised by unevenly divided opportunities. And as weaker groups in general end up in less desirable environments, the distribution of 'space' might preserve and reinforce social inequality in society (Sibley, 1995).

2. Neighbourhood Effects and Operating Mechanisms

There already is a large body of research done on the question whether living in disadvantaged neighbourhoods is associated with socio-economic outcomes of individual residents (see for a review Dietz, 2002; Sampson / Morenoff / Gannon-Rowley, 2002; Galster, 2005). In Europe, neighbourhood effects seem to be smaller (Buck, 2001; Drever, 2004), although more recently analyses of Swedish population data found quite strong neighbourhood impacts on employment status, social mobility and income (Musterd / Andersson, 2005; Musterd / Andersson, 2006; Musterd et al., 2007; Galster et al., 2007a; Andersson et al., 2007). In their latest contribution, Andersson et al. (2007) explored the relationships between individuals' incomes and various aspects of the neighbourhood household mix, namely: education, ethnicity, income and tenure. For all four dimensions, the effect of the absolute share, the relative share and the overall diversity of a specific group was examined. The analyses reveal that, firstly, for all dimensions, the proportion of disadvantaged groups has a stronger effect than the proportion of advantaged groups, and that, secondly, neighbourhood income mix is more important in explaining income differences than education, ethnicity or tenure neighbourhood mix. Although the ethnicity dimension is not the crucial one, as emphasised by the authors (Andersson et al., 2007, 656), ethnic concentration and diversity of one's neighbourhood is certainly a significant variable in someone's economic status; a factor not to be neglected. However, these 'neighbourhood effects' give little insight into the mechanisms that bring them about. Statistical studies show to what extent a certain neighbourhood context is associated with different individual outcomes, but neighbourhood effect studies are troubled with data related difficulties and methodological problems (e.g. Lupton, 2003). The same pitfalls apply to the current study, however, it contributes to the literature in two ways. First, by differentiating among four different ethnic groups, namely Turks, Moroccans, Surinamese and Antilleans. Second, by testing two theoretical mechanisms that might explain the association between place of residence and labour market participation.

The statistical relationship between place of residence and a particular individual outcome alone is not a 'neighbourhood effect'. Like Dietz (2002, 540), I would like to think of a neighbourhood effect as a social interaction that influences the behaviour or socioeconomic outcome of an individual. Lupton (2006, 60) labels these 'people effects', such as anti-social peer groups, weak family bonds and social networks to support education and child development, and a lack of role models, also called endogenous neighbourhood effects (Galster, 2005). Next to people effects, there are 'real' place effects, says Lupton (ibid.), such as local labour market, neighbourhood stigma and local facilities. These mechanisms that bring forth effects for individual residents but which lie outside the realm of the neighbourhood, are also called exogenous and correlated neighbourhood effects. I consider these effects to be 'people effects'. Because structures, after all, are brought about by individual action and social interaction (Giddens, 1984). The neighbourhood stigma, for example, or the extent to which neighbourhoods provide bad or good services, cannot be seen apart from the thoughts and actions of individuals. In that sense, every underlying mechanism is a product of social interaction and social relations, in- or outside the spatial context of the neighbourhood.

The most essential social neighbourhood mechanisms are: (selective) socialization, epidemic / social norms, social networks and stigmatization. Galster (2005, 10) describes these mechanism as follows. The first, socialization, refers to the change in attitudes and behaviours of individuals by means of contact with role models or peers (neighbours, for example), also referred to as contagion effects. In case of selective socialization, only some of the individuals are influenced. Not only direct contact, but indirect interaction as well, causes socialization, just by sharing the same space with role models or peers. The second mechanism, epidemic / social norms, is a special subset of socialization effects, characterized by a minimal threshold of members of a particular group. Only when a critical mass has been reached, than will their social norms begin to influence others. The third mechanism, social networks, is specified as a distinct process involving the interpersonal exchange of information and resources. And the last mechanism, stigmatization, occurs when actors (outside the neighbourhood) negatively stereotype residents and / or reduce the neighbourhood resources because of its household composition. In this mechanism, the threshold notion is important as well, because stigmatization only occurs when the percentage of a specific group of households in the neighbourhood has reached that critical mass.

It is important to note that the mentioned mechanisms might change the attitudes and behaviours of individuals for the worst, but also for the best. Although the main focus is mostly on the negative effects of ethnic concentration, it might increase opportunities for individual residents as well. With regard to social networks, for example, Portes and Sensenbrenner (1993) argue that ethnic minorities might profit from resources and support from spatially embedded social interrelations, also referred to as the ethnic enclave. Besides job opportunities and information on jobs, networks offer practical, social and emotional support. In the Netherlands, first generation immigrants in particular rely on their networks to find their way in Dutch society. Besides the use of networks for finding a place of residence in certain neighbourhoods, they also play an important part in finding a job (Pinkster, 2008). On the other hand, these contacts seldom provide the necessary information and chances for moving up the socio-economic ladder. For that purpose contacts outside the own social group, so-called weak ties, are often more important, as Granovetter (1974) showed us. There are indications that contacts with native Dutch operate as weak ties (Odé, 2002), but the possibilities of establishing 'ethnic bridges' are limited in ethnically concentrated neighbourhoods (Van der Laan Bouma-Doff, 2007a; Briggs, 2007). Thus, in stead of stimulating job information and opportunities through strong ties, ethnic concentration might reduce peoples' opportunities due to the lack of weak ties. The same distinction between possible positive and negative effects applies to socialization and social norms. Zhou and Bankston (1996), for example, showed that the tightly knit Vietnamese community of New Orleans fares well by the social norms of promoting discipline with regard to attending school, and Borjas (1998) as well mentions the transmission of norms for educational attainment as a positive effect of residential concentration of immigrants. There are, however, also possible negative consequences to be considered. Portes (1998) mentions four negative consequences of social capital: exclusion of outsiders, excess claims on group members, restrictions on individual freedom and downward levelling norms. Social interaction may thus socialize residents in a way that hampers labour market participation. A Dutch study by Pinkster (2008) shows that processes of collective socialization and social control do affect labour market behaviour of young women living in a poor, highly concentrated neighbourhood. She found, for example, that for some girls education is not considered to be a necessity and that they are not supposed to work, as their job is to raise children and to take care of the home. These norms restrict the work options of Moroccan and Turkish girls, even if they are allowed to work, like this girl cited by Pinkster (2008, 2598 – 9): "My father (. . .) didn't want me to take this job. He was worried about what the neighbours would say about me travelling late at night by myself. Such gossip would shame my family". One might think that these are family related effects rather than neighbourhood effects, however, as Pinkster correctly argues, because the socialization mechanisms that influence individual economic action are preserved and reinforced through the tight social control within the local social structures, they cannot be separated from the neighbourhood.

For a better understanding of neighbourhood effects the causal mechanisms are crucial, also for policymakers. Until now, the evidence base of social mix strategies of (local) governments has been quite weak (Andersson et al., 2007,

656). It is important, however, to understand whether it is social networks, for example, that help or hinder inhabitants, or rather the neighbourhood stigma that decreases the life chances of residents. Both neighbourhood effects require a different type of policy to be deployed, and in both cases the appropriate threshold should be determined. As Galster (2003) argues, the (disadvantaged or advantaged) group has to reach some critical mass of density over an area that is likely to become effective in shaping the behaviour of others (see also Crane, 1991; Buck, 2001). For policymakers this information on this critical mass is crucial in spatial planning and design, for example when the dispersion of affordable dwellings over the city and its region is concerned.

The preceding thoughts and theories result in a few notions on the empirical approach this study should take into account. A first step will be to simply test whether there are differences in labour market participation between similar individuals living in different kinds of neighbourhoods. If there are 'neighbourhood effects', two theoretical mechanisms will be explored: the contacts with native Dutch and the acculturation of 'modern' values. Let me start by saying that both operationalizations are far from perfect. As far as the first one is concerned, I am aware that contacts with native Dutch, or ethnic bridges, are not synonymous with social networks, or bridging ties. For studying networks, a more thorough network research is required. Unfortunately I only know to what extent ethnic minorities mainly maintain contacts with their own ethnic group or with native Dutch. Of course, members of the own group can form bridging ties as well. On the other hand, contacts with native Dutch can certainly be functional, for instance in learning to speak the Dutch language, of by improving one's labour marker position (Gijsberts / Dagevos, 2007; Odé, 2002) On top of that, the lack of contact with native Dutch is a popular explanation of negative neighbourhood effects in the public and policy debate, and therefore important to check upon. The operationalization of the socialization or social norms mechanism, namely the acculturation of 'modern' values, is far from perfect either. However, 'cultural integration', as the adoption of these values is also referred to, is considered to be important for immigrants' chances on the labour market as well. Studies, like the one done by Pinkster, show that views on female liberation, one of the dimensions of 'modern' views, indeed can form the operating mechanism behind restricted work options, be it to a certain extent. There is another problem with this operationalized mechanism, however, and that one has to do with the way the questionnaire is structured, but I will get to that later on.

Another important notion derived from the theoretical overview is that it is important to check for thresholds. Therefore the fact that a change in attitude sometimes requires the presence of a critical mass, will be taken into account in the analysis. In the next section, I will cover the data, and the methodological and measurement aspects of the study in detail.

3. Empirical Approach

3.1 Data

For the analyses I will use data derived from the Dutch SPVA survey 2002 (Sociale Positie en Voorzieningengebruik Allochtonen: Immigrants' Social Position and Use of Services), carried out by the Institute for Social Economic Research (ISEO) of the Erasmus University Rotterdam, in cooperation with the Social and Cultural Planning Office (SCP). The SPVA is a large-scale survey of the four largest ethnic groups in the Netherlands: Turks, Moroccans, Surinamese and Antilleans, who make up 67 % of the entire group of ethnic minorities (CBS, 2005). The SPVA respondents were selected by a stratified sample based on city of residence and ethnic origin. From municipal registers of thirteen cities, including the four major cities Amsterdam, Rotterdam, The Hague and Utrecht, households were selected randomly. Data were collected by means of face-to-face interviews by bilingual interviewers, using questionnaires which were translated if needed. Next to the heads of households, all other persons in the household over the age of 12 were asked to participate, but only in a shortened version of the survey. Because of that, certain crucial information is lacking for the other household members. I therefore selected heads of households for the analyses of this paper. Another selection concerns the age of the respondent. I selected respondents between the age of 18 and 50, because of the age dependent participation in education and work (due to cohort-effects, labour market participation significantly reduces after the age of 50). The remaining dataset contains data on 1,173 Turks, 1,056 Moroccans, 1,101 Surinamese and 869 Antilleans.

The zip code for each household in the SPVA is linked to population data from Statistics Netherlands (CBS) over the year 2002. As a result, we know the ethnic composition of each respondent's neighbourhood and therefore its level of ethnic concentration. As many scholars have pointed out thus far, such administrative boundaries are not the most perfect operational definitions of 'the neighbourhood' (Dietz, 2002; Sampson et al., 2002; Lupton, 2003). On average, 4,000 people reside in such postcode areas in the Netherlands, which might be too large in scale to accurately measure the variables of local neighbourhood affecting residents (Friedrichs / Galster / Musterd, 2003). It is yet unclear whether and how scale size influences the magnitude of neighbourhood effects, although a study of Andersson and Musterd (2006) showed that contextual effects on labour market performance are strongest at the lowest local level. The question of which scale matters most needs more attention in neighbourhood effect studies, but for now I am, just as many other researchers, dependent on the data at hand.

3.2 Method

In order to find out whether the level of ethnic concentration has additional effects on the labour market participation of ethnic groups, we need a multivariate analysis to control for individual background characteristics (Buck, 2001; Sampson et al., 2002). I will use a logistic regression design, in which the probability of participating on the labour market constitutes the dependent variable, and individual characteristics, such as gender, age, household situation and educational level as the independent variables. A multivariate design will not entirely account for the potential problem of neighbourhood selection, however. This selection problem concerns the fact that *certain* individuals who have *certain* (unmeasured) motivations and skills related to their own success and their children, are more likely to move to *certain* neighbourhoods than others. Bell (1958; 1968, referred to in Michelson, 1977) was one of the first who discussed such behavioural considerations. "He suggested that people evaluate themselves in terms of what they want to do most with their lives and then, when able, select neighbourhoods best suited to fit their needs. Bell called this process 'self-selection'." (Michelson, 1977, 17). In this case it is not (the social processes within or outside) the neighbourhood, but these evaluations that both affect choice of residence and labour market behaviour. Observed associations between ethnic concentration and labour market participation are thus biased because of this spatial selection process, even when all the observable characteristics are controlled for (Manski, 1993; referred to in e.g. Galster, 2005; Musterd et al., 2007). By including the residuals of a preliminary regression, Musterd et al. (2007) try to overcome this selection problem, also known as the omitted variable bias. They demonstrate that this particular bias is present, but that after correcting for it, the results do not change very much and that neighbourhood effects on economic outcomes do remain. Whether this approach enables us to solve the question of selection and endogeneity (the recursive influence of place of residence and individual outcomes) entirely, however, is still undecided. I will return to this matter in the results section.

After demonstrating the additional effect of ethnic concentration on labour market participation, I will try to unravel the mechanisms underlying these effects. If by including contacts and cultural orientation, effects of ethnic concentration are decreased or have even disappeared, it might be concluded that these processes are the operating mechanisms behind observed 'neighbourhood effects'. Although this approach is far from perfect either, the inclusion of variables that relate to social processes, might be seen as a contribution to the study of neighbourhood effects. Until now, studies have simply and solely used neighbourhood characteristics such as poverty or ethnic concentration as proxies for social processes through which neighbourhood effects might transpire (cf. Galster et al., 2007b, 731). The 'black-box' of neighbourhood effects can best be approached by intensive, ethnographic research, but the current study is nevertheless a small step ahead in researching neighbourhood effect mechanisms with extensive survey data. Moreover, the results can be generalized to the four largest ethnic groups in the Netherlands.

3.3 Measurement

The dependent variable is labour market participation, measured as having an employment contract of at least 12 hours per week. From the survey data I also derived the following individual characteristics: gender, age, immigration status (1st or 2nd generation), household situation, educational level of the respondent and both parents, language skills and place of residence. Gender is included as a dummy variable, in which male is coded 1 and female 0. Age is divided in three categories: 30 years or younger, 30 – 40 years and 40 years and older. Immigrant status is measured by country of birth and age of immigration. A person is considered to be a second-generation immigrant if he or she is born in the Netherlands or immigrated to the Netherlands before the age of six. Generation is included as a dummy variable, in which second-generation immigrants are coded 1 and first-generation immigrants are coded 0. Household situation contains five categories: singles, couples without children, couples with children, single parents and other household forms. The respondent's own education level contains four categories: no formal education, lower educational level (a lower vocational education or a lower general secondary education), middle educational level (a general vocational education, a higher general secondary education or a pre-university education) and higher educational level (a higher vocational education or university). In addition, the educational levels of the respondent's parents were included as dummies, in such a way that no formal education and lower education were coded 0 and middle and higher education were coded 1. The command of the Dutch language was measured by asking respondents whether they have troubles speaking Dutch, recoded in three categories: having troubles speaking Dutch always / often, sometimes or never. Finally, a dummy variable was included indicating whether the respondent is living in one of the big cities Amsterdam, Rotterdam, The Hague or Utrecht (coded 1), or in another, smaller city (coded 0).

Ethnic concentration, a variable which was matched to the individual data, was measured using the percentage of ethnic minorities living in the neighbourhood, or to be precise, in the postcode area. To investigate for thresholds, this percentage is divided into four categories: neighbourhoods containing less than 25% ethnic minorities, 25 to 50% ethnic minorities, 50 to 75% ethnic minorities and more than 75% ethnic minorities.

With regard to the possible operating mechanisms behind neighbourhood effects, the SPVA data contains information on the informal ties ethnic minorities have with native Dutch and their cultural orientation. The following question is used to measure contact: "Do you have more contacts in your spare time with (white) Dutch than with [own ethnic group] or do you have more contacts with [own ethnic group]?", on which the respondents could respond: more contacts with [own ethnic group], equal amount of contacts with both or more contacts with Dutch. The respondent was thus only asked about exclusive contacts (with native Dutch or his / her own ethnic group), while the actual contacts might be ethnically diverse. It was, however, not asked whether or not respondents maintain contact with *other* ethnic groups. In order to measure cultural orientation, respondents were asked to give their opinion on an extensive list of *Likert* items concerning values about individualization, authority, secularization and female liberation.[1] Regrettably enough, not all respondents were asked to give their opinion on this issue, just the head of household or the partner, in turn, as a result of which the number of respondents from which we know the cultural orientation is a lot smaller than in other cases. Nevertheless, a scale of cultural orientation was constructed, ranging from 1 to 5, in which a higher score corresponds to a higher subscription to modern values. Both ethnic minorities and native Dutch subscribe to these values to a larger or lesser extent; it is definitely not an 'ethnic' characteristic.

Table 1 summarises the descriptives of the used variables per ethnic group.

4. Results

Of the ethnic groups, Turks and Moroccans show significantly lower participation rates (respectively 50,1 % and 45,4 %) than Antilleans (59,4 %) and especially Surinamese (63,7 %). In addition, the first two ethnic groups live in concentrated neighbourhoods more often than the last two do. Ethnic minorities living in ethnically concentrated neighbourhoods indeed have significantly lower participation rates, although the association between concentration and participation is not that strong (the participation rates in the classified neighbourhoods are: 60,2 % (< 25 % ethnic minorities in the neighbourhood), 53,7 % (25 – 50 % ethnic minorities in the neighbourhood), 47,5 % (50 – 75 % ethnic minorities in the neighbourhood) and 44,7 % (> 75 % ethnic minorities in the neighbourhood) (Cramer's $V = 0{,}11$). Moreover, these differences might be entirely the result of differences in other individual characteristics, such as

---

1 The respondents were asked to react an statements like: Women are responsible for housekeeping; Acquiring an income is more important for boys than for girls; Women should quit their job when they have children; Men and women may live together without being married; A 17 year old daughter is allowed to live on her own; The opinion of the parents is still very important in choosing a partner for the child; Older relatives should have more to say in important decisions (for example about moving) than younger ones; In the Netherlands, the contact between men and women is too loose; If someone is in pain and has not got long to live, he or she is allowed to decide about ending his or her own life; It is very unpleasant if your son wants to marry someone of another religion, et cetera. The scale that has been constructed is a valid and a reliable one (30 % explained variance and cronbach's alpha = 0.88).

Table 1

Descriptives of the included variables (%, if not otherwise indicated)

		Turks	Moroc-cans	Surina-mese	Antil-leans
Work (dependent)	Employed	50.1	45.4	63.7	59.4
Gender	Male	71.6	71.7	43.3	43.7
Age	< 30	25.1	30.9	18.1	35.1
	30 – 40	44.6	42.6	39.0	35.9
	> 40	30.3	26.5	42.9	29.0
Generation	Second[a)]	8.9	11.0	15.4	12.9
Household situation	Single	8.1	12.7	26.7	34.6
	Couple, no children	13.3	11.6	11.4	11.5
	Couple with children	67.0	63.8	35.1	23.7
	Single Parent	9.0	8.4	23.6	26.0
	Other	2.6	3.5	3.2	4.1
Education (highest)	None	52.9	61.1	26.4	21.6
	Lower	21.4	12.3	29.4	30.0
	Middle	18.9	18.7	29.6	29.3
	Higher	6.7	7.9	14.6	19.2
Education father	Middle / Higher	3.8	4.0	16.9	28.7
Education mother	Middle / Higher	1.3	.8	11.8	19.0
Problems with	Always / Often	34.3	17.9	4.6	4.2
Speaking Dutch	Sometimes	40.7	40.8	11.0	25.4
	Never	25.0	41.3	84.3	70.5
Place of Residence	Within G4 cities	64.3	79.3	68.2	62.7
Ethnic concentration	< 25 %	35.8	23.0	44.5	53.2
	25 – 50 %	33.8	41.0	36.7	31.6
	50 – 75 %	20.0	27.0	13.5	12.1
	> 75 %	9.8	9.0	5.4	3.1
Contact	More with co-ethnics	74.0	64.6	38.4	31.2
	Same	20.5	26.7	38.7	31.7
	More with Dutch	5.5	8.8	22.9	37.1
Modern values	(mean, range 1 – 5)	2.57	2.45	3.15	3.24
Total *N*		1173	1056	1101	869

[a)] Second generation, born in the Netherlands or immigrated before the age 6.
Source: SPVA 2002 (ISEO / SCP).

immigrant status, education and language capabilities, which are also not distributed equally over neighbourhoods. For example, second-generation and higher educated immigrants, have more housing options and / or face less constraints in fulfilling their housing needs, thus, probably live in less-concentrated neighbourhoods. In order to control the relationship between ethnic concentration and labour market participation, such variables are taken into account in a logistic regression mode. Table 2 shows the results for the four ethnic groups individually. In the first step, only the different categories of ethnic concentration are built into the model, and in the second step all other features are built-in. Because of the empty cells problem, the last two categories of neighbourhood ethnic concentration are merged into one.

Table 2

Logistic regression analysis of labour market participation, odds ratios

	Turks	Moroccans	Surinamese	Antilleans
STEP I	Exp(B)	Exp(B)	Exp(B)	Exp(B)
Ethnic concentration (ref = < 25 %)				
25 – 50 %	0.786	0.769	0.770	0.855
> 50 %	0.753	0.582**	0.598*	0.861
STEP II	Exp(B)	Exp(B)	Exp(B	Exp(B)
Ethnic concentration (ref = < 25 %)				
25 – 50 %	1.010	0.884	0.879	1.161
> 50 %	0.943	0.501*	0.935	1.505
Gender (female)	0.197***	0.173***	0.450***	0.568*
Age 18 – 30 (ref)				
Age 30 – 40	1.190	0.933	3.973***	2.370***
Age 40 – 60	0.964	0.677	2.296**	3.443***
Generation (Born / raised in the NL)	0.956	1.171	0.791	0.732
Household situation (ref = Single)				
Couple without children	1.075	1.061	2.385*	2.966**
Couple with children	1.735	1.707	1.630	2.100**
Single mother	1.472	1.680	0.918	0.842
Other households	0.925	0.556	1.345	1.320
Formal education (ref = None)				
Lower educational level	2.145***	1.547	2.076**	1.618
Middle educational level	2.871***	2.515***	5.769***	3.101***
Higher educational level	2.970**	3.687***	8.947***	14.036***
Father Middle of Higher education	1.618	1.663	0.762	1.208
Mother Middle of Higher education	3.297	1.624	1.325	0.788
Problems Dutch (ref: Always / often)				
Sometimes	1.554*	2.994**	0.368	1.025
Never	2.356***	6.415***	0.941	0.844
Living in one of the big cities	0.865	1.371	0.981	0.865
Constant	0.672	0.319*	0.904	0.537
N included in analysis	864	707	746	660
Nagelkerke R^2	0.274	0.346	0.274	0.274

* = $p < 0.05$, ** = $p < 0.01$, *** = $p < 0.001$.

Source: SPVA 2002 (ISEO / SCP).

If we look at the effect of ethnic concentration in step I, we see that Moroccans and Surinamese both show negative effects, but only if the level of ethnic concentration exceeds 50 %, whereas no significant effects can be observed for Turks and Antilleans. The inclusion of all other explanatory variables in step II shows to what extent the observed effects are compositional effects, which is the case if the differences in background variables decreases the effect of ethnic concentration. This is clearly the case for the Surinamese group: after correcting for individual characteristics such as age and educational level, the odds on participating on the labour market are no longer effected by ethnic concentration. In contrast though, the Moroccan group still shows quite a strong effect of ethnic concentration. Thus, let us take two specific Moroccan individuals, with each a different ethnic concentration of their neighbourhoods as the only difference between the two; even if they match on all other features (for example: both men live in Rotterdam, are in their thirties, are not born in or immigrated into the Netherlands before the age of six, are both married and have children, are having a middle educational level, both parents not having such a education and both have no problems speaking Dutch), then the one who lives in the neighbourhood exceeding the level of 50 % ethnic minorities has a significantly lower probability of having an employment contract of at least 12 hours per week than the one who lives a neighbourhood with less than 25 % ethnic minorities. It is remarkable that only the Moroccan group is affected by ethnic concentration, and therefore further analyses should be concentrated on this difference. Before I look into the social processes that might be at work for the Moroccan group, let us first take a look at the other factors playing a part in explaining differences in participation rates.

For all four ethnic groups, gender and the educational level have the most explanatory power. Ethnic minority women, just as Dutch women, participate much less in the labour force than men do. In contrast, higher educational levels stimulate participation to a great extent, although the returns are higher for Surinamese and particularly higher for Antilleans, and lower for Turks and Moroccans. For the last two groups, the command of the Dutch language is very important as well. For Surinamese and Antilleans, on the other hand, there is an age-effect on the probability of participating, and both groups also show a household effect, in which especially couples without children tend to participate more (probably being double-income couples more often).

In sum, we may conclude that in explaining participation rates, neighbourhood ethnic concentration is of modest significance. Turks and Antilleans show no effects, and the observed effects for Surinamese are entirely attributed to compositional differences between residents. For Moroccans, however, living in ethnically concentrated neighbourhoods certainly is associated with lower participation rates. But the question still remains why. Are the lack of contacts with native Dutch and having traditional views underlying the observed negative neighbourhood effect?

When we look at the association between contact and concentration, however, we can see that for Moroccans this relationship is weaker than for the other ethnic groups. For them it is less important in which neighbourhood category they live (Table 3). The per ethnic group stratified multivariate analyses confirm this conclusion (Table 4). Taking into account the individual background of the residents (gender, age, immigrant status, household situation, education level, command of the Dutch language and place of residence), ethnic concentration indeed has quite a strong effect on the homogeneity of someone's informal ties, in the sense that ethnic concentration is assiociated with higher orientation on the own ethnic group, however, *with the exception of* the Moroccan group.

As a further means of control, I added the contact variable in the labour market participation model and, as expected, this did not change the effect of ethnic concentration whatsoever (results not reported).

Table 3

Crosstabs of contact by ethnic concentration (%)

		Ethnic Concentration Neighbourhood			
		< 25 %	25 – 50 %	50 – 75 %	> 75 %
Turks	More contact	64.2	73.8	87.6	83.3
	Same contact	27.2	20.5	10.3	15.8
	Less contact	8.6	5.6	2.1	0.9
	Cramer's *V* 0.149***				
Moroccans	More contact	54.2	65.4	72.1	63.4
	Same contact	32.1	26.0	21.8	31.2
	Less contact	13.8	8.6	6.1	5.4
	Cramer's *V* 0.104**				
Surinamese	More contact	25.3	44.8	55.8	57.6
	Same contact	39.8	40.0	34.0	33.9
	Less contact	34.9	15.2	10.2	8.5
	Cramer's *V* 0.216***				
Antilleans	More contact	23.4	34.8	51.4	46.2
	Same contact	29.3	36.6	30.5	26.9
	Less contact	47.3	28.6	18.1	26.9
	Cramer's *V* 0.183***				

* = $p < 0.05$, ** = $p < 0.01$, *** = $p < 0.001$.
Source: SPVA 2002 (ISEO / SCP).

Table 4

Logistic regression analysis of having predominately contact with own ethnic group, effect of ethnic concentration, odds ratios

	Turks	Moroccans	Surinamese	Antilleans
	Exp(B)	Exp(B)	Exp(B)	Exp(B)
Ethnic concentration (ref = < 25 %)				
25 – 50 %	1.616*	1.135	1.716**	1.446
> 50 %	2.416**	1.000	3.012***	2.186**
N				
Nagelkerke R^2	0.175	0.202	0.178	0.289

a: Controlled for gender, age, immigrant status, household situation, educational level, command of the Dutch language and city.

* = $p < 0.05$, ** = $p < 0.01$, ** = $p < 0.001$.

Source: SPVA 2002 (ISEO / SCP).

To conclude, the 'neighbourhood effect' for the Moroccan group cannot be explained by the fact that they might have less contact with native Dutch in ethnically concentrated areas than in less concentrated ones. The informal ties, 'restrained' by ethnic concentration, do not seem to be the neighbourhood effect mechanism underlying lower participation rates. At least, that can't be derived from the available data. This does not mean, however, that informal ties with native Dutch cannot be functional for ethnic minorities in general and Moroccans in particular. It merely says that 'confined' contact in ethnically concentrated neighbourhoods is not the operating mechanism.

The second theoretical link that I wanted to examine is the socialization / social norms mechanism. As stated before, its operationalization – the extent to which individuals subscribe to modern ('Western') values – is far from ideal, an additional problem being the number of respondents that filled in the questionnaire items on cultural orientation. Table 5 shows us that ethnic minorities living in ethnically concentrated neighbourhoods subscribe in a somewhat lesser extent to modern values such as individualization, secularization and female liberation, than their counterparts in other neighbourhoods. This time the association is the strongest for the Moroccan group. Also when this relationship is controlled for the influence of other individual characteristics, Moroccans and Surinamese both show effects of ethnic concentration on cultural orientation (Table 6).

So, do the, by ethnic concentration driven, more traditionally orientated values of Moroccans form the operating mechanism behind lower participation rates in ethnically concentrated neighbourhoods then? Are there some kinds of contagion effects in play in these types of neighbourhoods? The ethnographic study of Pinkster (2008) indeed shows that socialization mechanisms affecting labour market behaviour of young women living in a high minority neighbourhood, are preserved and reinforced through the tight system of social control within the local social structures. But, although the fact that 'neighbourhood effects' might very well be the result of socialization processes within the neighbourhood, there is more at stake here. Because when the cultural orientation is introduced into the labour market participation model, the effect of ethnic concentration, again, hardly changes (results not reported). Moreover, especially for the Moroccan group, the cultural orientation does not have any effect on labour market participation. In other words, Moroccans who participate on the labour market do not subscribe to modern values any more than those who are not.

Table 5

Cultural orientation by ethnic concentration

	Ethnic Concentration Neighbourhood				
	< 25 %	25 – 50 %	50 – 75 %	> 75 %	*Eta*
Turks	2.66	2.56	2.40	2.62	0.172
Moroccans	2.66	2.41	2.40	2.31	0.218
Surinamese	3.24	3.14	3.00	2.86	0.201
Antilleans	3.34	3.13	3.12	3.03	0.198

Source: SPVA 2002 (ISEO / SCP).

Table 6

Regression analysis of cultural orientation, effect of ethnic concentration, odds ratios

	Turks	Moroccans	Surinamese	Antilleans
	Exp(B)	Exp(B)	Exp(B)	Exp(B)
Ethnic concentration (ref = < 25 %)				
25 – 50 %	–0.015	–0.188***	–0.085*	–0.097**
> 50 %	–0.001	–0.173***	–0.138***	–0.052
N	884	836	1006	778
Nagelkerke R^2	0.209	0.266	0.267	0.289

a: Controlled for gender, age, immigrant status, household situation, educational level, and having predominately contact with own ethnic group.

* = $p < 0.05$, ** = $p < 0.01$, *** = $p < 0.001$.

Source: SPVA 2002 (ISEO / SCP).

To conclude, the neighbourhood effect on participation does not disappear by the inclusion of neither social contacts nor cultural orientation. The extent to which ethnic minorities predominately maintain contact with their own group is not the mechanism at work here, so it seems, and the same goes, be it to a lesser degree, for the acculturation of Western values. But then how can the effect be explained?

4.1 Understanding Spatial Selection: Beyond Exclusive Individual Choice Selection

As said earlier, the most important methodological problem in neighbourhood effect research is that observed statistical relationships might not be 'neighbourhood effects' but merely 'selection effects'. There will always be characteristics which are not measured but which do play an important part in choosing a home or a neighbourhood, or any other choice in life. The theory is, for instance, that ethnic minorities who 'want' to integrate, shall move out of concentrated neighbourhoods into less concentrated, white neighbourhoods. A first generation immigrant husband and wife, for example, who want their children to succeed in Dutch society, will move to a whiter neighbourhood, but at the same time pay more attention to the importance of language, of reading and getting an education. When their children appear to do well in school in that particular neighbourhood, it doesn't have that much to do with the characteristics neighbourhood, but with the ambitions of the parents. So, it's the (unmeasured) motivations, like dedication and the willingness to make sacrifices on behalf of their children's future (Galster, 2005, 16), which determine both their residential choice as well as their (children's) integration into core institutions like the education system and the labour market.

All kinds of sophisticated methods, econometric techniques in particular, have been constructed to counter the selection problem, such as sibling studies and instrumental variables for example (see for a review Galster, 2005; and recent efforts: Musterd et al., 2007; Gurmu, Ihlanfeldt / Smith, 2007; Maurin / Moschion, forthcoming). In spite of their great importance, these studies on the issue of selection might put just a little bit too much emphasis on the individual choice, at least in my opinion. Besides the fact that people's individual motivations and their 'integration desire' lead to the conscious choice for a given neighbourhood, there are also factors outside the individual that cause people to end up in certain neighbourhoods (Van der Laan Bouma-Doff, 2007b). Neighbourhood selection is of fundamental importance in studying and understanding neighbourhood effects. This does not revolve around individual selection effects alone (choice), but also around institutional selection effects (constraints / opportunities). The theory that ethnic minorities who 'want' to integrate also want to move to a whiter neighbourhood, is in my opinion only part of the story. The results from this current study show that a highly stigmatized and discriminated against group of people encounters limitations and constraints in all parts of society. The observed 'neighbourhood effect' for Moroccans might be better understood in the light of institutional selection. In any case, it is probably not just a matter of individual choice. Within Dutch society, Moroccans are the most stigmatized and discriminated ethnic category, as a result of which Moroccans are most likely to be confronted with barriers on both the housing *and* the labour market (Andriessen et al., 2007). This causes them to have less access to and a weak position in both core institutions in Dutch society, thus resulting in a statistical relationship between ethnic concentration and labour market participation.

5. Conclusion

This paper dealt with differences in labour market participation rates of four ethnic minority groups and the way these are associated with ethic concentration. A first step was simply to test whether there are differences in labour market participation between similar individuals living in different kinds of neighbourhoods. After that, two theoretical mechanisms were explored, namely the contacts with native Dutch and the acculturation of 'modern' values. Both are popular explanations for assumed negative neighbourhood effects, and part of the isolation thesis, which states that living in ethnically concentrated neighbourhoods hampers integration because it makes the orientation on Dutch society and contacts with native Dutch to a great extent redundant.

The results show that in general, ethnic concentration has no additional effect on participation on the labour market, *with the exception of* the labour market participation by Moroccans. For them, living in neighbourhoods with a population consisting of more than 50 % ethnic minorities, is associated with a lower probability of having an employment contract of at least 12 hours a week. The relevance of the study is that, with the available extensive survey data, I could include social processes, which might underlie the observed negative neighbourhood effect. However, the neighbourhood effect on participation does not disappear by the inclusion of neither social contacts nor cultural orientation. An explanation for the observed relationship might be that this not a neighbourhood effect but in fact a selection effect. Scholars generally attribute this selection effect to unmeasured individual characteristics, such as dedication, ambition and so on. The popular idea is that those who 'want' to integrate will automatically move to a whiter neighbourhood. Their successful integration is not caused by the whiter neighbourhood *per se,* but rather the result of their own, unmeasured motivations and skills. However, not just individual choice plays a part in neighbourhood selection. Institutional selection effects, shaped by constraints and opportunities individuals encounter, are of great importance as well, causing weaker groups to end up in less desirable environments. I argue that the statistical relationship between neighbourhood concentration and labour market participation by Moroccans largely exists because Moroccans are a highly marginalized, stigmatized and discriminated against ethnic category. Due to institutional selection mechanisms and certainly not simply by individual choice, Moroccans are confronted with barriers on both the housing and the labour market, resulting in less access to and a weak position in both of these core institutions.

Because weaker groups, in the Netherlands particularly the Moroccans, generally end up in less desirable environments, the distribution of 'space' reproduces and reinforces social inequality in society (see also Sibley,1995). However, in order to fully understand neighbourhood effects, we need to gain a better understanding of the residential choice process, especially by finding out the individual motivations and institutional mechanisms that lead to neighbourhood selection.

References

Andersson, R. / *Musterd,* S. / *Galster,* G. / *Kauppinen,* T. (2007): What Mix Matters? Exploring the Relationships between Individuals' Incomes and Different Measures of their Neighbourhood Context, Housing Studies 22 (5), 637 – 660.

Andersson, R. / *Musterd,* S. (2006): What Scale Matters? Exploring the relationships between individuals' social position, neighbourhood context and the scale of neighbourhood, Paper presented at the 36th Annual Meeting of the Urban Affairs Association, Montreal, April 19 – 22.

Andriessen, I. / *Dageros,* J. / *Nievers,* E. / *Boog,* I. (2007): Discrimenatiemonitor nietwesterse allochtonen op de arbeidsmarkt 2007, Den Haag: SCP.

Bell, W. (1968): The city, suburb, and a theory of social choice, in: Greer, S. et al. (eds.) The new urbanization, New York, 132 – 168.

Bell, W. (1958): Social choice, life styles and suburban residence, in: Dobriner, W. M. (eds.), The suburban community, New York, 225 – 247.

Bolt, G. / *Burgers,* J. / *Van Kempen,* R. (1998): On the social significance of spatial location: spatial segregation and social inclusion, Netherlands Journal of Housing and the Built Environment 13, 83 – 95.

Borjas, G. J. (1998): To Ghetto or Not to Ghetto: Ethnicity and Residential Segregation, Journal of Urban Economics 44, 228 – 253.

Briggs, X. de Souza (2007): Some of My Best Friends Are . . . , Interracial Friendships, Class, and Segregation in America, City & Community 6 (4), 263 – 290.

Briggs, X. de Souza (1998): Brown Kids in White Suburbs: Housing Mobility and the Many Faces of Social Capital, Housing Policy Debate 9 (1), 177 – 221.

Buck, N. (2001): Identifying neighbourhood effects on social exclusion, Urban Studies 38, 2251 – 2275.

Crane, J. (1991): The epidemic theory of ghettos and neighbourhood effects on dropping out and teenage childbearing, American Journal of Sociology 96, 1226 – 1259.

Dietz, R. D. (2002): The estimation of neighbourhood effects in the social sciences: an interdisciplinary approach, Social Science Research 31, 539 – 575.

Drever, A. I. (2004): Separate spaces, separate outcomes? Neighbourhood impacts on minorities in Germany, Urban Studies 41, 1423 – 1439.

Friedrichs, J. / *Galster,* G. / *Musterd,* S. (2003): Neighbourhood effects on social opportunities: the European and American research and policy context, Housing Studies 18, 797 – 806.

Galster, G. (2007): Neighbourhood Social Mix as a Goal of Housing Policy: A Theoretical Analysis, European Journal of Housing Policy 7 (1), 19 – 43.

Galster, G.(2005): Neighbourhood mix, social opportunities, and the policy challenges of an increasingly diverse Amsterdam, Wibaut lecture, Amsterdam Institute for Metropolitan and International Development Studies (AMIDSt), University of Amsterdam.

Galster, G. (2003): Investigating behavioural impacts of poor neighbourhoods: towards new data and analytic strategies, Housing Studies 18, 893 – 914.

Galster, G. / *Kauppinen,* T. / *Musterd,* S. / *Andersson,* R. (2007a): Does Neighbourhood Income Mix Affect Earnings of Adults? A New Approach using Evidence from Sweden, Journal of Urban Economics.

Galster, G. / *Marcotte,* D. E. / *Mandell,* M. / *Wolman,* H. / *Augustine,* N. (2007b): The Influence of Neighbourhood Poverty During Childhood on Fertility, Education and Earnings Outcomes, Housing Studies 22 (5), 723 – 751.

Giddens, A. (1984): The Constitution of Society. Outline of the Theory of Structuration, Cambridge.

Gijsberts, M. / *Dagevos,* J. (2007): The socio-cultural integration of ethnic minorities in the Netherlands: Identifying neighbourhood effects on multiple integration outcomes, Housing Studies 22 (5), 805 – 831.

Granovetter, M. S. (1974): Getting a job: A study of contacts and careers, Cambridge.

Gurmu, S. / *Ihlanfeldt,* K. R. / *Smith,* W. J. (2007): Does residential location matter to the employment of TANF recipients? Evidence from a dynamic discrete model with unobserved effects, Journal of Urban Economics, in press.

Laan Bouma-Doff, W. van der (2007b): Involuntary Isolation: Ethnic Preferences and Residential Segregation, Journal of Urban Affairs 29 (3), 289 – 309.

Laan Bouma-Doff, W. van der (2007a): Confined Contact. Residential Segregation and Ethnic Bridges in the Netherlands, Urban Studies 44 (5 / 6), 997 – 1017.

Lupton, R. (2006): How does place affect education?, in: Delorenzi, S. (ed.), Going Places. Neighbourhood, ethnicity and social mobility. London: Institute for Public Policy Research, 59 – 71.

Lupton, R. (2003): 'Neighbourhood effects': can we measure them and does it matter?, CASE paper 73, Centre for Analysis of Social Exclusion. London: London School of Economics.

Manski, C. F. (1993): Identification Problems in the Social Science, Sociological Methodology 23, 1 – 56.

Maurin, E. / *Moschion,* J. (forthcoming): The social Multiplier and Labour Market Participation of Mothers, The Journal of Applied Social Science Studies.

Musterd, S. / *Andersson,* R. (2006): Employment, Social Mobility and Neighbourhood Effects: The Case of Sweden, International Journal of Urban and Regional Research 30, 120 – 140.

Musterd, S. / *Andersson,* R. (2005): Housing Mix, Social Mix and Social Opportunities, Urban Affairs Review 40 (6), 761 – 790.

Musterd, S. / *Andersson,* R. / *Galster,* G. / *Kauppinen,* T. (2007): Are immigrants' earnings influenced by the characteristics of their neighbours?, Environment and Planning A.

Odé, A. (2002): Ethnic-cultural and socio-economic integration in the Netherlands. A comparative study of Meditterarean and Carribean minority groups, Assen.

Pinkster, F. M. (forthcoming): Localized social networks, socialization and social mobility in a low income neighborhood in the Netherlands, Urban Studies.

Portes, A. (1998): Social capital: Its origins and applications in modern sociology, Annual Review of Sociology 24, 1 – 24.

Portes, A. / *Sensebrenner,* J. (1993): Embeddedness and immigration: Notes on the social determinants of economic action, American Journal of Sociology 98, 1320 – 1350.

Sampson, R. J. / *Morenoff,* J. D. / *Gannon-Rowley,* T. (2002): Assessing "neighbourhood effects": social processes and new directions in research, Annual Review of Sociology 28, 443 – 478.

Sibley, D. (1995): Geographies of exclusion. Society and difference in the West, London / New York.

Uitermark, J. / *Duyvendak,* J. W. / *Kleinhans,* R. (2007): Gentrification as a governmental strategy: social control and social cohesion in Hoogvliet, Rotterdam, Environment and Planning A 39, 125 – 141.

Zhou, M. / *Bankston,* C. (1996): Social Capital and the Adaptation of the Second Generation: The Case of Vietnamese Youth in New Orleans, in: Portes, A. (ed.), The New Second Generation, New York, 197 – 220.

Schmollers Jahrbuch 128 (2008), 175 – 190
Duncker & Humblot, Berlin

Germans in Germany's Ethnic Neighborhoods

By Anita I. Drever*

Abstract

In contrast to most research on the effects on residents of living in an ethnic neighborhood, this paper explores how living within an ethnic neighborhood affects members of the *dominant* ethnic group – in this case Germans – rather than the minorities that define it. The results indicate that Germans living within ethnic neighborhoods are less well off financially than their peers in other parts of the city, and are more likely to be living in large buildings in need of repair. The analysis did not however suggest that Germans living in ethnic neighborhoods have fewer social contacts, or that they are more likely to be unemployed. Indeed, Germans living within ethnic neighborhoods reported levels of satisfaction with their housing and standard of living equal to Germans elsewhere. These results would seem to paint a rosy picture of the lives of German residents of ethnic neighborhoods, were it not for a notable absence of school-aged German children within these spaces.

JEL Classifications: J15, R21

1. Introduction

Researchers have spent nearly three decades exploring the patterns and consequences of residential segregation for *immigrants* in Germany. Until recently, these studies of immigrant settlement geographies and their attendant social consequences were nearly unanimous in their conclusion that immigrants living in Germany's densest ethnic concentrations had limited contact with wider German society. They were sharply divided, however, over whether this hindered immigrant integration, by limiting immigrants' contact with Germans who might help them acculturate (Hoffman-Nowotny / Hondrich, 1982; Esser, 1986), or whether ethnic neighborhoods instead helped to ease integration into Germany society thanks to information shared within immigrant communities regarding housing and job opportunities, and strategies for coping with everyday life (Heckmann, 1981; Elwert, 1982). Although both sides of the division concluded that neighborhood context was having an im-

* The author would like to thank Kenneth H. Orvis and anonymous reviewers for comments on an earlier version of this paper.

portant influence on minorities living within Germany's ethnic neighborhoods, they did not extend their research to the effects of such neighborhood context on persons of German origin.

Recently, researchers have questioned the degree to which ethnic neighborhoods organize or define the personal networks of their minority inhabitants (see Drever, 2004; Oberwittler, 2007; Drever / Hoffmeister, 2008). Advances in transportation and communication technologies arguably limit the influence of neighborhood of residence on social and career opportunities. This body of research has however similarly neglected to examine the degree to which living in an ethnic neighborhood might affect the social and economic integration of *Germans* living within them.

There is also a long-standing debate in the segregation literature regarding whether individual economic outcomes in minority neighborhoods are a product of internal neighborhood dynamics, or of neighborhood location relative to employment opportunities or of trends in regional economic growth and income inequality (see Ihlandfeldt / Sjoquist, 1998). Wilson (1996) and Kasarda (1989) believe that some minority neighborhoods in the United States are impoverished largely because they are geographically distant from areas of employment growth. Jargowsky's (1997) analysis indicates that the economic health of an urban region drives the expansion and contraction of impoverished minority neighborhoods. These analyses seem to indicate that the urban economy and neighborhood geography rather than discrimination or limited interpersonal networks are behind the deleterious conditions in some minority neighborhoods. Again, with the exception of Jargowsky (1997), these studies have tended to focus on minority outcomes in ethnic neighborhoods.

This paper addresses this gap in the literature by examining the social and economic integration of Germans living within the country's ethnic neighborhoods. Compared to the U.S., Britain, or France, Germany has few majority minority neighborhoods (Drever, 2004; Schönewälder / Söhn, 2007). Yet in many of the country's largest cities around 1 in 5 residents does not possess German citizenship. In these cities areas of distinct minority concentration – like Kreuzberg and Duisburg-Marxloh – have developed. How are tens of thousands of non-immigrant Germans – persons born in Germany with German citizenship – faring in these neighborhoods? Are they disadvantaged by their residential location?

The paper is organized around three research questions. First, what are the socioeconomic and demographic characteristics of non-immigrant Germans living within ethnic neighborhoods? In other words, who are the Germans who are living in these neighborhoods, and how do they differ from Germans living in other parts of the city? Second, to what extent do persons of German origin living in ethnic neighborhoods appear to be socially or economically isolated from the larger society? Researchers have argued that immigrants within Germany's ethnic neighborhoods have few relationships with native-born Germans and therefore have diminished economic opportunities and higher unemployment rates. Might the same be true for the Germans living in these same neighborhoods? Do Germans in ethnic neighborhoods have fewer social contacts, for example, or are they more likely to lack savings? Third, to what extent do the findings of previous research into housing quality in ethnic neighborhoods apply to the Germans living there? Research has shown that immigrants living in ethnic neighborhoods tend to be concentrated in poorer-quality housing (Drever, 2004). Might that be true for non-immigrant Germans as well?

2. Ethnic Neighborhoods in Germany

Many of the spaces presently recognized as ethnic neighborhoods in Germany were first settled by Southern and Eastern Europeans who had participated in Germany's post-WWII guest-worker program. Germany began importing labor in the late 1950s to address the country's labor shortage. At the close of the Second World War, Germany's economy and many of Germany's largest cities were in ruins and its occupiers were intent on attenuating the country's industrial base in order to hobble any future military ambitions. Fear that communism would become popular among impoverished Germans reversed the policies of its Western occupiers, however. Large loans to fund the reconstruction of the country's economic infrastructure were made through the Marshall Plan, and Germany entered a period referred to as its *Wirtschaftswunder* (economic miracle). During the 1950s, Germany's rapidly expanding economic base quickly absorbed the country's able-bodied male workforce (federal policies encouraged single-earner households so women were retreating from the labor force during this time). As a result, Germany implemented guest-worker programs to bring in workers from Italy, Spain, Portugal, Greece, the former Yugoslavia, and Turkey to alleviate the labor shortage.

Guest-workers, who began arriving in Germany during the late 1950s, were initially housed in dormitory-style housing near the factories where they were employed (O'Loughlin, 1987). But by the time the guest-worker programs were halted in 1973 because of the economic slowdown induced by the OPEC oil crisis, many of the 'guest' workers had acquired longer-term residence permits and formed a critical and stable part of the country's low-wage work force. As family-unification migration replaced worker migration in the mid-1970s, immigrants started moving out of the dormitories and into homes in the wider housing market that could accommodate their spouses and children. They mostly occupied Germany's least desirable housing: unrenovated *Altbau* (pre-World War I) apartment buildings in central-city areas, and working class housing near factory sites. These areas still remain important sites of ethnic residential concentration.

Today immigrants are also increasingly found in Germany's large social-housing estates (*Großwohnsiedlungen*). During the 1960s and 1970s, Germany's social housing was largely inhabited by middle and lower-middle income German citizens. As this housing stock aged vacancy rates rose and local social housing authorities accepted increasing numbers of non-citizens (Huttman, 1991). *Aussiedler,* persons of German descent from Eastern Europe and the former Soviet Union, also came to be concentrated in social-housing estates because their German citizenship facilitated their access to this form of affordable housing (Häußermann / Kapphan, 2000, 156).

Despite the fact that Germany is now home to 7.3 million persons without German citizenship, it has few neighborhoods that are more than 50 % foreign (Drever, 2004; Schönwälder / Söhn, 2007). This stems partly from the locally diverse nature of the country's housing stock – chic apartments in renovated, turn-of-the-20th-century buildings are a world apart and can fetch twice the rent of crumbling, coal-heated dwellings across the street. Apartment buildings constructed a century apart often stand within meters of each other in inner-city areas that were bombed during the Second World War.

German policymakers also attempted to actively engineer dispersed immigrant settlement patterns. A two-tiered system of quotas, enforced by the German address registration system, was enacted in 1975 to help prevent the formation of immigrant 'ghettos'. Cities whose populations were more than 12 % foreign could choose to ban further in-migration of foreign nationals, citing the argument that their social services were 'overburdened' (Rist, 1978; Leitner, 1987; Arin, 1991). Settlement bans could also be placed on particular neighborhoods within cities where immigrant concentrations were developing. Settlement bans could also be placed on particular neighborhoods within cities where immigrant concentrations were developing. The policies were not particularly effective as they did not apply to immigrants from European Community countries and immigrants from outside the EC could get around these measures by using the addresses of friends or family outside such neighborhoods on official correspondence (Rist, 1978). Though these measures may have helped stabilized the growth of ethnic neighborhoods they did not lead to their diminishment (Arin, 1991).

Immigrants in Germany today therefore tend to be scattered through many sections of the country's cities, but where they form concentrations it is in certain kinds of neighborhoods, especially those with turn-of-the-20th-century apartment buildings and in the *Großwohnsiedlungen* or large housing estates owned by local governments. Also, Germany's ethnic neighborhoods tend themselves to be ethnically diverse: in only 15 neighborhoods[1] in all of Germany do Turks – Germanys most numerous and arguably most disadvantaged

1 Schönwälder and Söhn's (2007) analysis was undertaken at the level of the *Innerstädtischen Raumbeobachtung.* These areas have an average of 8,880 inhabitants.

ethnic group – constitute more than 20 % of a neighborhood's total population (Schönwälder / Söhn, 2007).

In neighborhoods where immigrants are concentrated, previous research has revealed above-average levels of poverty, unemployment, and welfare dependency (Friedrichs, 1998; Haussermann / Kapphan, 2000; Schönwälder / Söhn, 2007). However as Schönwälder and Söhn (2007) point out there also many ethnic neighborhoods that are not economically disadvantaged. Further, some researchers argue that the social disadvantage measured in ethnic neighborhoods stems from the characteristics of Germans in these spaces, not immigrants (Bartelheimer / Freyberg, 1996; Buitkamp, 2001). The present paper explores the extent to which this appears to be the case nationwide in Germany, and the extent to which economic disadvantage might be tied to isolation and to dissatisfaction with one's standard of living, among Germans inside ethnic neighborhoods.

3. Data and Variables

3.1 The German Socio-Economic Panel

The German Socio-Economic Panel (SOEP) is based on data collected by the *Leben in Deutschland* (Living in Germany) survey administered on a yearly basis to nearly 25,000 persons in Germany. The dataset contains detailed socioeconomic, demographic, and housing information that can be used to assess several dimensions of the situation of Germans living within ethnic neighborhoods (SOEP Group, 2001). In 2004, a special-topic module dealing with social networks and trust was also included the *Leben in Deutschland* survey. The measures included in this module can be used to asses the degree to which Germans in ethnic neighborhoods might be socially, and hence potentially economically, isolated. The SOEP data are linked with 1998 – 1999 data collected from statistical offices in 16 West German cities with more than 300,000 residents. These data, derived from address registry data, indicate the proportion of persons living within a SOEP respondent's zip code area who are foreign citizens.

3.2 'Germans' versus 'Immigrants'

Statistical analysis forces the drawing of clear nationality distinctions, even in instances where no clear distinctions exist. Unlike the United States, where access to citizenship has long been granted to persons born within U.S. borders or with 5 or more years of legal residence, naturalization in Germany was until recently largely only open to persons of German descent. As a result, only a small number of the former guest-workers and their children acquired German citizenship during the latter part of the 20th century. On January 1,

2000, however, the laws were changed so that persons born in Germany to a parent who had been resident in Germany for eight or more years and who was in possession of a permanent residence permit were automatically granted citizenship at birth. Naturalization rates by both birth and application rose from 1 % to between 2 % and 3 % of the foreign population per year (Laux, 2005). According to the 2005 *Mikrozensus,* less than half of the population in Germany with a *Migrationshintergrund* (migration background) did not have Germany citizenship. This raises difficulties with regard to drawing the line between immigrants and non-immigrants. For the purposes of this study, however, Germans are defined as persons with German citizenship who were born in Germany. Person both with and without German citizenship born abroad are categorized as immigrants, similar to the 'foreign born' category often employed in US research on immigration.

3.3 Ethnic Neighborhoods

For the purposes of this paper, ethnic neighborhoods are defined as zip code areas that – according to Germany's local statistical offices – were more than 25 % foreign in 1998 and 1999. Unfortunately data on persons with a 'migration background' are not available at this level. The 25 % cutoff was chosen because according to the SOEP, a majority of persons living in zip code areas that are 25 % or more non-citizen feel they are living in an area with 'many foreigners' (see Drever, 2004). Zip code areas in Germany's largest cities contain an average of 17,700 persons and are similar in size to U.S. zip codes, which are commonly used in neighborhood research (see Osterman, 1991; Ross 2000; Wen / Christakis, 2005). This paper only looks at Germans living in cities of 300,000 or more persons. This is because an analysis of the entire German population inside and outside ethnic neighborhoods would largely be a comparison of Germans living in inner-city ethnic neighborhoods with the rest of Germany including the nation's farmers, small alpine town dwellers et cetera, leading to a conflation of neighborhood effects with city size effects. Similarly the analysis looks only at cities in western Germany because there are few zip codes with substantial numbers of immigrants in the eastern portion of the country.

4. Analysis

4.1 What are the Socioeconomic and Demographic Characteristics of Germans Living within Ethnic Neighborhoods?

Germans living in ethnic neighborhoods differ from their compatriots living in other parts of the city in a number of ways: Perhaps the most profound difference is a marked apparent reluctance among German families with children to live within ethnic neighborhoods (see figure 1). Inside ethnic neighborhoods, 79 % of German households do not have children, compared to 68 % outside: a difference that a chi square test finds statistically significant at the .01 level. These statistics on the number of households with children mask the even starker differences in the prevalence of school-aged children inside ethnic neighborhoods. While the proportion of Germans with pre-schoolers is equal inside and outside ethnic neighborhoods, the proportion of Germans with school-aged children in ethnic neighborhoods is about half of what it is outside. Immigrant children, by contrast, make up an equal proportion of the population whether inside or outside ethnic neighborhoods.

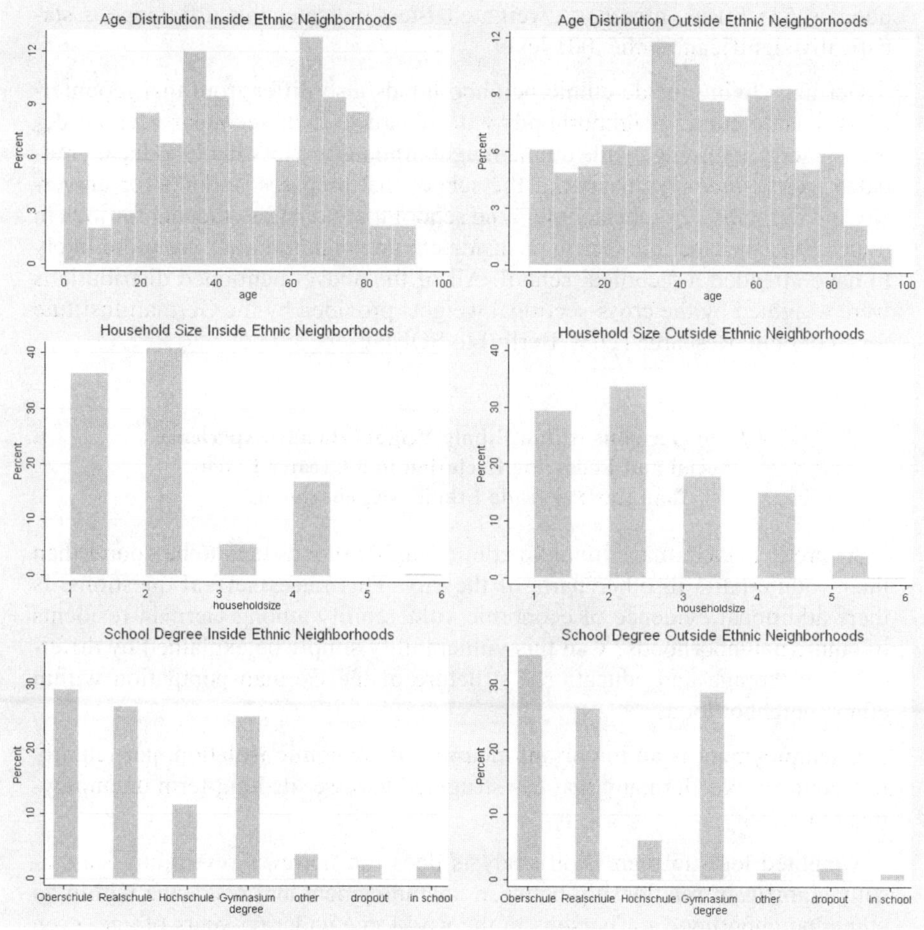

Source: SOEP, author's calculations.

Figure 1: Differences in economic and demographic characteristics for Germans inside and outside ethnic neighborhoods

Germans in their 20s and those over 60, by contrast, are over-represented in ethnic neighborhoods. Persons in these age groups tend to live in smaller households, a fact reinforced by the finding that nearly 80 % of all German households inside ethnic neighborhoods are inhabited by just one or two persons (see figure 1).

Because immigrants on average earn less than Germans (see Münz et al., 1997) one might expect average incomes of Germans in the neighborhoods where immigrants are concentrated to be lower as well. This is indeed the case. Net household income is 14 % lower among Germans living inside ethnic neighborhoods (2221 Euros / month) compared to outside ethnic neighborhoods (2535 Euros / month). A weighted *T*-test indicates this difference is statistically significant at the .001 level.

Germans living inside ethnic neighborhoods also differ from their counterparts outside ethnic neighborhoods with regard to their secondary-school degrees. Germans living inside ethnic neighborhoods are less likely to have graduated from *either* Gymnasium – the school that prepares students for university in Germany – *or* Oberschule – the school that prepares students for jobs in trades like construction. Germans inside ethnic neighborhoods are more likely to have attended a technical school. All of the above-mentioned distributions were weighted by the cross-sectional weights provided by the German Institute for Economic Research (DIW Berlin) to SOEP users.

4.2 Do Germans within Ethnic Neighborhoods Experience Social and Economic Exclusion to a Greater Extent than those Outside Ethnic Neighborhoods?

As predicted, Germans living in ethnic neighborhoods tend to be poorer than their counterparts in other parts of the city. This raises several questions. Is there additional evidence of economic vulnerability among German residents of ethnic neighborhoods? Can this vulnerability simply be explained by differences in the age and educational structure of the German population within ethnic neighborhoods?

Unemployment is an important measure of economic isolation, particularly in a country like Germany that has struggled to lower its long-term unemployment rate.

Weighted logistic regression analysis does not however reveal any statistically significant relationship between unemployment and residence within an ethnic neighborhood for persons in the workforce under 65 years of age, even without controlling for age and years of education (see table 1).

Arguably, economic vulnerability could instead afflict persons in ethnic neighborhoods who hold jobs but are worried about losing them. Survey respondents were asked to rate their security in their present job. This information was used to create a binary dependent variable 'job is secure / job is at least somewhat insecure' for logistic regression analysis. Again, employed Germans residing inside ethnic neighborhoods

Table 1

The influence for Germans of residence in an ethnic neighborhood on unemployment and job security

	Unemployment (*n* = 1504)		**Feeling one's job is secure (*n* = 971)**	
Constant	–2.28***	+1.86	+0.30***	–1.5**
Ethnic Neighborhood	–0.31	–0.20	–0.10	–0.12
Age		–0.02*		+0.02**
Years of Education		–0.26***		+0.08**
Prob > *F*	0.390	0.000	0.702	0.007

* = significant at the .05 level, ** = significant at the .01 level, *** = significant at the .001 level.
Source: SOEP, author's calculations.

Another measure of economic vulnerability is whether or not persons have savings that they can dip into when confronted with an emergency. Given the lower income levels among Germans within ethnic neighborhoods, it isn't surprising that this population is less likely to have a financial cushion for emergencies (see table 2). This difference disappears when age and years of education are added into the equation, however. This suggests the observed difference in savings levels is due to differences in human capital rather than neighborhood differences per se.

Table 2

The influence for Germans of residence in an ethnic neighborhood on emergency savings and social-housing consumption

	Possess no savings for Emergencies (*n* = 1974)		**Living in Social Housing (*n* = 1307)**	
Constant	–1.015***	+2.39***	–1.25***	+1.24
Ethnic Neighborhood	+0.41*	+0.34	–0.25	–0.17
Age		–0.03***		+0.01
Years of Education		–0.16***		–0.25***
Prob > *F*	0.026	0.000	0.260	0.000

* = significant at the .05 level, ** = significant at the .01 level, *** = significant at the .001 level.
Source: SOEP, author's calculations.

Dependence on government housing support in the form of social housing was not more prevalent among Germans in ethnic neighborhoods (see table 2). This finding is of interest because one might suppose Germans dependent on social-housing support might be driven into close proximity with persons of foreign origin. Germans in ethnic neighborhoods were also no more likely to feel their job was at risk indicating their employment situation is no more precarious than for Germans living outside ethnic neighborhoods.

In the literature on ethnic neighborhoods, concern is expressed that immigrants living within these spaces lack contact with the wider society (see Esser, 1986). How, then, are the Germans faring within these neighborhoods? Although German citizens are in the majority in most of Germany's ethnic neighborhoods, increasing numbers of these citizens are persons born abroad. Are persons of German origin experiencing social isolation when they live in spaces that are even more heavily immigrant than is indicated by official statistics?

Difference-of-means tests for the number of friends reported by Germans living in and outside ethnic neighborhoods indicate that living within an ethnic neighborhood does not diminish Germans' level of social contact (see table 3). Germans within ethnic neighborhoods had as many close friends as their counterparts outside ethnic neighborhoods. Four-fifths of Germans both in and outside ethnic neighborhoods also reported visiting or being visited by friends or neighbors one or more times per month. This is important, not only for the social well-being of the German population, but also because social contacts play a critical role in labor market integration. Even in Germany with its formal, tightly regulated labor market, approximately one third of all Germans find their jobs through networks (Drever / Hoffmeister, 2008).

Table 3

The influence for Germans of residence in an ethnic neighborhood on number of friends and visits with friends and neighbors

	Inside ethnic neighborhood	**Outside ethnic neighborhood**
Number of close friends	4.26	4.35
Visits with friends or neighbors one or more times per month	79.6 %	80.4 %

‡ Neither difference was statistically significant at the .05 level.

Source: SOEP, author's calculations.

Another measure of the health of peoples' social relationships with others is the degree to which they are trusting of people around them. Given the cultural differences between Germans and persons of immigrant origin, one might expect general levels of trust to be lower among persons of German origin living within ethnic neighborhoods. However, Germans living within ethnic neighborhoods were no more likely to perceive others to be untrustworthy than their counterparts outside these spaces (see table 4).

Table 4

The influence for Germans of residence in an ethnic neighborhood on number of friends and visits with friends and neighbors

	% in agreement inside ethnic neighborhoods	% in agreement outside ethnic neighborhoods
Generally people are trustable ($n = 2086$)	63 %	65 %
These days you can't depend on anyone ($n = 2082$)	38 %	37 %
When dealing with strangers it's better to be careful before one trusts them ($n = 2088$)	90 %	86 %
Most people would take advantage of you if given a chance ($n = 2069$)	41 %	45 %
Most people are willing to go out of their way to help you	41 %	37 %

‡ No difference was statistically significant at the .05 level.

Source: SOEP, author's calculations.

4.3 Is the Housing Quality of Germans Living in Ethnic Neighborhoods Compromised?

Another area of concern is the housing quality and standard of living experienced by Germans in ethnic neighborhoods. The literature on immigrant housing within ethnic neighborhoods indicates that immigrants often pay more for lower quality housing (see Kapphan, 1995). Further, given that many immigrant neighborhoods are in inner-city locations where housing units are more densely packed in space, one might assume this would negatively affect the standard of living in these areas.

As one would expect, only one in ten Germans residing in an ethnic neighborhood lives in either a single-family house or a duplex, in comparison to one in four persons living outside ethnic neighborhoods in Germany's largest cities. In fact, nearly half of all Germans living within ethnic neighborhoods inhabit buildings with nine or more units (see table 5).

Germans living within ethnic neighborhoods are also living in buildings they perceive to be in greater need of repair than Germans living outside these areas (see table 6). Though nearly equal numbers felt their building was in need of major repairs, many more Germans living in ethnic neighborhoods felt their building was in need of at least some repair. Given the lower income levels of Germans inside ethnic neighborhoods and the fact that much of the housing inside ethnic neighborhoods pre-dates the First World War, this comes as no surprise.

Table 5

The influence for Germans of residence in an ethnic neighborhood on number of friends and visits with friends and neighbors

	Inside ethnic neighborhood	Outside ethnic neighborhood
Single-family house	8 %	12 %
Duplex	3 %	15 %
Apartment with 3 – 4 units	7 %	13 %
Apartment with 5 – 8 units	34 %	34 %
Apartment with 9+ units	46 %	24 %
Skyscraper	2 %	2 %

$N = 2489$. $P = 0.000$.
Source: SOEP, author's calculations.

Table 6

State of housing repair for Germans living within versus outside an ethnic neighborhood

	Inside Ethnic neighborhoods	Outside ethnic neighborhoods
Building in good repair	59 %	70 %
Building needs some repairs	37 %	27 %
Building needs major repairs	4 %	3 %

$N = 2526$. $P = 0.0188$.
Source: SOEP, author's calculations.

Although Germans living within ethnic neighborhoods have lower incomes, live in higher density housing, and are more likely to live in buildings that need renovation, when asked about their satisfaction with both their housing and standard of living they expressed as much satisfaction as their wealthier counterparts outside ethnic neighborhoods. This suggests that Germans living within the country's multicultural neighborhoods are living there to at least some extent by choice, not because they are forced to by circumstance.

Table 7

Satisfaction with housing and living standard on a 0 – 10 scale for Germans living within versus outside an ethnic neighborhood

	Inside ethnic neighborhood	Outside ethnic neighborhood
Satisfaction with housing	7.49	7.51
Satisfaction with living standard	6.97	7.19

Source: SOEP, author's calculations.

5. Conclusions

The picture that emerges from this analysis of Germans living within the country's ethnic neighborhoods is one of a population that is somewhat economically disadvantaged but not isolated from the larger society. Germans living within the country's ethnic neighborhoods appear to have numbers of close friends and levels of social trust equal to their compatriots outside these areas. They are no more likely to be unemployed, to work in jobs with little security, or to live in social housing. Most tellingly, perhaps, despite their lower average incomes, more densely populated neighborhoods, and greater likelihood of living in housing in need of repair, Germans living in ethnic neighborhoods are as satisfied with their standard of living as persons outside these spaces.

Why? Ethnic neighborhoods are perceived as spaces of disadvantage and social isolation, especially for Germans. Why does the analysis herein largely contradict this perception? A variety of explanations is possible. Though a majority of persons living in a zip code that is more than 25 % foreign feel they live in an area where foreigners are heavily concentrated, it could be that economic and social isolation effects aren't observable until much higher levels of ethnic concentration are reached. This is unfortunately not something that can be tested using SOEP data as the sample size of persons live in more ethnically concentrated areas is prohibitively small. Another possible explanation is that that Germans living in ethnic neighborhoods are persons who *want* to be there, who value contact with diverse populations. This would appear to be supported by the contentment in overall standard of living expressed by Germans living within ethnic neighborhoods. Finally, it could also simply be that neighborhoods no longer play as vital a role in structuring the social and occupational lives of their cell-phone-carrying, automobile-driving inhabitants as they once did. This supports the assertion some theorists have made that trends in the wider urban economy have more effect on individual than neighborhood-level segregation or poverty rates (see for example Jargowsky, 1997).

Neighborhoods do not necessarily play only a minor role in everyone's life, however. While adults with easy access to transportation are free to pursue their careers and social lives in a real or virtual neighborhood of their choosing regardless of where they live, children largely spend their lives in, and experience life through, the neighborhood near their homes. Further, the local school system puts them into intimate contact with the children of the residents that surround them. German parents, in search of more child-friendly amenities and fearing for the educational future of their children, appear to be leaving ethnic neighborhoods when they reach elementary school enrollment age. One Kreuzberg school is even reportedly a *Deutschenfreie Schule* (German-free school).

It is problematic that Germans appear reluctant to raise their children in the city's ethnic neighborhoods even though the Germans remaining in these spaces appear content with their standard of living. Schools are an important engine of social and economic integration. If German parents are unwilling to remain in ethnic neighborhoods because they are reluctant to send their children to schools there, this does not bode well for the successful integration of the children of immigrants. Moreover, it is indicative of the extent to which the German school system has failed to accommodate ethnic-minority children. If the proportion of German children living within ethnic neighborhoods continues to lag relative to the population as a whole, this will be an important indicator not only of the degree to which German families feel disadvantaged in these neighborhoods, but also of the brightness of the future of Germany's newest generation of citizens of immigrant origin.

References

Arin, C. (1991): The Housing Market and Housing Policies for the Migrant Labor Population in West Berlin, in: E. Huttman (Ed.), Urban Housing Segregation of Minorities in Western Europe and the United States, Durham: Duke University Press, 199–214.

Bartelheimer, P. / *von Freyberg,* T. (1996): Ansätze zu einer Frankfurter Segregationsanalyse. Thesen und Trends, Widersprüche 60, 27–47.

Buitcamp, M. (2001): Sozialräumliche Segregation in Hannover. Artmutslagen und soziodemographische Strukturn in den Quartieren der Stadt, agis texte Nr. 23, Hannover.

Drever, A. (2004): Separate spaces, separate outcomes? Neighborhood impacts on minorities in Germany, Urban Studies 41 (8), 1423–1439.

Drever, A. / *Clark,* W. (2002): Gaining Access to Housing in Germany: the foreign minority experience, Urban Studies 39 (13), 2439–2454.

Drever, A. I. / *Hoffmeister,* O. (2008): Immigrants and social capital in a job-scarce environment: The case of Germany, International Migration Review, 42 (1).

Drever, A. I. / *Spiess,* C. K. (2006): Netzwerke sind bei der Stellenfindung von Migranten bedeutend, DIW Berlin Wochenbericht 22 / 2006, 327–331.

Elwert, G. (1982): Probleme der Ausländerintegration. Gesellschaftliche Integration durch Binnenintegration? Kölner Zeitschrift für Soziologie und Sozialpyschologie 34, 717–731.

Esser, H. (1986): Ethnische Kolonien: "Binnenintegration" oder gesellschaftliche Isolation?, in: J. Hoffmeyer-Zlotnik (Ed.), Segregation und Integration: Die Situation von Arbeitsmigranten im Aufnahmeland, Forschung Raum und Gesellschaft, Berlin, 106–117.

Friedrichs, J. (1998): Ethnic Segregation in Cologne, Germany, 1984–94, Urban Studies, 35 (10), 1745–1763.

Häußermann, H. / *Kapphan,* A. (2000): Berlin: von der geteilten zur gespaltenen Stadt?, Opladen.

Heckmann, F. (1981): Die Bundesrepublik: Ein Einwanderungsland?, Stuttgart.

Heckmann, F. (1998): Ethnische Kolonien: Schonraum für integration oder Verstärker der Ausgrenzung? Ghettos oder ethnische Kolonien?, Düsseldorf.

Hoffman-Nowotny, H. J. / *Hondrich,* K. O. (1982): Ausländer in der Bundesrepublik Deutschland und in der Schweiz, Frankfurt am Main.

Huttman, E. (1991): Subsidized Housing Segregation in Western Europe: Stigma and Segregation. in: E. Huttman (Ed.), Urban Housing Segregation of Minorities in Western Europe and the United States, Durham, 199–214.

Ihlandfeldt, K. / *Sjoquist,* D. (1998): The Spatial Mismatch Hypothesis: A Review of Recent Studies and their Implications for Welfare Reform, Housing Policy Debate 9 (4), 849–892.

Jargowsky, P. A. (1997): Poverty and Place: Ghettos, Barrios and the American City, New York.

Kapphan, A. (1995): Nichtdeutsche in Berlin-West: Zuwanderung, räumliche Verteilung und Segregation 1961–1993, Berliner Statistik 12, 198–208

Kasarda, J. (1989): Urban Industrial Transition and the Underclass, Annals of the American Academy of Political Science 501, 26–47.

Laux, H. D. (2005): Naturalization of Foreigners in Germany: Opportunities and Obstacles, Paper presented at the 2006 Annual Meeting of the AAG, Chicago (Illinois).

Münz, R. / *Seifert,* W. / *Ulrich,* R. (1997): Zuwanderung nach Deutschland, Frankfurt am Main.

Oberwittler, D. (2007): The Effects of Ethnic and Social Segregation on Children and Adolescents: Recent Research and Results from a German Multilevel Study, Wissenschaftzentrum Berlin Discussion Paper Nr. SP IV 2007–601.

Osterman, P. (1991): Welfare Participation in a Full Employment Economy: The Impact of Neighborhood, Social Problems 38 (4), 475–491.

Ross, C. E. (2000): Neighborhood Disadvantage and Adult Depression, Journal of Health and Social Behavior 41, 177–187.

Schönwälder, K. / *Söhn,* J. (2007): Siedlungsstrukturen von Migrantengruppen in Deutschland: Schwerpunkte der Ansiedlung und innerstädtische Konzenstrationen, Wissenschaftzentrum Berlin Discussion Paper Nr. SP IV 2007–601.

SOEP Group (2001): The German Socio-Economic Panel (GSOEP) after more than 15 years – Overview, in: E. Holst / D. R. Lillard / Th. A. DiPrete (eds.): Proceedings of the 2000 Fourth International Conference of German Socio-Economic Panel Study Users (GSOEP2000), Vierteljahrshefte zur Wirtschaftsforschung 70 (1), 7 – 14.

Wen, M. / *Christakis,* N. A. (2005): Neighborhood Effects on Posthospitalization Mortality: a Population-Based Cohort Study of the Elderly in Chicago, Health Services Research 40, 1108 – 1128.

Wilson, W. J. (1996): When Work Disappears, New York.